DATE DUE

DEMCO

Also by David Rieff

Going to Miami

David Rieff

Los Angeles

Capital of the Third World

Simon & Schuster

New York   London   Toronto   Sydney   Tokyo   Singapore

SIMON & SCHUSTER
Simon & Schuster Building
Rockefeller Center
1230 Avenue of the Americas
New York, New York 10020

1 2 3 4 5 6 7 8 9 10

Library of Congress Cataloging-in-Publication Data is available

ISBN: 0-671-67170-7

This book is for Ariane Zurcher

Contents

· · · · · · · · · · · ·

Part III

A civilization progresses from agriculture to paradox.
                    —E. M. Cioran

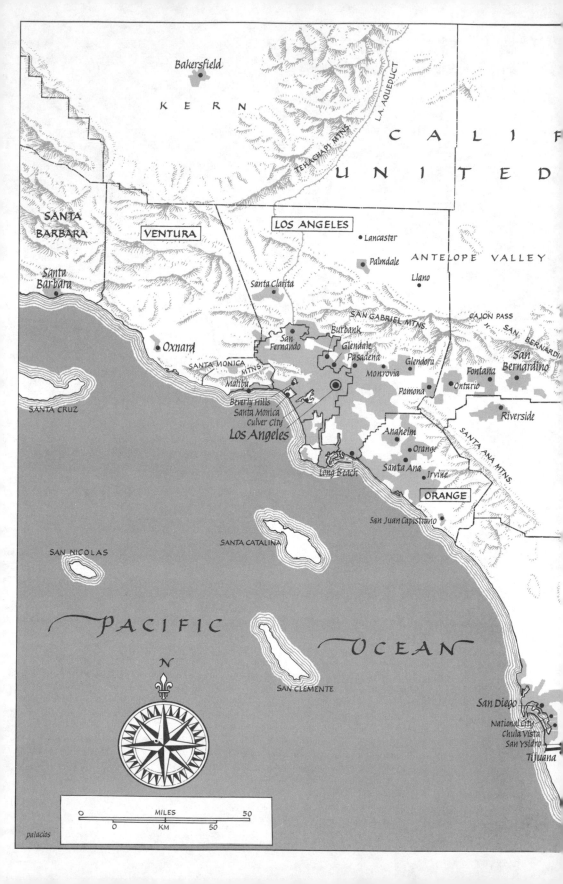

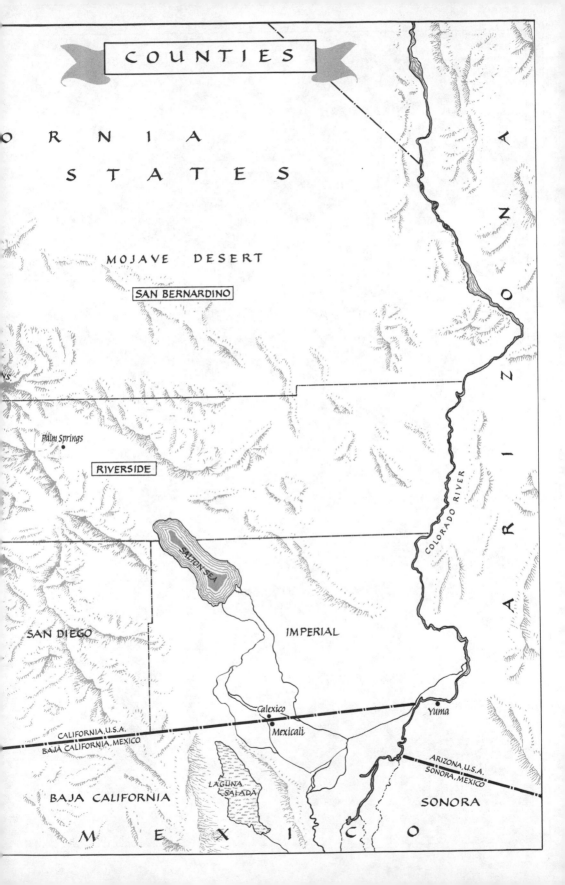

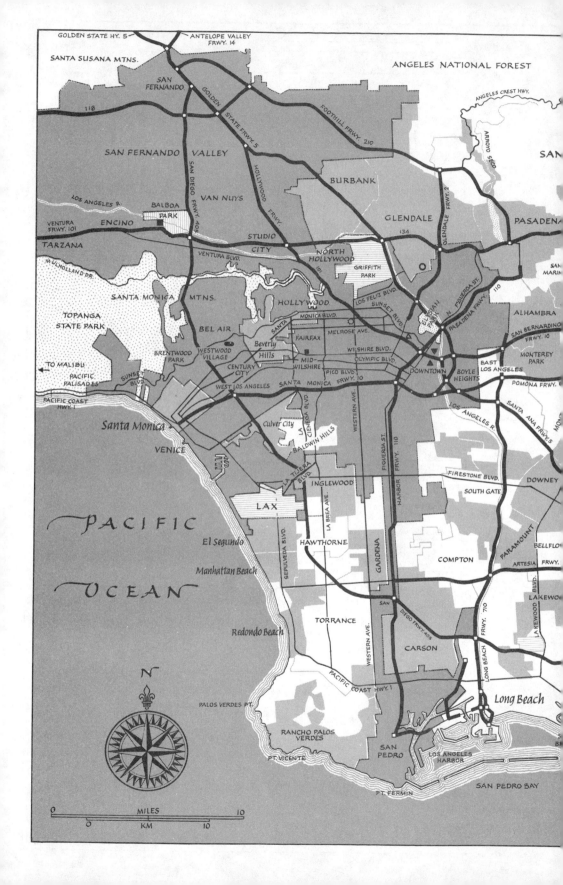

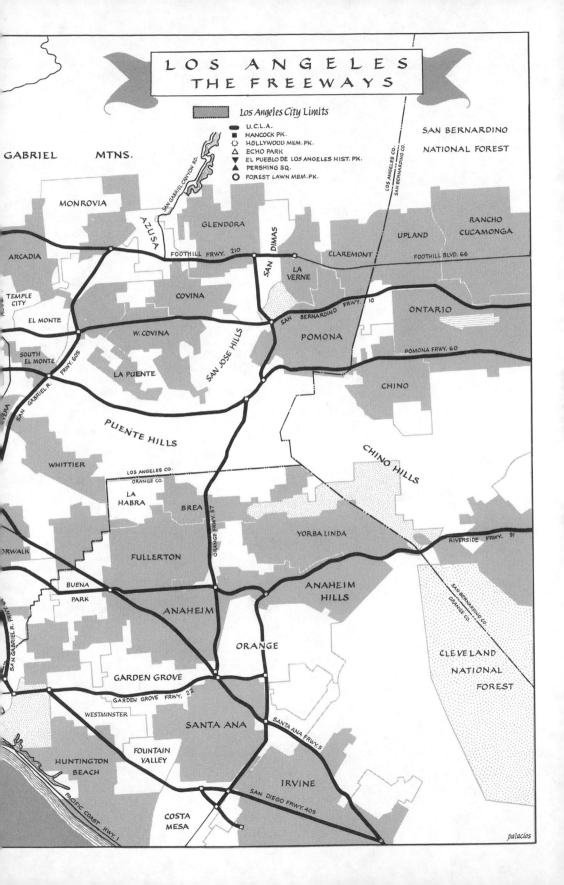

Prologue

. . . .

It is jarring to be planning a trip somewhere, to have, as the French aptly say, already departed, morally speaking, only to find that your friends all seem to believe you are going somewhere else. This is even more troubling when the two destinations in question are, in fact, one and the same. When I began to tell people in New York that I would be staying in Los Angeles for a while, and hoped to write something about the city, they seldom waited another sentence before beginning to discourse on the subject they presumed me to have taken on. Which is only to say that in the month before my departure for the West Coast, I heard more Hollywood stories and more L.A. jokes than I knew what to do with. There were not, it appeared, any other subjects of note that could possibly concern me, anyway. This consensus was not encouraging. L.A. was not just a familiar subject; it verged on being a tapped-out one, or so I was assured. Repeatedly.

Here are some of the things my friends said about the project:

"Is there really anything new to be said about Hollywood?"

"You're really going out to do a script, right?"

"Didn't John Gregory Dunne already write a book about one of the major studios? I've got a copy I could lend you if you need it."

"Don't do it. You think you're going out there to write a book about the industry, but it's money that always wins out in Los Angeles. You'll end up trying to become a screenwriter or, worse, a script doctor and never do another serious piece of work again. That's the way things go out there."

"Didn't some Englishman just write a good book about all that? I think it was called *Los Angeles Without a Road Map,* or something. I'm not quite sure if it was fiction or nonfiction, but I read a piece of it in *Granta.*

"I never figured you for a sun-worshipper."

"[Obscene joke about two starlets deleted.]"

Then the familiar jokes would kick in, those tired old chestnuts about Southern California that people on the East Coast, particularly in New York, cannot to this day quite restrain themselves from taking out for an airing from time to time. These soon began to run together in my head, like an assemblage of outtakes culled from Woody Allen's representative put-down of Los Angeles in his film *Annie Hall.* The people I knew in New York, especially, it seemed, those who had moved as adults to the city from the West Coast, seemed to draw their opinions from the same inventory of drearily reductive images that Allen relied on. Los Angeles as automotive wasteland. Los Angeles as a smog-smeared, lobotomized universe of fast food, endless car trips, and airheads of both genders and every known sexual orientation, most especially, I was told, chastity. Los Angeles, where the psychiatrists met the surfers, and where all the hairdressers who did not become producers at least *had* producers. All this was seasoned with bits of gleeful doomsaying. What did I know of the Los Angeles of Charles Manson and the Hillside Strangler? The Los Angeles of black street gangs, with their "colors" and their assault rifles? The Los Angeles of mudslides, canyon fires, and maddening Santa Ana winds? The future epicenter of that earthquake that was sure to strike California one of these days?

I mention these views because even now they continue to surprise me. It would be self-regarding to imagine that my friends were incapable of holding ill-informed opinions, but on no other subject can I recall hearing people I care for and admire advance opinions so automatically or in such intellectual lockstep. Such attitudes were beneath them, I thought, kneejerk responses rather like the support American liberals gave to the Sandinistas before the chastening wind of Mrs. Chamorro's victory. One moment, I would sit listening as friends affirmed the intractable complexities of some "situation" in the world, only at the next moment, the subject of Los Angeles unwisely having been raised, to find myself treated to views of such innocent, stereotypical rigidity that a late-night television comic would have thought long and hard before including them in his routine. The private life was complicated; New

York was complicated; German reunification was complicated; and Lord knows the Middle East was complexity itself. But it seemed that Los Angeles, a city of seven million human beings in a region twice as populous, could be ostentatiously reduced to a few pop clichés. Utter the words "Los Angeles" and usually scrupulous Jekylls would turn into jeering Hydes. It was all very puzzling.

Such derision was not based on ignorance alone. The people who were describing L.A. in this cliché-ridden way often knew the city well (some, as I say, had even grown up there), and many went often to the West Coast on business. Nor was it a simple matter of New York chauvinism, although it was hard not to feel that for quite a few well-educated New Yorkers bashing Los Angeles was not just a matter of the traditional rivalry between the two coasts (now heightened by the anxiety, increasingly prevalent in the East, that L.A. might no longer care very much about what people thought in Manhattan), but also one of the last remaining bigotries that could be maintained without guilt. There was a touch, in all this L.A.–bashing, of the bitter old joke that anti-Catholicism is the anti-Semitism of the intellectuals, or of the lamentable habit of people who would never dream of uttering the word "nigger" speaking easily of "rednecks" and "white trash."

There was something else as well. The more I listened (or, more exactly, was lectured), the more convinced I became that when people outside of Southern California spoke of L.A. they were not speaking of a real place at all. In most of the country, but particularly in New York, the name Los Angeles did not refer to a city any more than the name Hollywood referred to a neighborhood within that city. What they were talking about was a fantasy, a place that existed everywhere except in real space, and that was populated with myths rather than with citizens. Even people with fairly subtle ideas about American urban geography, people who could rattle on knowledgeably about gentrification in Cincinnati or the expansion of Chinatown in San Francisco into previously Italian North Beach, kept confusing Hollywood and Los Angeles. Perhaps it was easier that way. For while I am doubtless being severe with my friends, I do not believe that they would have spoken so reductively, in the language of a Borscht Belt shtick rather than as they customarily did, had they really been able to conceive of Los Angeles in anything other than mythic terms, and frightful ones at that.

Here are some of the jokes about Los Angeles that people told me before I left New York:

"Their idea of reading is a long personalized license plate."

"Don't forget to buy that beachfront property in Nevada while it's still affordable."

"L.A.'s only contribution to civilization is being able to make a right turn on a red light." This actually comes from *Annie Hall,* a case of life imitating kitsch, although I am fairly sure that the person who told it to me did not remember where she had heard the story.

"Just be sure to peek behind those facades every so often. Everything in L.A. is a stage set, up to and including the mountains. Those Santa Ana winds they all complain about are probably produced by a huge wind machine out at the Paramount sky lot."

"Wasn't it Los Angeles that Gertrude Stein had in mind when she made that crack about there being 'no there there'?" And I received a hurt, doubting look when I said, as repressively as I could, "No, it was Oakland."

"How are you going to know when you've gotten there, anyway? The whole place is just a hundred suburbs masquerading as a city."

And I kept thinking that these were very old jokes, the products of a world that no longer existed. To begin with, they only made sense if there continued to be some kind of dialectical relationship between New York and Los Angeles. After all, there is nothing particularly funny about making fun of the antithesis, that is, of L.A., unless the thesis, New York, still burns brightly as an ideal of city life. But New York, as all of us who live there know—however quiet we keep the news—is a specter of what it once was, and grows dirtier, more desperate, and more expensive with every passing year. It hardly exemplifies anything these days, except perhaps the bleaker assertions of Thomas Hobbes.

In Dashiell Hammett's *The Thin Man,* Nora Charles says to Nick, "Those were the good old days," and Nick replies (it is the 1930s), "No, these are the good old days." And now they were gone in Manhattan, well and truly gone. Indeed, it was probably as much a psychoanalytic question as anything else, a textbook case of repression, why it never seemed to occur to my friends that a city in which it was impossible to walk three blocks without encountering a homeless person, in which racial bitterness had deepened to a point almost beyond even the imagination of healing, and in which people's lives were regulated not so much by the dictates of their schedules as by a more intrusive calendar of water-main breaks, subway floodings, and building collapses was not a place whose residents had any business making fun of other cities' shortcomings, much less, however implicitly, of appointing themselves the high arbiters of the cosmopolitan.

But what group of people who have been winners once have not confused their success with the materialization of some deeper entitlement? Even today, some thirty-five years after they had to give most of it up, many people in England have still not taken in the fact that they live empireless and in Europe; in a Europe, moreover, whose engine is united Germany. To hear New Yorkers talk, one might think that they still live in the city of Dorothy Parker, Edmund Wilson, the Jewish intelligentsia of the forties and fifties, and the international art world. To point out that although New York was indeed the capital of the international avant-garde for most of the second half of the twentieth century —which, in any case, wasn't really so very long, something that was becoming clearer as the millennium loomed—and of finance capitalism for a good deal longer, there was nothing inevitable about this, is to be met with blank stares, but it's true. The artists and intellectuals that made the postwar city came because of Hitler (they might well have remained in Paris and Berlin otherwise) and stayed on because of money and habit. As for Wall Street's preeminence, that had as much to do with America's domination of the postwar world as it did with the particular adeptness of the great New York banking and brokerage houses. In any case, the world occupies its capital cities as a renter rather than an owner, and even when it buys it is usually prepared to sell and move on, even if that means taking a loss.

The Sunbelt had leached New York of much of its money; crime had made the experience of daily life, even for its most pampered residents, an anxious, vigilant affair; and high rents had made it impossible for many of the aspiring painters, actors, dancers, and writers to live any place decent, and, if they came at all, to remain unless they were immediately successful. Perhaps it was all this bad news that was making New Yorkers so provincial. What had become difficult to imagine in New York was not so much that the world was changing, but that outside the city change actually could be for the better.

Either way, the changes were coming. That summer I left for Los Angeles, the newspapers were filled with news of Gorbachev. By the time I returned, the Communist world had fallen apart, and Germany was one nation. "It will be so nice," remarked a cynical Italian friend, "to live in New York now that it has become such a backwater." And an English poet, commenting on the decision of a mutual friend to become the American correspondent of a British Sunday paper, said with a sigh, as a parent might contemplate the latest injury of an accident-prone child, "I would have thought Berlin would be a more interesting assignment just now." The importance of New York was anything but a question of justice. Except, that is, in the perverse sense of that marvelous *New Yorker* cartoon of a few years back, in which a small fish is being consumed by a medium-sized fish, which, in turn, is being eaten by a very large fish. The small fish is thinking "There is no justice in the world"; the medium-sized fish is thinking "There is some justice in the world"; while the very large fish thinks "The world is just."

Even putting aside the fact that people always have a hard time getting used to unfamiliar arrangements, and factoring out, as well, the Augean stables' worth of hype that had always made any rational consideration of the relative positions of New York and L.A. such an unalloyed nightmare, it seemed plain that New York was about to change sizes. The city that H. G. Wells had described (his travel book about America, written in 1906, is an object lesson in how romanticism clouds thought) as "lucid, an image of unclouded intelligence," and that even Gertrude Atherton, who did so much to pioneer a distinctly "Californian" sensibility in the 1880s and 1890s, conceived of as "the concentrated essence, the pinnacle of American civilization and achievement," was unlikely, a hundred years later, to again astonish the world. Perhaps it would adjust to its diminished role—as Paris had done successfully, and London halfheartedly—or perhaps it would not. What seemed sure was that, as for an actress after forty, hereafter only certain roles would be available.

The great lesson of New York's decline was that the curtain comes down just as surely on historical periods as it does on individual lives. In theory, of course, it should not be surprising that the cultural and financial division of the world that was the direct result of the Second World War is no more permanent than the political arrangements of post-1945 Europe, but it is, just the same. Twenty-five years ago, John Updike quipped that the problem with New Yorkers was that they believed that anyone who lived anywhere else "was, somehow, kidding," but in 1990 it was surely New Yorkers who were in fact deluding themselves.

And what could be said about New York seemed to me to apply also to America as a whole. In retrospect, Reaganism had been less a period in which the United States reassumed the mantle of empire than one in which new empires—Japanese finance, the European Community— began to take their proper role in the world. How fitting that the last years before the end of the Cold War, that is, the last period of the frozen bipolarity of the American-Soviet rivalry, should have been presided over by a man who had starred in Hollywood movies about the Second World War, and who could still sway a crowd by re-creating some of his better roles.

To be sure, it was impossible to predict that Communism would collapse so swiftly, or that the economic profligacy known as Reaganomics would transform the United States from the world's principal creditor to its largest debtor. What was clear, though, long before the events of 1989 swept the East bloc away, was that the era of American hegemony was ending. And when the Soviet empire did collapse, Americans were dismayed to discover that what was, by any definition, a great victory had left them with little money and less confidence. They could go on affirming, as Ronald Reagan had done in the 1980s, that it was morning in America, or talk themselves into the idea that the military victory over Iraq really signified something lasting. But after the momentary euphoria, these mantras of superiority persuaded few people inside the fifty states and almost no one outside them.

Mostly, people were talking about American decline. If they were reactionaries, they tended to quote from Allan Bloom's *The Closing of the American Mind.* If they were moderates, they usually preferred Paul Kennedy's *The Rise and Fall of the Great Powers.* (Only radicals, for whom, self-evidently, the decline of the United States was less disturbing news, had no single "pillow book.") Administration officials, and their supine handmaidens on Capitol Hill, might continue to talk about military power, conjuring up narcoterrorism and Middle Eastern warlords as the new threats to American security, but, viscerally at least, most people understood that the real danger was economic. It was not expeditionary forces or Stealth aircraft that represented success but rather the German and Japanese cars one saw in the automobile showrooms, and the appliances that all seemed to be manufactured in East Asia. It was as if half a lifetime of discourse, assumptions, and beliefs had been knocked into a cocked hat. Even Reaganism had been a last fling, a binge paid for on credit, one of whose principal beneficiaries, oddly enough, had been New York, which, during the 1980s, enjoyed a fantastic boom. By 1990, however, that was all over. Drexel Burnham Lambert had folded, and the city itself was facing bankruptcy.

It was because I felt that the whole world was changing faster than I could possibly understand, that we had crossed not just into a new historical moment but into an entirely new epoch, that I kept looking for a vantage point from which I might see things more clearly. For a time, I occupied myself sedulously clipping every newspaper story I could find about these new circumstances. The one about the Big Eight accounting firm that was now having all its back office work done in Manila. The ones about the new assembly plants that were springing up in the Caribbean and in the so-called Maquiladora zones along the U.S.– Mexican border. The one about how baseballs were all manufactured in Costa Rica these days, and the one about the new collaboration that had been hammered out between Mitsubishi and Daimler-Benz at a secret meeting in a hotel in Singapore.

I clipped stories about fax machines, home work stations, and all the other technological innovations that were so radically transforming the whole idea of place. I clipped all the stories about the movements of capital that were just as radically altering the idea of the nation-state. The only part of the daily newspaper that made any sense at all was the business pages. There was no talk of flag there. I read about companies moving not just "offshore," a term of art meaning where labor was cheap and labor unions impotent, but to Europe or Asia. "Europe right now," said an official of Hewlett-Packard, as he announced the move of the company's personal computer group from Sunnyvale, California, to Grenoble, France, "is a little more attractive because of the investments pouring in." Here was the denationalization of the world treated as a fait accompli, a context in which one had to follow the Tokyo and Frankfurt stock exchanges as diligently as the Dow-Jones average. Meanwhile, the news pages themselves made less and less sense. The disastrous and the picturesque might still make the most eye-catching stories but, apart from exacerbating one's own sense of personal insecurity, they told one next to nothing about these great new times.

Just what was a nation in this age of a fully mobile, denationalized international market? Just what was a nation when vast numbers of immigrants were on the move, making every society in the developed world what the social workers liked to call, with their usual anodyne imprecision, multicultural? And what did it mean to be an American, when it was obvious to anyone with eyes to see that the new immigrants were not being assimilated as they had been during the last great wave of immigration to the United States at the turn of the century? Nothing was melting, except, conceivably, the public school system under the heat of the demands being placed upon it. What was it to be an American in the age of the yen, the deutsche mark, the Swiss franc, and, soon, the hard ECU? Talk about the center not holding. . . . After all, nobody got up one balmy afternoon on the Capitoline Hill sometime in the fifth century and said that the Roman empire was over and the Dark Ages had begun. Had something equally important taken place without any-one quite having realized it? More and more, the answer seemed to be yes.

I walked through the streets of New York, and of half a dozen other American cities as well, and the colors of the skin of the people I passed were ones that had not been present in the America of my childhood. I saw racial types and heard languages that had never before been present on the American continent. And yet most people I met seemed to take it for granted that every busboy in New York was Chinese, and that all the official signs were now written in Spanish as well as in English. Talk about the victory of the private life. . . . It was not that I expected to hear that these changes represented something awful, but I did expect them to be noticed. Could anyone seriously imagine that changes of this magnitude would leave the United States as it had been before?

And yet everyone I knew was taking the transformation of their own country in stride. To be sure, the last twenty years had so seriously compromised the idea of public community that perhaps this wasn't as surprising as I thought. The draft had been abolished (would that go down as the real accomplishment of my generation of anti–Vietnam War activists?), and my friends had long ago abandoned the public schools. These new people could not afford the places where we all ate, and danced, and exercised. So in some ghastly sense, they were both ubiquitous and invisible at the same time. You didn't have to notice them unless you wanted to. Often, I would sit in a restaurant and be literally unable to follow the conversation going on around me, so mesmerized was I by the Laotian busboy, or the Peruvian parking lot attendant, or the Haitian dishwasher—our new fellow countrymen. Who are they? I thought. Who are we? I thought.

So I did not know anymore what a nation was, or a family, or a boundary, or a decent life. The future had come to seem as odd and incomprehensible as those stars that frightened Pascal, as vast and as cold. As 1988 became 1989, and then as 1990 made of the millennium a palpable, disturbing certainty, I felt as though I was losing my grasp on what I knew and yet was unable to learn this new idiom the future was imposing. One could hide from all of this, travel, whether externally, through journalism or holidays, or internally, through drugs, alcohol, or affairs of the heart, but in the end there was no getting away.

I had little hope that there was an answer waiting out there on the West Coast that I could capture and bring home with me. Still, I felt that after so many false starts it was at last time to pay some close attention to the tragedy at hand—that tragedy called time, that tragedy called history. There was nothing further to keep me in New York: America might or might not be in decline, but New York's decay, however obvious, was, equally obviously, a special case. Above all, I wanted badly to find out whether this overwhelming sense I had of things becoming *different,* both in the country and in the world at large, would bear the test of a less abraded proving ground. And so I fixed on Los Angeles, looking to California as Americans have done so often in their dreams, as the place where the American future might possibly be working itself out, and made my plans for departure.

It seemed like a perfect time to arrive. Los Angeles had always been a place where expansive rhetoric about the future was a commonplace of civic life, but even by that standard the current mood was even more unconscionably upbeat than usual. A city-sponsored partnership, the L.A. 2000 Committee, had just issued its final report, where it was baldly asserted that "just as New York, London and Paris stood as symbols of past centuries, Los Angeles will be THE city of the 21st century." It would have required principles of iron to resist that capitalized "the." I felt as though I had found America again, or, rather, what Europeans, in particular, had always imagined America to be: vulgar, naive, energetic, and persuaded of its own special mission. I did not doubt—my befuddlement had not made me that credulous—that the reality would turn out to be quite different, but what was abundantly clear was that, in Southern California, anyway, American capitalism was still full of juice, and in no way inclined to hide its light under a bushel just to indulge those tapped-out notions of decorum that the northeastern establishment, both financial and cultural, persisted in holding on to, a shredded spar at a shipwreck.

When I finally left New York, I was as apprehensive about finding a legible American future in Los Angeles as I was about not finding one there. LAX, the Los Angeles International Airport, was not an auspicious start, and had more the quality of a showcase in an underdeveloped country than of American exceptionalism. An enormous portrait of the sitting mayor, Tom Bradley (the international wing of LAX, I later discovered, is actually named after him), greeted the arriving passenger, and, beneath this garish idol, a chiseled phrase welcomed visitors to Los Angeles, "home of the 23rd Olympiad," an event by that time some five years in the past. In the baggage claim area, there were the same bilingual signs one saw in New York, and the sounds not only of Spanish, but of Chinese and Persian as well. After a while, during the interminable wait for the luggage to arrive, I felt as if all languages, the ones I spoke and the ones I could not make out a word of, had fused into an undecipherable mass. Not only couldn't I understand, I couldn't think.

But then the bags came, and I walked out of the claim area into a perfect July day, clear and warm, with a bright, consoling sun. It had been 104 degrees in New York earlier that morning, and suddenly I remembered the old joke that if the United States had been settled from west to east, then the Northeast would now be a game park. Then a gray BMW glided toward the curb, and my old friend Allegra got out. Gorgeous Allegra, pausing to adjust her sunglasses and stare, irony and affection playing across her features, over the sunroof at me. "Welcome to L.A.," she said. The old stereotypes are always best, I think, at least when you first arrive.

I We have already done so much that people call impossible. However, if the bumblebee knew the theory of aerodynamics, he would not be able to fly. But the bumblebee, being unaware of scientific truths, goes ahead and flies anyway. If it is possible, we will do it here.

—Tom Bradley, Mayor of Los Angeles

. . . .

1. The Last American Dream Worth Having

· ·

It had been more than twenty-five years since I had last spent more than a few consecutive weeks in Southern California. For me, it was far more of an antiworld, an imaginary alternative not only to New York but to Europe, than a real place, although I had known it well as a child. Then, Los Angeles had been the lesser pole of attraction in the bicoastal custody settlement that had followed my parents' bitter divorce in 1958. I would spend the school years with my mother in Manhattan and the summers (this arrangement was later truncated to parts of the summers) with my father in California. I don't remember many incidents from that time and, I suspect, never wanted to. Indeed, one of the most distinct memories I retain from my childhood is my conscious effort, with each birthday, to forget as much of what had happened the year before as I could. This only changed in my early teens, when the prospect of a parole into adulthood (or out of puberty, anyway) finally seemed imminent. The past had swallowed up California with the rest of my childhood. Or so I thought.

But no sooner had I returned for an indefinite stay than the light, and the air, and the smells began to jog my memory. I began to rediscover Los Angeles as Allegra and I drove around just as surely as, by writing, a writer discovers a subject. On a quiet street in Westwood, near the UCLA campus, I asked Allegra to stop, having realized with a start that I had spent all of August in 1961 in the house on the corner. Later, I was convinced that I had made the whole thing up, but, perhaps surprisingly, I found that I had been right.

More than anything, I began to remember how easy life had seemed in Southern California in that distant country called the early sixties. I had always thought that this sense of material comfort that backlights all my childhood memories of Los Angeles had more to do with the fact that, at the time, my father's situation on the West Coast was infinitely more comfortable than my mother's back in New York. Now I was less certain. To be sure, middle-aged Californians today too easily offer up their doubtless idealized memories of the fifties and sixties as counterpoints to a rougher present, but this is by no means the whole story. That suburban cornucopia existed, all right, and those who contemplate its existence in mocking disbelief don't know what they are talking about.

That was the moment when, for the first time, masses of Americans—not all, to be sure, but not few either—began to live a kind of life that only the rich had tasted before. It is venal snobbery to pretend otherwise, rather like the Colorado joke that defines an environmentalist as someone who built *his* A-frame in the woods ten years ago. Wherever they sprouted, from Long Island to San Diego County, those suburbs gave people better lives, whatever the price exacted in conformity. In California, this suburban vision came with the additional pleasures of fruit trees, rosebushes, eucalyptus trees, and four kinds of palms. Should people really have minded that much of this flora was exogenous to the region? Most of us were newcomers as well; newcomers dreaming of ease and things, which is not the worst definition of an American, nor as reprehensible as the critical thinkers, themselves richly endowed with possessions and leisure, believe.

Twenty-five years later, I found it as strong as ever west of the San Bernardino Mountains, and south of the Tehachapis, maybe stronger, that golden dream of Southern California. It was hard not to feel as if I were simply taking up where I had left off, back there in the strong, enveloping sunlight of childhood. Allegra drove, drove in that particularly western way where the drive itself is as compelling a social occasion, and as welcome a social context, as the destination toward which we were making our leisurely way. There was no sense of the ride being an interruption, as there commonly is even in cities like Atlanta or Miami, cities where people are every bit as dependent upon their cars as they are in greater Los Angeles. Rather, the trip itself seemed as convivial a way of meeting and talking as half an hour in a bar or café.

Allegra drove. Past gleaming new buildings that now surrounded the airport like canyon walls. Past strip malls, gas stations, and convenience stores. Past supermarkets the size of football fields that seemed to punctuate the long boulevards at fifteen-block intervals. After a while, the Northeast started to feel every bit as cramped and mean in my memory as Californians had always said it was. I suddenly remembered one of my playmates in Westwood asking incredulously, as Labor Day loomed, "You mean you're going back *there*?" And as I contemplated all this apparent luxury, Allegra interrupted my reverie to observe that we were skirting a fairly tough neighborhood and that I should see a lot of gang graffiti on the walls of the housing courts along La Tijera Boulevard.

"There's gang stuff all over the place here," she said, and, soon after, we turned sharply. A few minutes later, we had left the houses behind and were crossing along the edge of the old SoCal oil patch, with its nodding pumps moving as comically, and, it appeared, as gainfully, as Disney characters. I would discover that every Angeleno had a slightly different route for getting from LAX to the city, that none involved the freeway, which was judged to be too crowded and too unpredictable.

The green oil derricks, bobbing up and down like toy dinosaurs, in turn gave way to residential boulevards. There were the same run-down housing courts that had been omnipresent near the airport, but, interspersed among them, one began to see fine examples of Spanish and ranch-style houses that are almost the emblem of middle-class L.A. as people live it, rather than as it is depicted on television—not opulence, but genuine comfort. We were in a middle-class black neighborhood called Baldwin Hills. By now, the downtown, with its skyscrapers and its giant construction cranes, loomed on the horizon. Before long, we were turning off La Brea Avenue onto a small street, and moments later Allegra pulled into her own driveway. The air smelled of roses and barbecue smoke. The silence was all but absolute. "We're about a block and a half south of Wilshire Boulevard," Allegra said, and I read into our proximity to this major commercial street far more significance than she possibly could have intended.

During those first few days in Los Angeles, I fell in love with the city all over again. It is, in any case, a famously pleasant place to visit. Its horizontality, and the absence of any efficient and fast system of public transportation, means that unless one is poor or chooses to go to those parts of the city where the poor live, it is easy to forget that anyone in L.A. isn't middle-class. In most American cities, the homeless and the dangerous impinge on the daily experience of the prosperous and the striving. In L.A., apart from the downtown where few middle-class people live, and the beaches of Venice and Santa Monica, where thousands of homeless people make their lives, they do not. One could argue about the real nature of racial segregation in the city, but there was no question that the class segregation was well-nigh absolute.

Allegra lived in the mid-Wilshire district, an area of L.A. that, while unquestionably middle-class, was by no means one of the city's more sought-after addresses. Multiracial—the park at the end of the street was constantly filled with Mexican children celebrating *piñata* parties, and Asian teenagers trying to get some privacy from their families—the neighborhood was too far east to be attractive to most white, middle-class Angelenos, or "people from the Westside," as they were euphemistically known in L.A., not least to themselves. And yet, mid-Wilshire was so much more comfortable than any equivalent area in New York, say, or Chicago that it was often difficult to understand why these regions hadn't in fact become game parks, whatever the original direction of European settlement in North America. I soon grew accustomed to waking up to the sounds of birds, and falling asleep in silence—without the familiar music of breaking bottles, the scream of ambulances and police vehicles, or some madman's curses echoing up into my bedroom from the street below. I should add that my apartment was in a part of New York that was far grander than where Allegra lived in L.A.

There were few surprises (except, perhaps, how familiar everything soon came to seem) but many pleasures. The sight of fresh California produce, so much . . . well, bigger than the fruits and vegetables one saw in the East. The cleanliness of the streets. No matter how often I reminded myself that the sidewalks were clean mostly because the sidewalks were empty, I could not get over my relief to be in a city where the streets did not look like souks or obstacle courses. And along these streets were not just the fast-food joints like Sky's and Bob's Big Boy that everyone associates with Los Angeles, but restaurants that were every bit the equal of New York's, and better still of San Francisco's, where American cooking amounted to little more than a fair copy of Europe or a pastiche of some synthetic cuisine that never existed in any real country, all virgin olive oil, kiwi garnishes, and implausible combinations. For me, only the sexual seemed less interesting in Los Angeles than I had anticipated, but then wet dreams about Southern California have become such a national cliché that I should perhaps attribute my reaction to pure snobbish contrariness.

What seemed most important was that L.A.'s pleasures and ambitions still made sense. Certainly, little else did in an America that had become so nearly illegible to itself, so riven now by faction and special interests as to be almost ungovernable, and scared witless by Japanese enterprise. In the rest of the country, people were talking despairingly about how to stave off inevitable decline, but in L.A. they were still talking about becoming number one: the number-one city in America, the number-one economy in the nation, the new center of the developed world. Americans always used to talk that way, but had now grown accustomed to hearing this kind of triumphalist chitchat from the Japanese—with whom, it was said, we had traded places. But in Los Angeles, local boosterism was alive and well, emanating not only from the usual suspects at the Chamber of Commerce, the Pacific Stock Exchange, or the senior management of the *Los Angeles Times,* but from people like Allegra's friends, who were mostly ex-radical types still uneasily reconciling themselves to jobs in public-interest law, journalism, or government.

"Look," said Peter, a political consultant for left-wing Democratic candidates, who had also worked briefly at City Hall, "the economy of Los Angeles is now so diversified that even the severest of recessions would not do it much lasting harm. If California were an independent country, it would have either the seventh- or the tenth-largest GNP in the world, depending on which set of statistics you believe. We've got everything here: agriculture, aerospace, the entertainment industry. We've even got oil, although I hardly recommend to my candidates that they stress that side of things for all the obvious reasons. We've got cheap labor from the other side of the Mexican border, and cheap capital from the other side of the Pacific. And we don't have any hangups about Europe. Business looks to the Pacific first here. They know that's where the real growth is going to be in the twenty-first century. With Europe uniting, they'll have everything they need, anyway, except raw materials, whereas Asia . . ." His voice trailed off. "Did you know there are a hundred million middle-class people in India?" he asked me.

Peter was quick to add that he was not sure he saw all of this as a good thing. The New Left was a banked fire within him, but its embers still smoldered on. Months later, he would tell me that he sometimes daydreamed, during his morning commute to his office, of a cataclysmic stock-market crash that would sweep everything away once and for all. "But you know," he said sadly, "when we had the one in 1987 it barely caused a ripple out here. Sure, it eventually led to Drexel Burnham collapsing—you can see their empty building off Wilshire in Beverly Hills—but L.A.'s as solid as ever. The junk-bond market can collapse; it doesn't need the junk-bond market. The Cold War can end; it doesn't need the Cold War. The mix is just too damn competitive."

It was a religion. There was a month when I could not go anywhere in Los Angeles without meeting someone who might as well have been on the city payroll, so enthusiastic and uncompromising was the pitch.

There was Darci, a legal secretary who, on the way to shopping expedi-
tions to the Irvine Ranch, an upscale supermarket on the edge of West
Hollywood, used to give me long and loving lectures on the superiority
of California produce. There was Dan, who knew everything there was
to know about the German refugee community that had settled in Los
Angeles in the late thirties, and who took me on long drives that started
in Pacific Palisades, the neighborhood where Thomas Mann had lived,
passed through Westwood, where so many had found work on the UCLA
faculty, and ended at the old studio lots—those that were still standing,
anyway—where Fritz Lang and Douglas Sirk had made their American
pictures and the former members of the Berlin Philharmonic had recorded background music before rushing off in the evenings to play
Schoenberg at the Wilshire Ebell Theater. I heard people praise the
beach, the business acumen, and the ethnic mix. I heard people praise
the weather and dismiss the smog. They could not have been more
different from one another. What they had in common was a passion for
Los Angeles and a generous pleasure in showing it off.

Curiously, it was as I drove around the city with this platoon of Virgils
that I first came up against another reality of life in Los Angeles, one
markedly at odds with the triumphalism my new acquaintances all
shared. The freeway system had always been the paradigmatic symbol
of the good life L.A. promised. Now it was paralyzed with traffic; constantly, it seemed, not just during the morning and evening rush hours.
I soon noticed that everyone seemed to avoid these celebrated arteries
whenever they could, opting instead for what looked like the positively
pre-Californian solution of the surface streets.

As far as I could see, the region that had contributed the expression
"life in the fast lane" to the American language was reduced to exploring
the more extravagant connotations of the word "gridlock." Indeed,
Darci later told me, with a certain perverse pride I thought, that when
Steve Sax, the long-time Los Angeles Dodgers second baseman, was
traded to the New York Yankees, East Coast reporters at his first press
conference had asked whether he would miss Southern California.
"Sure," he replied easily, "but I won't miss the traffic jams." Conscious
of the New York area's overburdened highways, the reporters all
laughed. "No, really," Sax said seriously, "you people back east don't
know anything about real traffic."

The brute volume of cars on the road had steadily extended the
amount of time it took to get from one part of Los Angeles to another.
Again and again, as we sat stalled in traffic, my companions would seem
as mystified as they were frustrated. Angelenos have always had the
unsettling tendency to conflate time and space when they talk about

travel, as often as not measuring distances by describing how long it took them to drive from point A to point B. Now all their calculations were out of whack. In the 1970s, most agreed, the phrase "It's about twenty minutes" had accurately enough described most ordinary trips. But now, even adding ten minutes to the total didn't guarantee anything. The new estimate was frankly ironic: you got there when you got there, those were the new rules of the road in Los Angeles. Certainly, no one I drove with agreed with the authors of *The City Observed,* the best architectural guide to L.A., when they wrote that "for many of us the freeways are Southern California's grandest public artworks," or, if they did, they preferred to contemplate these masterpieces from the safety of the city's boulevards and streets.

"I think we'll just go surface tonight," my Los Angeles friends would tell me again and again. And although they invariably spoke in tones of edgy wonder, and tended to present the decision, each time they made it, as an exceptional one, it was clear that the freeways had grown so impacted that what had once been the eccentric, much-derided choice of that small minority of L.A.'s drivers who found the highways intimidating had become, over time, the only sane way to move around the city during larger and larger swatches of the day. In due course, we would set out along wide and relatively unimpeded streets, occasionally pausing, as we crossed an overpass or skirted a freeway interchange, to stare worriedly down at the clot of red taillights stretching back toward the line of the horizon, or at the undulating sea of white headlights that appeared to be moving, at least from a distance, with such stately decorum that they might have been a funeral cortege of epic dimensions.

Instead of saying, "Why don't we go for a drive?," a phrase that had regularly punctuated the California segments of my fractured childhood, people tended to demand querulously why there was so much traffic, as if all these new cars had descended mysteriously, a plague of Datsuns, to blight the pristine landscape of their California dream. As often as not, my companions would attempt to discern, as we sat stuck, idling in the fast lane of some freeway at some formerly uncluttered hour of the day—eleven in the morning, say, or nine-thirty at night—some anecdotal explanation for the tie-up. "It must be the night game down at the Coliseum; after all, Stanford's in town," Darci might say, whereas Dan, resolutely cultural to the last, would attribute the event to L.A.'s newfound artistic vitality. "Is there something on at the Music Center tonight?" he would ask. When all else failed, everyone fell back on the old local standby, the solemn pronouncement "There must be an accident up ahead."

But, of course, it almost always turned out that the Music Center was dark that night, and that the USC football team was playing *at* Stanford, while rarely if ever was the mysteriously heavy traffic accounted for by the deus ex machina of a smashed and twisted car and the sight of a wrecker's bright, revolving light flashing from the shoulder of the road. There were traffic tie-ups all the time for one simple reason: there were now too many cars in Los Angeles to fit on freeways that were never built to accommodate them all.

The final report of the L.A. 2000 Committee, for all its boosterism and utopian confidence in the ability of more planning to solve almost any problem, had put the matter starkly. "Even with the completion of the first phase of Metro Rail and light rail projects," the committee declared, "96 percent of us will still travel by car. At the same time, distances between home and work are increasing along with the number of drivers, which is multiplying faster than the population, with the result that the average morning rush-hour speed on the entire freeway system in the year 2000 is forecast to be 17 miles per hour, or roughly half the speed in 1980." The committee's recommendations included an enormous expansion in public transportation as well as a considerable expansion of the freeway system itself, but it was hard to see where the money was going to be found to pay for such programs in a part of the country where, as the report itself conceded before reverting to upbeat form, land was no longer either cheap or plentiful, and where the voters traditionally concerned with keeping taxes low might approve a highway bond issue but were unlikely to support a public transportation network few would ride on a bet.

Certainly, no one I talked to really seemed imaginatively prepared to give up their cars or even use them sparingly. Driving, after all, was one of the main points of living in Los Angeles, not only because it was so spread out, and had, in fact, been designed for the automobile, but also because the freeway system was just what John Gregory Dunne had called it: "More an idea than a roadway." The alternatives being proposed—carpooling, leaving one's car in some municipal lot and then continuing downtown by train—had little appeal, and the RTD, L.A.'s public bus system, took forever. "Look at Miami," more than one person told me grimly. In Miami, a Metrorail system had been constructed at great expense, garnished with public art, and opened to the residents of Dade County. They stayed away in droves, to paraphrase the old Goldwynism. Today, the pristine, empty cars of this system can be observed whirring along on their elevated tracks, while, on the congested roadways below, commuters inch their way along in brutal rush-hour traffic. And this is Miami where, it should be noted, people are much less enamored of their cars than is the norm in Los Angeles. No, a likelier outcome than the widespread use of light rail is that Angelenos will just grumble and go slowly, just as most people who live in the great cities of the Northeast have adapted to a level of filth and insecurity that they would never have imagined tolerating twenty years ago.

It was on the freeways that I first heard a note of what was instantly recognizable to me as an "eastern" sourness insinuating itself into people's everyday conversations. I heard endless, bitter wisecracks about just how life-diminishingly long it took to get anywhere at all in L.A. County, let alone its surrounding suburbs—the five-county area that advertisers and television newscasters preferred to call "the Southland."

The Harbor Freeway, people told you, was really the longest parking lot in the world. The warnings that Caltrans, the state agency that administered the freeway system, regularly posted about mudslides *actually* meant that traffic was about to speed up, not slow down. Or so people said, sighing elaborately, as if on the off-chance that their ironizing had not been broad enough. And did I know that by the time the high-speed rail link was built, the one that would get you from downtown Los Angeles to the Las Vegas strip in three and a half hours, it would easily take eight to drive from central L.A. to the farther suburbs of the San Gabriel Valley? The tone was far more Manhattan island than Manhattan Beach, California.

This view of the traffic jams as an affliction, a natural calamity like the canyon fires that regularly destroyed some of the nicest houses in the Los Angeles hills, or, among the more socially conscious, as one more symbol of the idiocy of capitalism, tended to mean that people almost never spoke of the proximate cause, housing. No one can spend very long in Los Angeles without talking more about real estate than is entirely good for the spirit. I was in town no more than half a day before receiving my first lecture on the astronomical rise in housing prices— or "values," as most people preferred to say—that had made almost every property on the Westside worth triple or quadruple what it might have fetched a decade before. But this inflation and the transportation mess were events joined at the hip.

As prices rose during the 1980s, middle- and lower-middle-class families trying to get into the housing market for the first time found themselves obliged to buy in relatively cheaper areas like San Bernardino County to the east, Ventura County to the north, and Orange County and even the northern edges of San Diego County to the south. The L.A. 2000 Committee estimated that Los Angeles County itself was steadily becoming more job rich and housing poor, with two thirds of the new jobs to be found in the city itself and in adjacent northern Orange County, and 60 percent of the new housing located elsewhere in greater

L.A. The freeway system is a sensitive register of such change, and it appeared that all these new commuters were putting pressure not just on their own areas but on the entire grid. The real reason for many of the tie-ups, it turned out, was not necessarily an event close at hand but might well be something going wrong twenty miles away. And the truth was that all one had to do was drive around L.A. for a few days to see that what the committee was predicting as one possible dire outcome had already largely occurred.

Of course, when people in Los Angeles lamented the lack of affordable housing in the city proper, they were not being entirely honest with themselves. The real estate market might have boomed (one realtor told me matter-of-factly that she doubted whether any family not comprising what she referred to as "two professionals" could afford a decent house anywhere in West L.A.), but actually there were plenty of nice houses on the market. The problem for many buyers was that they were to be found in black middle-class neighborhoods like Baldwin Hills. Some whites, of course, would never even have considered living in a black neighborhood, whether out of damnable racism or legitimate fear for their own, and, more important, their children's safety, it is not for me to say. But what was striking was the large numbers of whites I met who could bemoan their inability to find an affordable place to live within fifty miles of their offices without ever acknowledging the existence of a Baldwin Hills—a case, it seemed, not simply of invisible men but of invisible neighborhoods as well.

Black people noticed, to be sure, but their voices counted for no more that summer I arrived in Los Angeles than they did in the rest of the United States that year. When white people thought about blacks at all, they conjured up crack addicts, unwed mothers, and teenage "gang-bangers." Middle-class blacks were barely acknowledged, except, occasionally, as a group whose existence disproved the claims of black militancy. This was true in L.A. even though the city had been governed by a black mayor for the previous seventeen years. I suspect I would have been just as oblivious had not a black reporter at the *Los Angeles Times* mentioned Baldwin Hills and the commuters to me. What had started as a helpful tip was soon revealed as a source of deep, if restrained, anger. "I'd like my white friends to say the name once in a while, at least, even if they don't want to live there," she said, her voice rising. Her friend interrupted: "You know, sometimes I think the only reason most white folks who live in L.A. have heard of Baldwin Hills is because they can't avoid all the signs when they drive surface out to the airport."

For most white people I came to know in Los Angeles, even those who were most sympathetic to black concerns, a commute was a commute and the black grievance was the black grievance, a question of apples and oranges. Most younger suburbanites, who had never even lived on the Westside, and now did not really hope to, barely considered the city of Los Angeles at all, except as a place to work or, if one dared brave the traffic, to come to for dinner, a sporting event, or a concert downtown. And since downtown Los Angeles, no matter how much it had been built up over the past decade and a half, was still a pretty uninteresting place after dark, most people stayed close to home, which in reality meant farther and farther away from the city.

Who could blame them? Indeed, what was remarkable was not the desire to go home and stay in the suburbs at the end of a long day, but the quirky pride that so many seemed to take in the amount of driving they did. Like Wall Street lawyers, who, during the heyday of the mergers-and-acquisitions fever of the 1980s, liked to boast about the hours they put in behind their desks, the new breed of L.A. commuter reveled in the numbers they were piling up on their odometers. "It can take me up to three hours to get downtown from my house in Irvine," the journalist Robert Scheer told me, almost gleefully, then added, "It's okay; I get a lot of thinking done in the car, and, of course, I have a phone now."

It was an old Los Angeles conceit, this belief in the automobile as haven in a heartless world and of the freeway as the untrammeled frontier. What was new was that, try as optimists like Scheer might do to transform its meaning, this new congestion was steadily pecking away at both constituent parts of the Los Angeles mystique: velocity and ease. After all, it was one thing to spend six and a half hours in a car cruising down the open road, but three hours plus to Orange County each way? Bumper to bumper? That, even for a Californian, is an acquired taste, to say the least.

In the 1960s, Reyner Banham, whose book *Los Angeles: The Architecture of Four Ecologies* remains the most sinuous and eloquent appreciation of the city, had described the freeways as "the place where [Angelenos] spend the two calmest and most rewarding hours of their daily lives." An enthusiastic proponent of Los Angeles, whose fundamental characteristic, for him, as for so many other devotees of the city, was the psychic freedom that its vaunted mobility and vast spaces provided, Banham was on to something essential about the spirit of L.A. From 1934, when the Arroyo Seco Freeway was built, connecting the city of Pasadena with downtown L.A., through the early 1960s, when Governor Edmund G. "Pat" Brown presided over the completion of the greatest highway network since the German autobahns of the 1930s, the free-

ways had been the emotional center of the city, far more defining of its
character than its central business district. Now, what Banham had celebrated, the Los Angeles "all of whose parts are equal and equally accessible from all other parts at once," was changing fast. The long-neglected
downtown was sprouting skyscrapers as fast as the crews could put
them up, while the freeways themselves were not only gradually becoming impassable but were even beginning to show their age.

They were not even that peaceful anymore. It was not just the freeway shootings, although those months in 1988 when a few of the city's
more excitable motorists began to take potshots at strangers whose
understanding of the rules of the road differed from their own marked a
Rubicon of sorts. "It was funny not to feel safe in your car," Darci
recalled. Even Banham himself had remarked presciently that the act of
coming off the freeway would be analogous, in older, more pedestrian-
friendly cities, to coming inside from outdoors. The mile or two that
might remain of the journey counted, he wrote, "as no more than the
front drive of the house." Banham's error lay only in positing an America
fundamentally at peace with itself. What the freeway shootings did was
to remind anyone who had not yet heard the news that in America
nowadays the urban outdoors can be lethal.

The people who live in the desperate black slums of Compton and
South Central Los Angeles did not, of course, need these lurid accounts
of gunfire at the interchanges to bring home to them just how unsafe
life had become. In their neighborhoods, so-called drive-by shootings
(in a city as spread out as L.A., even the muggers and hitmen had to
work from their cars) had become nightly occurrences, as gang members, aboard what were, in effect, mobile gun platforms, roamed the
graffitied streets and the run-down housing courts. The fire from their
assault rifles punctuated the balmy Southern California evenings so regularly that when I asked a group of teenaged girls in a Compton housing
court whether a night passed *without* the sounds of shots being fired,
only one girl timidly answered, "Last Thursday was quiet," and she was
hooted down by her friends. Those girls knew to venture cautiously in
what Banham, had he lived to see it, might have had some difficulty in
describing as anyone's front drive. And even the real indoors could be
dangerous. Many people I met spoke casually of intermittently sleeping
on the floors of their apartments lest they be blown away in their beds
by a stray round.

Not that this bad news from the slums had anything but the remotest
chance of sinking in. Rather like rainwater falling on drought-parched
land, or white people listening to black people's grievances, Los Angeles
appeared unable to absorb what was going on in its poorer precincts. It
was not the fault of the press coverage. The information was there, if

anybody on the Westside wanted it. Indeed, if anything, the local television stations were overly concerned with the daily body count in Watts or in the Mexican barrios of East Los Angeles, home to a million souls, with and without their documents. Moreover, the fear of the South Central gangs and the fear of drugs were constantly being stirred up by Los Angeles officials, notably by the current chief of police, Daryl Gates, and his predecessor, Ed Davis. Telegenic antigang strikes like Operation Hammer were played up in the evening newscasts whenever they were underway. There was even the ludicrous spectacle of Nancy Reagan, who, shortly after the Reagans returned home to California, donned a flak jacket and watched, her face set in its customary amiable rictus, as an LAPD SWAT team battered down the front door of a so-called crack house. She said nothing, not even the phrase "Just say no" that had been her husband's administration's main contribution to the drug war, but stood, a diminutive figure surrounded by photographers, as helicopters whirled overhead and beefy cops brought the dealers and the addicts, one by one, toward the waiting prison vans.

"This is Vietnam here," the head of the Los Angeles District Attorney's Hardcore Drug Unit told the *Los Angeles Times*. But if this added to the psychological unease of people in West L.A.—and one's impression was that it did, sometimes radically—it affected their daily lives only glancingly. Whatever the night sounds like in South Central, or among the homeless who congregate on Fifth Street downtown, the streets are quiet in Santa Monica, and the only things that smell smell nice, like the ocean and the eucalyptus trees. On more occasions than I like to remember, I would sit in some Westside living room, surrounded by lovely objects and by people with soft voices, and watch video clips of the day's mayhem in Compton or Boyle Heights. Though I would will myself to believe in the reality of these images, I often found myself only half doing so. The comfort around me was too strong, the horrors on the screen too removed, too weightless. They might as well have been taking place on the moon.

Through the good offices of a friend who worked at the paper, I began to use the *Los Angeles Times* building on Spring and First streets as a base. Every morning, we would drive downtown—surface, naturally—first passing the beautiful trees and even more imposing mansions of Hancock Park before crossing into Korean and finally poor Salvadoran immigrant neighborhoods. This horizontal world of mini-malls, dilapidated houses, and small apartment buildings would suddenly give way to the gleaming verticality of downtown L.A. Once inside the *Times* building, my friend would hurry off to his morning meeting, while I would repair to a seldom-used office in the City-County department.

As in most modern offices, there were few private spaces at the *Times.* Only senior staff worked in rooms with doors and walls that extended to the ceiling. Everyone else worked in modules, where there was no privacy. My office, which was the domain of two reporters at the paper who were not only senior enough to command a door but senior enough to be almost always on the road on assignment, was mainly a refuge for die-hard smokers (smoking was banned in the building, although there was a little rooftop enclosure where the weak-willed could repair for a cigarette). Otherwise, I was alone, free to read clips, make calls, or leave and stroll through the busy workspaces like a flaneur along a great boulevard. The *Los Angeles Times*'s founder, Harrison Gray Otis, had said, "Los Angeles wants no dudes, loafers, and paupers; people who have no means and trust to luck." He had given, I thought, as I surveyed the buoyant activity around me, a perfect definition of a writer.

The paper was doing its best to report what was actually going on in the city. What was then called the City-County bureau at the *Times* was no more prized an assignment than it would have been at any other newspaper with national pretensions, but it was still more than possible —what great novels were contained in every section of each day's newspaper—to get a fairly accurate sense of what was going on. Still, though its talented bureau chief, Bill Boyarsky, might delve into the real workings of L.A. city government, and a great reporter like Robert Scheer might write eloquently about the Jews of L.A. or the new multiracial realities of formerly lily-white Orange County, the general mood in Los Angeles was more accurately reflected by the *Times*'s style section, or its real estate pages, which every week featured the house a local celebrity had bought or renovated. Even more important was the decision to feature different local news in separate editions of the paper. The *Times* was divided into "zones," which meant that people on the Westside never even heard about many things that went on in the San Fernando Valley or in East Los Angeles. Ostensibly, this was a way of serving the community and, of course, of assuring advertisers that they would reach their target markets, but it was also an astonishingly effective method of fragmenting any possible citywide sense of community as well.

The mood at the paper was every bit as triumphalist as the conversation among Allegra's friends. It was an article of faith at the *Los Angeles Times* that L.A., as Mayor Bradley had put it, "stood at the brink of a great destiny." "We in Los Angeles," he continued, "are determined to lead the state and the nation into the twenty-first century." On the business pages, one regularly read assertions that L.A.'s growth could go on forever, no matter what transpired in the rest of the world. On the cultural pages, one read about L.A.'s new museums, now so rich that

they, alone among contemporary museums, seemed able to buy anything they wanted, whatever the Japanese might bid. The Getty in Malibu, for example, had acquired van Gogh's *Irises* in the same year that it
had bought a Pontormo, a Rembrandt, and a Renoir. Only the news and
opinion sections seemed to hold out, the grumpy naysayers at the inves-
titure, and when, in early 1990, the whole paper was redesigned as "a
faster-format, easier-to-read *Los Angeles Times,*" it was hard not to wonder how long it would be before these sections as well gave Los Angeles
the news it clearly wanted to hear. And what that was, above all else, it
seemed to me, was the ironclad guarantee that New York and Chicago
were all washed up, and with them all those old European notions of
hierarchy that the East has always represented to westerners. It was
California's turn now.

You found it everywhere, that fierce braggadocio, asserting California's ascendancy over the rest of the country that, by now, must be the
oldest new idea in American life. As far back as 1912, the developer and
railroad magnate Henry Huntington had given it its classic formulation:
"Los Angeles," he predicted, "is destined to become the most important
city in this country, if not the world. It can extend in any direction as
far as you like; its front door opens on the Pacific, the ocean of the
future. The Atlantic is the ocean of the past. Europe can supply her own
wants; we shall supply the wants of Asia." Of course, people in Southern
California have been repeating this capitalist mantra throughout an
American century whose dominant orientation was resolutely Atlanticist. In the 1980s, however, for the first time, promise and reality started
to look as if they might coincide after all.

Within a few weeks of my arrival in Los Angeles, I began to think that
the most interesting thing about the city might well turn out to be not
how much but how little had changed there. The population was certainly adapting to the bad news. If there was more smog, then, almost
unconsciously I thought, they stayed in more. And while it might be
harder to get around—and nobody liked driving as much as they had in
the past—everyone was still as enthusiastic as ever about the automobile itself. There was pessimism about the country, and about the future
in general for that matter, as there was in the country as a whole, but
Angelenos remained upbeat about themselves and their city, as if L.A.
were an independent country and they themselves were immune from
the ravages of time. In a hundred different ways, crudely and with great
subtlety and deftness, they were saying that Southern California was the
place to be. And however much I might try to dismiss these claims, both
in conversation and in my notes, this optimism never ceased delighting
me.

What an extraordinary city it was, more a religion, really, than a place fixed in time and space. The bad news had an anecdotal, ephemeral quality, while the good news always seemed to signal a prophecy fulfilled. That golden dream, the set of images and expectations by which Californians had always made sense of themselves, continued to prevail. As the state's leading contemporary historian, Kevin Starr, had put it, "Los Angeles did not just happen or arise like so many other American cities out of existing circumstances—a harbor, a river, a railroad terminus. Indeed, for a long time it had none of these. Los Angeles envisioned itself, then externalized that vision through sheer force of will, springing from a Platonic conception of itself, the Great Gatsby of American cities."

And no one whom I encountered in Los Angeles in all the time I spent there ever wholly relinquished this conception of the city as the center of the California dream, the capital of America's America. The businessmen in the California Club and the poorest Salvadoran immigrant alike wanted it so. Even the radical critics one met at UCLA or read in papers like the *L.A. Weekly* agreed that what they too often called the postmodern had reached its apogee in greater Los Angeles. This most laissez-faire of cities turned out to be, on closer examination, a society made up almost entirely of true believers. They had found the future, no matter how much they might disagree about what that future was. They had found the dream.

When in Los Angeles, begin with dreams. The finite city might have been transformed over the course of the past twenty-five years, but the fantasy Los Angeles—that blond ideal of eros, Arcadia, material wealth, and American exceptionalism—had not only kept pace alongside it, but seemed to have won the race without even breaking a sweat. Perhaps it had to, perhaps the race was fixed, for, as Joan Didion once remarked about her native state, things had better work out in California "because here, beneath that immense bleached sky, is where we run out of continent." And if it turned out that this last frontier had been settled to the groaning extreme of overpopulation, this last copybook had been blotted, and this most potent of American dreams finally overwhelmed by that temblor measuring eight on the Richter scale that is also known as history, there was a pretty good case to be made for ignoring the possibility, just as most Californians ignored the possibility that, sooner or later, a real temblor would devastate their city.

Who could blame them? Despite the traffic, despite the pollution, despite the crime, life for people in Los Angeles who had money in their pockets still resembled to an astonishing extent what envious outsiders had always imagined it to be, a dream . . . just a bright, wonderful California dream.

2. There's No Time Like the Future

· ·

I struggled to maintain my skepticism. In dreams begin responsibilities, as the poet said. But the truth was that treating Los Angeles as a dream seemed to breed a degree of verbal extremism so pronounced that it repressed thought. It was not just the boosterism, though there was plenty of that all right. But for every banker, real estate CEO, or downtown businessman insisting that L.A. was the city of the future, an equivalent number of apocalypse-minded academics, heads stuffed with the latest mad French fads, were forecasting capitalist meltdown. Everybody was ready with a prediction, whether it was a secretary in the San Fernando Valley prophesying a race war, or the urbanist preaching the redemptive potential of the home (suitably rewired and plugged in, of course) as workplace. Such fanaticism went with the territory. One could think anything one liked about L.A., it appeared, except that it was just another city.

People talked far more about the future than they did about the present, let alone the past. "I'm here because L.A. is where things are going to work out," a broker told me as we sat in his office in the Security Pacific tower in the downtown business district, staring out at the city. He meant capitalism. "This is where the contradictions of the

American empire are finally going to come to a head," said a radical journalist over cappuccino in Westwood. He meant capitalism too, with a dash of race war. But they shared a sense of expectation, the belief that "in the year 2000," a locution they used with abandon, "things" would be different. "It's worth sticking around for," the writer assured me solemnly as we parted.

For a city that is usually described as being fanatically anti-intellectual, these accounts were surprisingly abstract and willed. Certainly, they did not correspond to my own sense of human motivation. The millenarian talk about L.A.'s future resembled nothing so much as the paradisiacal language that so many people use in Los Angeles to describe their decision to relocate to Southern California. In reality, of course, the reasons that impelled most middle-class people, whether in 1925 or 1990, to move to L.A. (as opposed to entertaining fantasies about living there) have been the same ones that invariably inform a step as rare and serious as pulling up stakes and going someplace unfamiliar and far away: the lure of a better job, an accident of biography, the rigors of the affective life. Southern California was and remains the most heavily mythologized place in America, even by those who live there and really should know better, but it is a concrete place as well. One has only to look at the pathetic runaways who flock to Los Angeles from all over the United States only to find, instead of stardom, the inexorable cruelties of a big city and who, too often, end up in a life of prostitution on the streets of Hollywood (the neighborhood, that is, not the fantasy) to see what happens to those who are unable to separate myth from reality.

But if there was much that was wrong about treating Los Angeles in this abstract, metaphorical way, there was something true about it as well. Any decision to pull up stakes (and that image, with its allusions to temporary encampments and voyages as yet uncompleted, is instructive in itself) resonates peculiarly in the minds of Americans. For all that we imagine ourselves a practical people, it would be inconceivable for a European, let alone an Asian, to share our romantic ideas about the moral enhancement that each displacement brings. For, say, a French girl to decide to leave her home in the provinces and try her luck in Paris is almost purely a calculation of cost and benefit, with the added fillip of media hype. For Americans, similar decisions have always had the quality of an imperative, a living out of one of the nation's central myths. Every American schoolchild used to learn Horace Greeley's injunction, "Go west, young man," and Abraham Lincoln's father's instruction to his son that "when you see the smoke from your neighbor's chimney, it's time to move on."

A myth, to be sure, but one with vast consequences. A nation as pledged as America has been to this idea of newness is bound to have little imaginative sympathy for the traditional notions of a city, with its boundaries, fixed hierarchies of space and status, and the visible remnants of the past carrying their implacable intimations of mortality. To be an American has always meant being able, precisely, to exercise one's right to opt out of the continuum of history, choosing isolation over community, and one's desires over one's obligations. In the grand rhetoric of Emerson, it is to be "a seeker with no past at his back." More prosaically, the notion is embodied in the great American expression "Don't fence me in." Inevitably, this model of utopia depends on solitude and space to spare and is as contemptuous of any particular place as it is of the past. Perhaps this is why Americans have been so oddly complacent about the decay of their older cities. If New York or Philadelphia doesn't "work" anymore, it must be time to move on.

The exception in all this language of mobility is the house, and, often, the garden. The idea of the dream house is largely an American invention. "For the first time in history," Dolores Hayden has written, "a civilization created a utopian ideal based on the house rather than on the city or the nation." In Los Angeles, people talk obsessively about their homes (they did so long before skyrocketing prices made such conversation a matter of financial as well as affective interest) in a way that they rarely do about their neighborhoods. They are proud of L.A. as an abstraction, but they love their gardens. At moments like these in Los Angeles, one really does start to think that when Jefferson wrote "the pursuit of happiness" he really must have meant private property after all.

If Southern California contains a world of dream houses, none are quite so dreamy in the end as that ultimate residence, the automobile. Was it the association of the idea of freedom, which, in the American context, has been synonymous with a conception of autonomy verging on the autarkic, with that of mobility that made the American love affair with the car persist long after traffic conditions had made the actual experience of driving anything but fun? Certainly, the promise of the automobile was not transportation so much as solitude and independence, two ideas that dance in lockstep across the stage of the American imagination.

Those who continue to wonder why Americans so obdurately resist mass transportation, or, for that matter, the humbler expedient of carpooling, miss the real point. Individual transportation has been as much a part of this American utopian ideal as the house with its backyard, or as the nuclear family—both of which are radical alternatives to every settled or communal notion of human society. So the mere, brute fact of traffic jams, like that of divorce, or even of alienation itself, only means that reality does not measure up to the ideal. What ideal ever did? By now, the most optimistic Americans have learned that lesson. In Los Angeles, people greet their new immobility with resignation. A Brookings Institution Fellow named Anthony Downs was speaking for many when he suggested that the only thing to do was "buy a BMW with comfortable seats, a high-quality sound system and car phone and enjoy it as best you can."

Cowboys don't ride buses. The act feels like a demotion from one's Americanness, just as sharing one's car with a stranger feels like an only marginally less drastic curtailment of one's autonomy. Traffic jams or no traffic jams, every car trip is a kind of miniature version of the fresh start that moving, on a deeper, more serious level, is felt to represent. This is true in most parts of the United States, but nowhere more so than in Los Angeles, which, after all, did not become the car-oriented, horizontal city it is today by accident, but rather, almost from the first, defined itself, in the words of an early L.A. civic manifesto, as an "extensive" rather than an "intensive" place. Steven Spielberg's animated film *Who Framed Roger Rabbit* presents a watered-down version of the old left-wing contention that big business conspired to destroy L.A.'s public transportation. The truth, as the L.A. historian Scott Bottles demon-strates in his remarkable book, *Los Angeles and the Automobile,* is starker. People preferred their cars and, from the first, the suburban ideal that L.A. embodied was what Bottles rightly calls "an autotopia."

To rely on a system like light rail, which, as recently as 1986, the then governor of California, George Deukmejian, referred to as "an exotic form of transportation," meant relying on the state, or, at least, on the community, and that is not what people came to Los Angeles for. If Americans soon translated the Calvinist idea of spiritual isolation into a quest for physical isolation, Los Angeles is to some extent the grafting of this notion onto the idea of the city. And if the elementary experience of all traditional city dwellers was walking, the most elementary thing any visitor to L.A. learns is that, except in a few neighborhoods, it is quite impossible to walk there and only barely possible to cross one of the boulevards before the light changes and the traffic begins to move again. One can only walk a certain distance, but, as an L.A. disc jockey used to say, "The freeway is forever."

Thus, the freeway comes to seem superior to the neighborhood, just as the suburban shopping malls replaced the downtown business hub as centers of commerce, and, in the end, of social life as well. On a certain level, Los Angeles has always held out the promise that, within its gen-erous and presumably expanding confines, the liberties of space would confound the tragic determinism of time. If Kevin Starr is right to call L.A. the Gatsby of American cities, this is not only because, like Fitzgerald's character, the city has constantly reinvented itself, but also because it has stood as the civic embodiment of the writer's famous remark that there are no second acts in American lives. Not when you can hop in the car, anyway.

To this day, Americans continue to cast their biographies as one long drama of breaking free: from family; from the old neighborhood or the old hometown; from behaviors like smoking, as much as from inherited beliefs like Christianity; these days, from marriage; in some widening circles, from sex; and, in dreams at least, from death itself. No one and nothing should be able to fence an American in, which may explain why of all the horrors of Communism it was an image like the Berlin Wall, the realization that in Communist countries people were not allowed to *leave,* that proved the greatest goad to popular anti-Communism. It was as if the prospect of being prevented from living as one chose was far less disturbing than the idea that one could be prevented from going where one wanted to.

In America itself, every change of address, every new postal code, brought with it the secret hope of transformation. And while these were old ideas in American life, predating by many decades the massive influx into California, what has always made the state a unique paradigm of these hopes was that only there could residents acquire, practically at the same time as their new drivers' licenses, a ready-made language— one that was, for all intents and purposes, the official ideology of California (which otherwise prided itself on being free of ideology)—for belittling the practical reasons for having come, and for transforming what had surely been a personal and practical decision into something metaphysical. The state motto, it should be recalled, is "Eureka," "I have found it," and its resonance is far more up-to-date than the original reference to the Gold Rush of 1849.

In Los Angeles, at least until fairly recently, once the immigrant (or, more accurately, the white immigrant, whether native-born or foreign) threw down roots, it was possible—indeed, it was almost expected— for the person in question to execute a complete break with the past, both in personal and in communal terms. Not for L.A. the rough-edged, unabashedly ethnic politicking of the East. A Mayor Curley of Boston would have been inconceivable, as would, no matter how racially polarized the city has grown in recent years, a demagogue like New York's former mayor Ed Koch. Nor did Los Angeles, even after its original Mexican Californio and Anglo settler populations had been leavened by Jews and Irish and Okies, long maintain white ethnic communities like those in the Northeast and Midwest. Rather, the movement was all in the opposite direction.

To be sure, Hollywood (the community, this time, not the neighborhood), which was, after all, the only major American industry to be founded and to remain largely controlled by Jews, might retain a nostalgic appetite for bagels and cream cheese at Cantor's delicatessen in the Fairfax district or at Nate 'n Al's in Beverly Hills, but that was where it ended. The real point was always Americanization, often complete with name changes, nose jobs, and intermarriage. And only within the hierarchy of the Catholic archdiocese did Irish Los Angeles really endure intact. For most of its history, L.A. has been a city where not only were differences and communal identities supposed to melt away, but, more remarkably, actually did melt away. "I didn't know what a Jew was until I went east to the University of Chicago," my mother once told me. She had lived in L.A., at the edge of the Valley, graduating from North Hollywood High School in the late forties, and I doubt that her experiences were all that peculiar among assimilated Jews of that place and time.

All this was possible, of course, because the city of dreams had always been a city of strangers as well. One did not shuck off identity with such impunity in New York or Boston. One was known, and the claims of the community were as gripping as the claims of the self. In Los Angeles, things were different. According to the census of 1950, fewer than half the residents of the Los Angeles basin had lived there for more than five years. If anything, the proportion of newcomers has only increased since then. Thus, one of the cardinal experiences of living in L.A. has always been one of spatial as well as temporal disjuncture between past and present, between Los Angeles and everything that goes under the name of "then" and "elsewhere." I am not, of course, speaking of those old pioneering California families. For them, the past is tangible enough. When such people speak, even today, of the astonishing beauty of the western landscape, they are thinking most often of the sacrifices of their ancestors. But unlike some of the agricultural regions of California, Los Angeles is not really their creation; it was the migrants, the newcomers, who built modern L.A. and imbued it with the magic of their intense, permissive dreams.

Dreaming of freedom, what they got was the freeways. Even today, when the frenetic construction of the last decade has finally flecked the flat bowl of the Los Angeles basin with some discernible landmarks— the skyscrapers of downtown, of Westwood, and of Century City—the most common experience of a motorist on the freeway is one of geographic confusion. Look away from downtown, and the sight through the windshield is still most likely to be an undifferentiated panoply of beautiful trees and less beautiful low-lying buildings. At first glance, one could as easily be in Watts as in Beverly Hills, in Los Feliz as easily as in Boyle Heights; it is often impossible to tell without reading the road signs. An illiterate would have to spend years making careful reconnaissances before being sure of the geographical markers. Even for the fully alphabetized, there is the nagging feeling that to enter the freeway is to move onto some enormous Möbius Strip, a series of contours that turn back on themselves.

I used to drive for hours through a city all of whose markers seemed hidden, a world of pure horizontality where the past was abolished and the future had become an unreal category. Trancelike, I would drive from the mountains to the beach, sometimes getting lost—and when one is lost in L.A. it can take hours to regain one's bearings, literally hours—but more often driving in a state of exalted neutrality. Sealed from the sounds of the road, sealed from the weather, with even L.A.'s bright, insistent light transformed by tinted windshields and the sunglasses on my face, I felt a sense of empowerment at times so overwhelming that it frightened me. Here was a rush as strong as cocaine. I felt ten feet tall, as if my individual existence had for once escaped its narrow bounds.

What was all this talk about limits, anyway? In moments like those, farcical to recount but no less powerful for the retrospect ironizing, it really did seem as if everything were up for grabs, as if reality were just what Southern Californians in their more overweening moments occasionally claimed it was: whatever you wanted it to be. I expect that part of this rush of feeling came from the fact that I had not driven a car in a long time, and so the experience had a freshness and a power for me that it would not have had for people who have never lived without their automobiles. But then, they tend to forget what an empowerment driving really is, and what Promethean knowledge. It is the most radical and nihilistic of solitudes.

Angelenos were never going to give up their cars, no matter how bad the traffic jams got. The urban planners could talk about it until they were blue in the face. "Someone has got to bite the bullet on the freeway issue," said Ken Topping, the city planning director, but his use of a word as vague as "someone" gave the game away. To be sure, responding to federal pressure, the state had set up the Air Quality Management District of Southern California, which had promulgated a plan calling for a cleaned-up, virtually smog-free Los Angeles by the year 2010. But while its director, James Lents, made bellicose noises about cracking down on polluters, a close look at the details, particularly at the postponement of compliance dates for giant polluters like California Edison, suggested that the rhetoric of the great cleanup was just that, rhetoric. And while Angelenos consoled themselves with this latest vision of utopia, they would hold on to their cars.

The clichéd portrayals of Los Angeles as the home to armies of cheerful amnesiacs absorbed in endless projects of self-improvement, smiling their goony smiles and murmuring "Fer sure," and "Have a nice day," and "Reel good" at the slightest provocation, utterly miss the point of how radical L.A.'s premise was from the beginning. Had Americans always wanted to emancipate themselves from the past? Very well, here at last was a place where it would actually be possible to do so. The first condition of paradise, the Spanish writer Julian Marias once wrote, is to find a place where there is "space to spare and where history is scarce." Eureka!

Simply because, more often than not, people in Los Angeles spoke in catchphrases did not mean that they had nothing of interest to say. Outside of Southern California, however, all people could hear was this witless verbiage, an idiom that did, indeed, borrow phrases from therapies and TV sitcoms with the avidity of a Reagan-era savings and loan CEO on a spree. People smiled condescendingly at the cornball boosterism, and winced delightedly—*schadenfreude* has always been the Northeast's middle name—at the vulgarity. As a result, they made the classic mistake of confusing erudition with intelligence. The irony was that, if anything, L.A.'s boosters were understating the importance and fascination of their city.

The garishly loony side of life in Southern California had always been good for a laugh or two. As far back as 1921, a local commentator was already bemoaning the fact that Los Angeles was "the most celebrated of all incubators of new creeds, codes of ethics, philosophies—no day passes without the birth of something of this nature never heard before." Twenty years later, an Episcopal church fact-finding report concluded sadly that "traditional habits do not reach people in this community." How could they have? Los Angeles, if it has been about anything, has been about rejecting the authority of all tradition, replacing it with what still seems, to many people who live in the city, like the democratic promise of the automobile. Even mired in traffic—and people in Southern California, by some estimates, spent 1.2 billion hours per year idling in their cars and used up 750 million gallons of gasoline doing so—the automobile remained as radical an idea, as, well, the United States of America.

All the fabled California cults, whether malign like Charles Manson, sweet like the Hindu gurus who, in the forties, had made converts of writers like Aldous Huxley and Christopher Isherwood, venal like Aimee Semple McPherson, or just plain unspeakable like Werner Erhard's est, were really far less radical, when you stopped to think about it, than one ordinary resident of the Los Angeles basin, driving alone on a freeway, unencumbered by spouse, children, or relations, through neighborhoods that, unless he has lived or worked there, are more like empty spaces than real places to him. All around him are other, similarly occupied people. Not only are they strangers to each other, but, by any objective yardstick, they are of little significance to the world as a whole, unlikely to gain even an Andy Warhol–like fifteen minutes in the limelight.

But as they drive, they are all stars. Perhaps the radio serves as the sound track, or perhaps they simply enjoy the ride. There has never been anything like this in the history of the world: every man and woman an Icarus. But the sun has not melted their wings yet, even though, as one wag put it, in Los Angeles "ecology is constantly struggling to keep up with mythology." Call it consciousness or false consciousness, mindlessness or bliss, nobody could have imagined that it would be possible to so completely decontextualize people, or that the internal combustion engine would make this atomization seem like a gift. Freedom has come in many guises, but only in L.A. is it synonymous with velocity—the velocity of a car on a freeway, the velocity of human expectations.

3. Los Angeles as Will and Idea

· ·

The people in New York who had been so spiteful about Los Angeles before I left believed, or, at least, affected to believe, that L.A.'s upbeat facade necessarily masked some deeper anguish. "They think life is fun," Kyra, a Soho restaurateur, told me grimly. "Well, it's not fun. It's hard, and sad, and messy, and above all short."

"Look at all these self-help groups," she went on. "You just know something is wrong with a place where everyone is constantly piling into their cars and going off to some meeting where they'll sit around with a bunch of people as cretinous as themselves and all love each other so much that maybe they really will stop drinking themselves to death, or gorging like pigs, or falling in love with the wrong airhead instead of the right airhead the way they should."

"Maybe it works," I said. We were talking on the phone. It was some time since we had last spoken.

"That's not the point," she answered testily. "The point is that what they're doing is a fucking misunderstanding of what life is all about. It's like that bumper sticker you see in Beverly Hills, the one that says 'Whoever has the most things when they die wins.' They don't get it! It doesn't matter what you have when you die, you're still dead."

She paused. I stared out into the yard. The ground was littered with kumquats.

"I suppose there'll be a pharaoh cult soon," she continued, "to go along with all the reincarnation. Shirley MacLaine will help you channel into the BMW you left parked in Upper Egypt in 1800 B.C. 'Honey, do you have my keys?' 'No, dear, you left them in Luxor when the Hyksos came, don't you remember?' "

We said good-bye unhappily, with exaggerated politeness.

Where Kyra was right was that, at last count, there were twenty-seven groups in Los Angeles devoted to helping people "get over" various obsessions, whether interpersonal or pharmaceutical. They were all more or less strictly modeled on Alcoholics Anonymous, which, though it was founded in the late thirties by an Akron surgeon named Bob Smith, and, of course, has branches throughout the United States, has been more successful in California than anywhere else. "Nowadays, the assumption is that if you aren't recovering from some addiction or another, you must still be practicing it," Dr. Judith Stevens-Long, a psychology professor at Cal State–Los Angeles told a reporter for *Los Angeles* magazine. The doctor went on to observe that "recovery is especially hot in Southern California." The spin-off groups—Overeaters Anonymous, Impotents Anonymous, Gamblers Anonymous, Depressives Anonymous, Cocaine Anonymous, and the like—presented addiction as the last remaining impediment to perfect "wellness." This, of course, was what set Kyra's teeth on edge, but my objection had been sincere. Was the idea really that much more preposterous than the American conceit of the City on the Hill? It just came without the transcendental trappings, with more talk and less language.

If anything, Kyra's complaint was the same sort of objection Europeans had been voicing about American ways since the days of Mrs. Trollope, who, during her American tour, had complained that in their self-indulgence her hosts had "piled their fires too high." Listening to Kyra, I was reminded of a moment in the early seventies, when the jogging craze first caught on in New York, and an English friend had voiced an amused disdain.

"Who on earth," he asked, letting the syllables out as slowly as air under water, "are all these semi-naked people running around in the street?"

As it turned out, he could not let go of the subject. A few days later, we met for dinner and I remember him telling me that he had gone to Central Park to observe them in their native habitat.

"I had the fantasy that I saw the angel of death all done up in a black track suit, invisible to everyone except to me, running alongside the panting figures and occasionally whispering in their ears: 'You can't put it off, you know; you can't put it off.' "

An Italian friend had been more straightforwardly indignant when she realized that, one by one, her American friends were all in the process of giving up smoking. "What has gotten into you people?" she demanded. "Do you all imagine you will live forever?"

The fear of death was part of it, a big part, but it was by no means the whole story. Americans . . . it was useless to try to explain this to Europeans . . . Americans just genuinely believed that they didn't have to remain in whatever shape—moral, physical, psychological—they found themselves. Emerson had said it a hundred and fifty years ago: "We are affirmative," he wrote. "[Europeans] live under obstructions and negations."

The how-to books that crowded onto the best-seller lists so insistently that many newspapers had been forced to establish a separate category so that other nonfiction even registered with the public were not simply about how to do a given thing better but also how to be, well, another person. And it was not as if Europeans were not following suit. The parks of London and Munich are now almost as clogged with joggers as the parks of San Francisco. Recently, the French government even announced new and punitive taxes on liquor and cigarettes. "This is not the United States," a French reporter snapped angrily when asked for her reaction. She was right, of course, though not in the way she imagined. In France, reform came from above, from a government rightly caught up short by the realization that 20 percent of the deaths in France were attributable to alcohol and tobacco. In contrast, in America —vulgar, democratic America—the pressure almost always has to come from below, and only recently have government regulations begun to catch up with popular attitudes.

Today, in West Los Angeles, it is not uncommon for a smoker invited to someone's house for dinner to call in advance to see if it will be okay to light up. Just as the office plazas of Century City are filled with disconsolate white-collar workers puffing on cigarettes as furtively as high-school kids in a campus stairwell, so I found West L.A. dinner parties interrupted by pariah smokers, forced to go onto the patio or outside in the garden to inhale a few lungfulls of tar and nicotine. Even marriages could be strained by this "tobaccoism." One evening, I offered a cigar to an acquaintance. His wife had been in the kitchen, gossiping with the host. When she returned to the table and found her husband puffing contentedly on a corona, her face hardened mulishly. "I'd never have married you," she said, "if I'd known you did *that*."

This L.A. cult of health, which, by 1990, had become as much as anything else a cult of abstemiousness, was one more example of implacable, ahuman American optimism. You might not be able to put "it" off, but why not see what it was like to do things that *other* way, to experience everything differently. There was, it seemed to me, a grammatical confusion. In Los Angeles, people were less obsessed with growing older than with being newer. Rather like their cars, I thought, and then worried that I was giving in to that old American pastime of making the city's strange newness the butt of the nation's jokes.

From the time when Ogden Nash had written his poem "Don't Shoot Los Angeles," meaning, of course, "I'm doing it for you," to Norman Mailer at his most unoriginal calling it "the queen city of plastic," Americans outside California had consistently missed the point. What they were really observing in L.A. were not manifestations of some anomalous nuttiness, but rather the American newness itself in all its blatant glory. Los Angeles had never apologized for itself, but now it finally seemed comfortable, assured, at times even complacent, rather than defiant. Even the eastern media establishment was catching up. Had the last "fruits and nuts" story actually been filed? Perhaps they could be stored next to all the wisecracks about the shoddiness of all things "Made in Japan" that, between World War II and the defeat in Vietnam, had provided such surefire laughs to millions of Americans.

In *The Day of the Locust,* a book that easterners like to quote from whenever they want to put down L.A., Nathanael West, who understood that fire rather than earthquakes was the real Los Angeles nightmare, imagined the city ablaze. He evoked "a great bonfire of architectural styles ranging from Egyptian to Cape Cod colonial . . . ," inhabited by cultists of all sorts, economic as well as religious, "the wave, airplane, funeral and preview watchers—all those poor devils who can only be stirred by the promise of miracles and then only to violence." Take away West's anger and disgust for the city (feelings that few people who made their livelihoods—as he did and for too long—writing film scripts, are ever freed from; the studios were, are, L.A. at its most repulsive), and what is left if not America itself? For if it is anything, the American self-image has always been an anthology of peoples and styles, a haven for economic refugees and political dissenters; in short, a land of people seeking, if not always the New Jerusalem, than at least a City on the Hill.

The question that I kept asking myself, the longer I spent in Los Angeles, was whether this was a self-conception that could weather the lean times that were closing in. In many parts of the country, they had arrived already. It was one thing to preach the gospel of exceptionalism in an age when, for all manner of political reasons, America really had been exceptional, and quite another to succeed in maintaining such a belief in an era that would certainly be one of relative decline and possibly of other, bleaker conditions. To say that the past is of no account when the present is coming on like a marvelous display window is all well and good. But what happens when the City on the Hill turns out to be located in a red-lined area, or, worse, if the Tokyo bankers started to foreclose? Abstemiousness is all well and good when it is a matter of personal choice. When it's compulsory, it is known by other names.

"I wouldn't be so quick to write this place off," Allegra said. We had been sitting for hours in an espresso bar on Beverly Boulevard, speculating gloomily about what would happen in America over the next few years.

"The funny thing about Los Angeles is that it has always made its own luck," Allegra said.

And the economic news did seem to have little to do with the world that surrounded us that night. Spotless cars were parked along a spotless curb. Suddenly, it seemed difficult to imagine that anything would ever go truly wrong in golden Los Angeles. That this was a view we could have at least partly refuted by the simple expedient of driving a few miles east did little to dam the feeling of complacency that evenings in West L.A. so easily engender. At that moment, the city really did seem like the place its early boosters had dubbed the "New Eden." And if that sounds like the work of some early advertising copywriter, there is a reason: it was. Southern California, after all, was, from the first, not so much settled as sold.

"The history of Los Angeles," Carey McWilliams wrote in his extraordinary account of Southern California, *An Island on the Land*, "is the history of its booms." When you drive around greater Los Angeles, it is hard to keep in mind the fact that the city has no natural advantages, being semi-arid and without either a natural harbor or any proximate sources of fresh water. And yet the actual experience of driving around Los Angeles is of being in a garden. The lemon trees bloom, the sprinkler heads discharge their opulent spray over green lawns, the palms rise vertiginously skyward. How could Angelenos *not* believe that they can change their lives when the city in which they live is such a triumphantly successful product not of some long collaboration of history, geology, and commerce, but rather of the will and idea of its leading citizens, of General Otis, of Henry Huntington, of E. H. Harriman of the Santa Fe Railroad, and of A. W. Ross? It was Ross who, long before most people realized that L.A. would wind up a car-borne city, created the first commercial center expressly designed to attract motorists. Located on a strip of Wilshire Boulevard that Ross promptly dubbed "The Miracle Mile," the property had been nothing more than a two-lane dirt road abutting a beanfield when Ross acquired it in 1925.

The men who undertook the great projects of city-building in Los Angeles did so almost entirely as speculative ventures. When Henry Huntington's uncle, Collis, the president of the Southern Pacific Railroad, decided to extend his railbeds south to Los Angeles in the mid-1870s, there was a tourist boom all right, but it was in Northern California. No one had the slightest reason to believe that L.A. would prove as enticing as San Francisco. The northern part of the state was already both prosperous and famous thanks to the Gold Rush (so famous, in fact, that Karl Marx could speak wonderingly of the "speed" and "shamelessness" of capitalist centralization in a region where capitalism had been all but unknown a century before). In L.A. there was . . . nothing.

Not for long, though. Once track had been laid, the Southern Pacific, joined, a few years later, by its competitor, the Santa Fe, began a relentless publicity campaign shilling the region's purportedly ideal climate and its boundless opportunities, at least for those whom General Otis was pleased to call "first-rate men," and, presumably without ironic intent, "hustlers."

In 1888, Otis placed the affairs of Los Angeles on a more organized footing when he pushed a bill through the City Council authorizing the creation of a Chamber of Commerce. Thereafter, it was this implacable body that would sponsor a vastly effective (and commensurately costly) national publicity campaign that made Los Angeles a famous city throughout America. By then, the country was inured to products being advertised, but no American municipality had ever before thought to sell itself as if it were a patent medicine. By 1900, as Carey McWilliams commented sardonically, L.A. was "the best advertised city in America."

The Chamber did more than pay for handbills and sponsor traveling carnival shows. It subsidized cultural events, festivals, and even magazines. Perhaps the most prominent of these magazines was *Land of Sunshine,* the brainchild of one Charles Fletcher Lummis, a Harvard-educated writer and amateur anthropologist (he had studied under Charles Eliot Norton) who became the leading member of Otis's Southern California cheerleaders at the *Times,* where he served as city editor. More honorably, it might be thought, he was the man who, as chief librarian of the city, gave the Los Angeles public library its first coherent shape.

To be sure, real estate developers in American cities had sold their properties using every manner of hucksterism and hype. However, before the rise of the Los Angeles of Otis and the railroad barons, no American city had ever been sold, lock, stock, and barrel, like one immense, hypertrophied subdivision. Nor had the leading citizens of Boston, New York, Chicago, or even San Francisco, even at their most grandiloquent, ever believed that the boom was the normal, not to say normative, condition of a great city's economic life. Presumably, they were familiar with a word that Otis preferred to ignore, despite or perhaps because of his checkered past (he had already failed as a newspaper publisher in Santa Barbara and was working as a government agent in Alaska when he succeeded in acquiring the failing Los Angeles *Daily Times*): bust. And yet, although the early twentieth-century history of L.A. is, of course, as much a cycle of booms and busts as that of any other municipality, Otis never faltered. For him, the severest recession was nothing more than a temporary impediment to the city's inexorable forward progress.

In this, as far as I could tell, the people who ran Los Angeles in 1890 and those who were running it today, the CEOs of corporations like Arco, Pacific Telesis, First Interstate Bank, Southern California Gas, and Rockwell International, were almost entirely of the same opinion. Indeed, to read the early history of L.A. and then to compare it with the contemporary city was to be constantly reminded of how little had changed, or, as Otis might have put it, how much had come true. Certainly Otis, had he been alive, would have had no trouble joining his corporate brethren on the board of the L.A. 2000 Committee, although, like many of them, he might have hedged his bets by endorsing, as James P. Miscoll, a Bank of America vice president, had done, the even more growth-oriented report of a business group called the Southern California Research Council.

"You don't get it, do you?" a lawyer at the downtown firm of Munger, Tolles, and Olsen, a transplanted New Yorker, had told me—more in sorrow than in anger—at the end of a long dinner in which I had pressed him to at least acknowledge that there was no guarantee that L.A.'s prosperity would last. "This city is recession-proof nowadays."

He paused.

"Barring a complete collapse of the capitalist system, that is," he added, as he signaled for the check.

To ensure the growth of the city, claims were continually advanced for Los Angeles that would never have carried conviction in older, more historically determined cities. Apart from the weather, the first thing that usually strikes visitors to L.A. is the friendliness of ordinary people. After a while, I began to wonder whether these good manners were due less to the innate virtues of the place, as locals insisted, or to the serenity that mindlessness affords, as people who dislike L.A. like to pretend, and more to the salesman's creed of keeping up a smile through thick and thin. After all, a place that starts with a For Sale sign around its collective neck always has to be on its best behavior in case a prospective buyer happens to drop by. And Angelenos have something of the same imperviousness to all negative comments that successful real estate brokers are so prone to exhibit when someone points out that the house they are showing you only has one closet, or the owner's teenage son has left Satanic memorabilia all over the kitchen counters. Seen in that light, the famed California "mellowness" and equanimity may be just one more spin on the cruder imperative of "Do anything, just don't blow the sale."

The darker accoutrements of the salesman's creed were present from the first. No American capitalists in the late nineteenth and early twentieth centuries can be said to have welcomed the rise of trade unionism. Ambrose Bierce, in his *Devil's Dictionary,* even ventured to define "grapeshot" as "the answer the future is preparing for the demand of American socialism." But in few cities was the nascent labor movement as ruthlessly suppressed as it was in Los Angeles. During the height of the labor wars, Otis drove around town in a limousine with a cannon bolted to its hood. In the words of the radical L.A. historian and activist Mike Davis, the downtown establishment "erected the open shop on the bones of labor, expelled pioneer Jews from the social register, and looted the region through one great real estate syndicate after another." Even now at the *Los Angeles Times*, any effort to unionize is sedulously resisted. Today, of course, the method of choice is pay increases and health benefits rather than scabs and court orders, but kinder and gentler though it unquestionably is, the iron will of L.A. businessmen to have it their own way remains unchanging.

In the first decade of the century, it must have been touch and go in this Los Angeles that had arisen as if by parthenogenesis. Perhaps this accounts for Otis's implacable boosterism, and for his unbending iron will. More than a plutocrat or a press lord, he reminds one of the great European nineteenth-century colonialists—Stanley, say, or Lugard. They, too, were monstrous by any humane standard, but in sheer animal terms, great and unforgettable just the same.

The risks that Otis ran were, in some curious way, opportunities as well. L.A.'s newness, even its paucity of natural resources, had the paradoxical effect of endowing Otis and his friends with the freedom to give full rein to the pursuit of their own appetites. From the beginning, the city fathers went after whatever they thought Los Angeles required to enrich itself, rather than trying to capitalize on what it already had or what lay close to hand. Thus, if San Francisco's prosperity was, in large measure, due to its marvelous natural harbor, the investors of L.A., having understood that harbors were worth having, created a man-made one for the city. The whole process was backwards. Whereas cities like New York (or Paris, or London, or Amsterdam, or even Ur of the Chaldeans for that matter) had flourished thanks either to a natural resource or some topographical or political advantage, L.A. made growth itself the engine of success rather than its consequence. In effect, the city's rise changed the very grammar of capitalism. Perhaps this was what Marx had in mind when he spoke of that distinctively Californian "shamelessness."

Even when New York was in its heyday, there was always talk in the drawing rooms of the fate of imperial Rome. The patrician Henry Adams may have been a voice in the wilderness, his nostalgia for the yeoman America that the Gilded Age had obliterated anything but disinterested, but in the 1880s he was by no means alone in understanding that all gilded ages only *seem* to last for an eternity. A genius he may have been, but in retrospect it is the spirit of Los Angeles, with its unholy mix of Emerson, John D. Rockefeller, and motion pictures, that may now be reckoned as truer to the essence of whatever genius America has possessed. Adams yearned for the past; the quintessential American happily dispenses with any piece of the past that does not benefit him in the present.

As I drove around Los Angeles, the sheer allure of the city seemed to make my rather feeble attempts at skepticism seem like a futile nonsense. One could recite the poet's lines about footprints on the sands of time until one was blue in the face, but the only footprints on the sand that I was seeing were on the Venice beach, and the bodies that had made them had fine tans and finer smiles. No one in Los Angeles, that first summer after my return, gave a damn about the vanity of human wishes. Only about vanity.

It is hardly surprising that history in Los Angeles is still construed either as a series of myths or as a tabula rasa. To be sure, the myths are traded in periodically to match the temper of the times. Helen Hunt Jackson's novel *Ramona,* that idyll of California life in the days of the Spanish dons, was known to every schoolchild in the state as late as the 1930s and is all but forgotten today. But in East Los Angeles and in ethnic studies departments at schools like Cal State—Northridge, Mexican-American militants have fashioned new myths, particularly a notion of an Aztec or mestizo nation in Southern California that they call Aztlán. Like all California self-conceptions, Aztlán posits only a mythic past, a dynamic present, and a rosy future. "Aztlán was the place of origin of the Aztecs of MesoAmerica," wrote the Chicano activist and scholar Rudolfo Anaya, "the place of the seven caves recorded in their legends. The Chicanos had returned to Native American legend to find the psychological and spiritual birthplace of their ancestors." What is most interesting about declarations like Anaya's is that the question of whether these caves were the *historical* birthplace of their ancestors is a matter of little concern.

As with all the California myths that preceded it, and despite its ambition to be anti-gringo, Aztlán is quintessentially Californian: the metaphor is everything, history the least important component, and hyperbole the sole rhetorical stance. The early publicists for California were equally interested in spinning legends. "California stands forth a veritable empire of the sun," wrote one of them in a typical passage. "It is as a land of sunshine that she is dreamed of throughout the universe. . . . In the poetry of her Pantheism, the sun god is California's titular deity." Obviously, the writer was not suggesting that temples of Baal be erected on Wilshire Boulevard, any more than Anaya was arguing that the Native American myths he and his comrades had resurrected were historically accurate. But in California, people have always wanted to distinguish between history and reality, and believed that the latter was not fixed but plastic. When Anaya argued that "Aztlán is real because myth is real," he was appealing to something beyond history, a card that trumps history. General Otis would have hated Chicano activism, but he would have understood the game.

Still, Otis and his corporate descendants have gone in more for the tabula rasa, for the past entire as memory hole. This idea of California as "the great exception," as Carey McWilliams dubbed it, as "dream," or as the shape of things to come remains the quasi-official ideology of L.A. As for history, language itself seemed to be taking care of that. It was in Southern California, after all, that the expression "That's history" was born, a phrase that simply means that something—a person, a relationship, a career, even a night out—is now over and need never be recalled again.

History, it appeared, was the province of historians and almost nobody else. To be sure, left-wing activists in L.A., who were themselves mostly academics and journalists, were interested in what had actually happened in the past. With them, one could discuss the defeat of the original Mexican inhabitants, the breaking of the unions, and the rest. Chicanos, understandably enough, at least insisted that the story of Los Angeles was not only a triumph or a miracle, but a tragedy as well, particularly for their ancestors. But as often as not such talk took place in the most idyllic of circumstances, on UCLA's gorgeous campus, or the coffee bars along the fashionable bit of Melrose Avenue. And even talk about the unreality of the California dream was, itself, a form of homage to its authority.

As for those arias to the California dream, they may have been clichés, but they were no less eloquent for being so. Listen to Mayor Bradley's stock campaign speech during his 1986 gubernatorial race:

> I remember when my parents moved to California, when I was six and my mother told me we were going to a place where it didn't matter what your name was or where you lived. She told me California was a special place where people judged you on what you did, and nothing else. So I worked hard and studied hard. I've always believed California is a very special place. I know what it's meant to me. It's a place where if you work hard, if you treat people like you want to be treated, you can set your goals high and not only dream dreams, but you and your children can then go out and realize them.

Trite they no doubt were, but Bradley's words are exactly what people in Los Angeles have been encouraged to think about their lives for generations now. The story he is spinning out is that of the L.A. everyman, from the departure from that unspecified but presumably less special place, toward a destination where the past would, by definition, no longer signify, and in which identity would be purely the product of one's deeds. Bradley's California is at once just and prosperous, but although he all but takes the prosperity for granted (it is described as being "there," rather like the fruit on a lemon tree), his certainty that it is a just place—a complicated assertion even for a successful black politician in America—depends on the view that the state, not just the people who flocked there, had emancipated itself of the country's historic burdens just as surely as migrants to California, like Bradley's own family, hoped to emancipate themselves from their personal ones.

And, of course, the California that Bradley is conjuring up is one where, crucially, dreams are simply a happier version of what, in less ecstatic language, would be referred to as ambitions. That said, Bradley was quite right, particularly given the exalted nature of Californian expectations, to phrase his reminiscence as he did. For had he, or any other California politician for that matter, actually employed a word like "ambitions," the spell would have been broken instantly. After all, every adult in his or her right mind knows that ambitions can be thwarted or may well have been unrealistic from the start. It is that magical word "dreams" that removes the whole argument from reason and from history.

With things going the way they were for Americans in the summer of 1989, as the realization sank in that the boom of the Reagan years was more likely to be a last banquet for the American century than a new beginning, it should have come as no surprise that people turned once more to the one place where the American future still looked bright and a fresh start still seemed possible. If the dream had come to dust in the rest of the country, what else was there to do but follow the familiar pattern, and light out, psychologically if not actually, for Southern California?

4. Premature Truths

· ·

Belief and salesmanship: they have never been easy to separate in Los Angeles.

The only other area of the United States in which, historically, municipalities have advanced such outlandish claims for themselves—claims that pronounced all other parts of the country passé, irrelevant to the future Americans manifestly deserved—was the towns and cities of South Florida, a region that began to come into its own in the second decade of the twentieth century. Already in 1889, Jules Verne had written his eerily prescient novel *A Journey to the Moon,* in which he imagined California and Florida vying acrimoniously for the privilege of launching the first rocketship into the heavens. Much as Marx appears to have done in London, so Verne in Paris seems to have had the impression that these two American states had abandoned the decorum in which finance capital still preferred to clothe itself at the end of the nineteenth century.

The state that secures the rights to the moon launch, Verne's narrator recounts, will leave the rest of America at the starting gate to the future. One can easily imagine George Merrick, the developer of Coral Gables, Florida, bidding against General Otis for the privilege of underwriting such an event. Both men wanted to persuade the rest of the world that only on their property would the American dream be fulfilled, and what better selling point than playing host to the first extraterrestrial car trip. People would be battering down the doors to buy houses, which, after all, was the purpose of the whole exercise. Had not Stephen Bornson, who, in 1931, was the California State Real Estate Commissioner, observed, "I see California as a deluxe subdivision—a hundred million acre project"?

"If a town site was located in a river bottom," Carey McWilliams wrote about the Los Angeles of the boom of 1887, "the promoters contended that sandy soils were the best in Southern California. If it was located in a desert, then it was being planned as a health resort; if it was located on a hillside, then it was the view that was being sold. Towns located in swamplands near the coast were, of course, laid out as 'harbor cities.' " In Los Angeles, he concluded, the word "real" was synonymous with "real estate." And what was meant by this was, almost exclusively, the single-family house. Even in the period when public transportation functioned in Los Angeles, it was to carry people to and from their houses, not apartments.

In Miami, of course, most multi-unit buildings were hotels rather than private dwellings. Even more than Los Angeles, the whole city had been envisaged from scratch. There, too, real estate speculators and a generation of newly minted plutocrats paid writers who were far more talented than the likes of Lummis and Charles Nordhoff (Damon Runyon and the young Ben Hecht were among the scribblers who did a stint shilling for Miami) to concoct fantasies about the region's bountiful present and limitless potential alluring enough to entice tens of thousands of buyers to invest in properties that were rarely what they were cracked up to be. It didn't seem to matter. But if William Jennings Bryan's quip that "Miami is the only place where you can tell a lie at breakfast and have it come true by evening" wasn't wrong, it was incomplete. Another such place did exist: it was called Los Angeles.

Rather than presenting an authentic version of the history of their respective regions, which would have meant allowing in all the tales of murdered Indians, expropriated farmers, cynical wars, and slave and coolie labor that would have been so bad for sales, South Florida and Southern California opted for a kind of pleasant, amorphous Mediterraneanism. Some history was necessary to the pitch since, even in those more credulous times, appeals to weather and visions of an earthly paradise were not by themselves enough. At their dimmest, these come-ons took the form of references, commonplace in both Miami and Los Angeles until well into the 1930s, to the "New Greece" or the "New

Italy." More accurately, both areas ballyhooed their links to the Spanish colonial past, even as they glossed over the way that past had actually segued into its Anglo present.

Miami's claim was spurious, of course. It could not have been easy for a city that was founded in 1896 to make all that much of a case for its historic links to Ponce de León, no matter how many streets Merrick and his colleagues named after him. The position in Los Angeles was entirely different. There, White-Anglo-Saxon-Protestant settlers had displaced a Mexican population that had been resident in Southern California for several hundred years. If this new white L.A. was to establish any relationship with the past, that link would ever be fraught with the intensity that the usurper so often feels towards the people he has displaced. Underneath the romance of Mexican California as evoked by Helen Hunt Jackson's *Ramona* and Lummis's more down-to-earth efforts to promote the building of houses in L.A. in the style of the Spanish missions, complete with stucco walls, bricks made of adobe, and red-tiled roofs, there was disquiet. To name a street Las Palmas was one thing; to name a boulevard after Pico, who was the last Mexican governor to rule before California seceded and declared itself a republic under the bear and the lone star emblem, was quite another.

Even before the renewal in Los Angeles in the 1960s of an enormous Mexican presence, a name like Pico, to those few Angelenos who retained a sense of the past, was less a euphonious publicity stunt, a capitalizing on some hazy notion of "old" California, than an attempt to reconcile the irreconcilable. It was as if Claudius and Gertrude had named a street in Elsinore after Hamlet's father. And while it goes without saying that no one in Otis's time, and only a prescient few (most notably Carey McWilliams) before the 1960s, conceived of a Mexican "return to Aztlán," the ghosts of these Californios were a kind of subtext to the otherwise oblivious triumphalism of Southern California, no matter how assiduously the state would try to domesticate these memories in such bland monuments as Pio Pico State Park, the governor's old ranch that sits at the north edge of Mexican East L.A., or in El Pueblo de Los Angeles State Park, the re-creation of "Old L.A." that sits at the far edge of downtown on Olvera Street, and is now as much a lure for illegal aliens from El Salvador down on their luck as for tourists.

Such ironies were not in the game plan. It was neo-Spanish architectural motifs rather than live Hispanics that were meant to add spice to the images both of Florida and of Southern California. The same neo-Moorish fantasizing can be found in both regions. If its most exuberant expression in the Southland (San Francisco, which most Angelenos have always viewed as a pseudo-eastern city—while residents of the Bay Area return their dislike of L.A. with interest—was never deeply affected by this style) is Myron Hunt and G. Stanley Wilson's Mission Inn, a grandiose hotel in Riverside, east of L.A., complete with catacombs and its own mini-Alhambra, it has analogues galore in Addison Mizener's preposterously kitschy and improbably appealing renditions of the palaces of Seville and Cordoba that line the Florida coast from Boca Raton south to Coconut Grove.

In a few instances, Miami and Los Angeles even share versions of the same *faux*-Spanish buildings. The most beautiful hotel in Miami, the Biltmore in Coral Gables, has a near twin, particularly in its interior design and ornamentation, in the Biltmore on Pershing Square in downtown L.A. Not surprisingly, both were put up in the mid-twenties by the New York architectural firm of Schultze and Weaver, a firm noted for its uncanny ability (it was also responsible for the Nacional Hotel, the third of its knock-offs of the Giralda Tower in Seville) to ape the style of great Spanish colonial architects like Churriguera while at the same time modifying them to suit the requirements of the Jazz Age. These hotels, like the elite clubs whose buildings were often the work of the same architects (Schultze and Weaver designed L.A.'s Jonathan Club shortly after it did the Biltmore), were less the work of individual entrepreneurs than collective undertakings of the business establishment, and the amorphous Mediterraneanism of their design was an integral part of the selling of Los Angeles.

The feudal arcadia represented by these fantastic re-creations of Californio palaces had about the same relation to reality as Helen Hunt Jackson's evocation, in her novel, of the old Franciscan priest in his mission, Father Salvierderra, coming to the aid of the heroic Indian couple, Alessandro and Ramona. Although Jackson was, in fact, an ardent campaigner for Indian rights, her sentimental prose was quickly appropriated by people whose only feeling for the aboriginal populations of Southern California was that they lent the otherwise barren landscape a certain aura of romance. The missionaries are portrayed repeatedly, in the popular literature of the time, as enthusiasts, and it is hard not to feel that they are really being presented as spiritual precursors of the Otises and Chandlers, the only difference being that the latter were freebooters of money rather than of faith.

"In imagination we can see them still," wrote one of General Otis's publicists of these first Franciscans to reach San Francisco Bay, "that little band of immortal pathfinders, dumb with wonder on the brown and windy hill." This writer, one John Steven McGroarty, a columnist at the *Los Angeles Times*, ends his book, *California*, by making the comparison explicit. Writing of Father Serra, he calls the Franciscan "the first and greatest character of which California can yet boast—her first missionary, her first merchant, the first of her empire builders." It is significant that late nineteenth- and early twentieth-century boosters of Los Angeles emphasized the missions rather than the Spanish colony, and, indeed, emphasized that it was Spain and, later, a secular Mexican government that, motivated by greed and anti-clericalism, moved to close the missions and sell off their properties. By harking back to a golden time, rather than an immediate past, Angelenos could forget about how the region had been taken from Mexico by force. Writing in 1911, McGroarty spoke of Father Serra's "dream." It was a case of having your idyll and subdividing it too.

In fact, this City Council view of the missions, in which selfless Franciscans ministered to grateful Indian flocks, is almost certainly false. Father Serra and his comrades in Christ appear to have been as dedicated to compelling the Indians to work in mission enterprises as they were to attending to their spiritual requirements, and if, as some have asserted, Helen Hunt Jackson intended her book as a sort of California *Uncle Tom's Cabin,* the problem was that old Father Salvierderra was as much Simon Legree as savior.

This kind of revisionism (and the mere mention of Father Serra to a Native American in California can cause a near riot, even today) was of course unheard of in the first decade of the century. This was a period in which amateur archaeologists buzzed industriously around the state, pillaging Indian gravesites and carting the bones off to Stanford University. In 1907, the owner of the Mission Inn (the commercial possibilities of these sites having been apparent almost from the start in Southern California), Frank Miller, put up a cross on a nearby hill to honor Father Serra. Henry Huntington, who had resigned as vice president of the Southern Pacific Railroad after his uncle's death, and was amassing a second, still grander fortune in land speculation and in his new venture, the Pacific Electric Railway Company, L.A.'s first brush with the rigors of a commuter rail system, was in attendance, as was General Otis.

A few years later, in 1912, Huntington would underwrite the *Mission Play,* a sentimental drama chronicling Father Serra's "dream" and the rise and fall of the missions, written by none other than John Steven McGroarty himself. The rich in Los Angeles before the First World War could have given lessons in class solidarity to the budding trade union movement had they not been so busily engaged in suppressing it, and it comes as no surprise that McGroarty was an important early investor in several of General Otis's real estate schemes, notably the San Fernando Mission Land Company. The success of that venture—at the time, the Valley was not yet part of Los Angeles—was largely dependent on the

ability of the Chamber of Commerce (or at the *Times,* the two institutions exemplifying, in those days, anyway, the principle of a distinction
without a difference) to convince people to settle so far from downtown L.A., and on Huntington's railway to extend its reach, through the
private right-of-ways it already controlled or could acquire, across the
length and profitable breadth of those arid surburban tracts.

Clearly, the *Mission Play* was art in the service of mammon in a way
that had probably not been seen since the decline of portrait painting.
What can safely be said of figures like Lummis and McGroarty is what
someone remarked of the five settling missionary families of nineteenth-
century Hawaii: "They came to do good, and they did very well indeed."
But it would be naive to imagine that works like McGroarty's were
simply exercises in crafted venality, and even more of a solecism to
underestimate the mythological force they exercised, and the way they
influenced generations of Californians between the First World War and
the early 1950s. The *Mission Play* was performed 3,200 times in its
own theater, the Mission Playhouse in San Gabriel. Even today, many
middle-aged Californians can recite, if by now only in embarrassed giggles, great, bathetic chunks of McGroarty's dialogue. The piece, and,
along with it, an image of what it meant to be a Californian, stuck, if not
by dint of truth then at least by dint of repetition.

"Read *Ramona,*" my mother advised me, shortly before I left for Los
Angeles. "It's still one of the keys to the place." Don't forget to read
Ramona, don't forget to bring your sun block. She was right, as it turned
out. Both were essential parts of the Southern California puzzle, the
dream of an uncomplicated past that could be carried forward, almost
literally ad infinitum, as important as the pursuit of pleasure, or the re-
creation, within a city and its surroundings, of a convenience-laden
simulacrum of the natural paradise.

The fact that people in Los Angeles have nearly forgotten these founding myths does not mean that they have disappeared. The most obvious
distinctions between hype, history, and myth are difficult enough to
maintain when people know some history; when everything has been
forgotten, or, at least, seems to be in the process of being forgotten, the
situation is all but impossible. Intelligent people in the United States
usually blame this amnesiac confusion on television, and backdate it
only to the fifties, to the golden age of suburbia, the founding age of
Disneyland. "Thirty-five years ago," runs a Disney promotional piece
about the first theme park in the L.A. suburb of Anaheim, "Walt looked
over this land and saw not two hundred acres of dusty orange groves,
but the happiest place on earth." But, in fact, the pitch is one that

McGroarty could have written, and what seems remarkable about a phenomenon like Disneyland is less its originality than its indebtedness to the language of boosterism, transformation, and fulfillment that was the hallmark of early twentieth-century Southern California.

The Spanish names that the Anglo founders of Los Angeles chose as street names, as much as the Spanish architectural styles that they favored for both civic and residential architecture, were chosen consciously. Though they were clearly inspired by genuine Spanish colonial buildings like the hotel that Governor Pico had erected on what became North Main Street, these buildings were as much grafts on the landscape as the (imported) eucalyptus trees that shaded the better neighborhoods of early twentieth-century L.A. It was, in fact, an early world's fair, the 1915 California–Panama Exposition in San Diego, that definitively established Spanish Revival architecture as the quasi-official style of the region. This style, which was also known as churrigueresque, was largely the brainchild of the New York architect Bertram Grosvenor Goodhue. In his pitch to the L.A. Board of Supervisors, Goodhue promised to create a building that would evoke "the romance of the old Spanish civilization."

The Goodhue-designed buildings (he died in 1924, having installed himself in Santa Barbara, where his practice thrived, and his Los Angeles Central Library building project was completed by an associate, the local architect Carlton Monroe Winslow) and their stylistic clones were, if anything, a scaled-down rendition of the even more opulent Hispanicism the City Council originally had in mind. In 1925, the Allied Architects Association had proposed a plan for a central administrative district for the city that was to involve the restoration of the Old Plaza, the historic center of Spanish- and Mexican-era Los Angeles. Between the Plaza and the new, Babylon-inspired City Hall (the building boasts an actual ziggurat at its top), there was to be an interconnected series of plazas surrounded by low-lying buildings constructed in the same Spanish Revival style. They would have names like La Rambla and El Paseo. But if this was an attempt, as Reyner Banham once put it somewhat romantically, to confer a "cultural immortality" on Hispanic Los Angeles, the city fathers' idea as to the actual Mexican residents of the Old Plaza area was quite different: where possible, they were to be driven out entirely.

Thus, at the same moment that L.A. boosters were producing reams of purple prose concerning the Spanish colonial heritage, and commissioning buildings to match, Mexicans were being forced east across the Los Angeles River. "It is quite likely," wrote the sociologist and muckraker G. Bromley Oxnam in 1920, "that the Mexicans now situated around the Plaza and in the Macy School District will be forced to go to other parts of the city within the next five years." This population was made up not only of descendants of the original inhabitants of the pueblo of Nuestra Señora la Reina de los Angeles de Porciuncula, but also of tens of thousands of unskilled Mexican workers who had been recruited by Huntington's Pacific Electric Railway to lay the track of the interurban railway that connected an already far-flung city. Huntington's agents would go down to El Paso, Texas, and then bring the laborers east to Los Angeles.

But even though Los Angeles, by the early twenties, already had the biggest Mexican population in the United States, few of the Anglo visitors, residents, or new migrants seemed to notice. "We do not have a varied group of different kinds of nationalities in Southern California," asserted Charles P. Bayer of the Los Angeles Chamber of Commerce in 1926. If you left out the hundred thousand Mexicans, that is. Then, as today on the Westside of L.A., Anglo residents were at once aware that it was Mexicans who performed most menial jobs, and yet they could act as if these people, once they finished working, went home not to the Old Plaza, or, as now, to East L.A., but to another planet.

The downtown Mexican neighborhoods, including one west of the Old Plaza which had been home to refugees who had fought in the Cristero rebellion against the self-proclaimed atheistic Mexican revolutionary government and had fled north after their defeat, were as much an impediment to profit as they were an embarrassment to the Chamber of Commerce's vision of an all-white Los Angeles. The *Los Angeles Times*'s Harry Chandler was determined that the proposed new railroad hub, Union Station, be located next to the Old Plaza. The Chandlers owned much of the land in the immediate vicinity, land whose value would multiply if the Mexican barrio gave way to the commercial hub. In due course, thanks in large measure to a fantastically successful promotional campaign undertaken by the *Times,* the Plaza site was approved in a referendum.

But, as has so often been the case in Los Angeles, history was rewritten at practically the same moment as the land was being redeveloped. The Plaza referendum was approved in 1926. By 1929, the Mexican population was largely relocated in the Boyle Heights section of East L.A. and in Watts, not yet the famous black ghetto but a Mexican colonia. What had been simply called the Plaza district, or, disparagingly, Sonoratown, had been redone. The Old Plaza was refurbished, and Olvera Street, which had been the main commercial thoroughfare of colonial Los Angeles, had been made over as a so-called Mexican Marketplace. Both were absorbed in an entity known as the Pueblo de Los Angeles

State Park, about whose potential as a tourist draw the Chamber of Commerce was extremely bullish.

In other words, Olvera Street was a theme park, perhaps the first such confection in the world. Before that, theme parks were transient phenomena, erected for the duration of a world's fair or national exposition and struck immediately after the closing ceremonies. People think of theme parks as Walt Disney's invention, but actually Olvera Street's creation antedates that of Disneyland's by a full thirty-six years. As is so often the case in Los Angeles, one repeatedly discovers that what seems at first glance like a radically new idea, something not just modern, but, to use that indispensable, if barbarous, catchword, postmodern, usually turns out to be one of L.A.'s older tropes.

"Sure L.A. is a make-believe town," Allegra said one morning at breakfast, as I told her glumly of my visit to Olvera Street, which seems today not only sordid and depressing but, paradoxically, like the *least* Mexican place in Los Angeles. "The interesting point is that it has always been a make-believe town, and that the illusion is not just a silly game but has a purpose behind it. It's just too easy to call this place a city of surfaces."

She brightened. "Or if you do, remember these are the only surfaces to which money clings like gnats to flypaper."

In driving the Mexican inhabitants out of downtown, and then erecting a simulacrum of their presence in the void they had left behind, Los Angeles was simply practicing its imperial vocation, for, from the start, its famous dreams have been, more often than not, dreams of conquest. The story has it that on the eve of the Spanish-American War, William Randolph Hearst cabled his correspondent in Cuba, the celebrated Richard Harding Davis, demanding more reports from the battlefields. When Davis honorably protested that there was, in reality, little fighting to chronicle, Hearst responded memorably. "You take care of the stories," he fired back, "I'll take care of the war."

Something of the same constellation must have existed between hired mythmakers like McGroarty and Lummis—"God made Southern California," Lummis had once explained, "and he made it on purpose"—and the great business tycoons who quite literally stopped at nothing to fashion a metropolis out of such an improbable array of constituent parts. It is too easy to reduce a figure like Lummis either to the venal or to the arrogant impulses which doubtless fueled his activities. A man of his times, with all the racist feeling those times encouraged, yes. But if Lummis profited from, say, the cult of the missions, he was also responsible for the preservation of most of the better colonial buildings in Southern California that still remain. The tycoons themselves were another story, grander and more awful at the same time. When one reads about them, they can remind one of Renaissance princes at one moment, while at others their machinations have all the blatant wickedness of villains in silent-era serials like *The Perils of Pauline* who were always tying the blameless heroine to the railroad track, as a locomotive approached in the distance, belching black smoke. The only difference was that in real life, these villains owned the railroad and, alas, Pauline got squashed as flat as a pancake.

Still, though one may quail at the ruthlessness of these men and give all one's sympathy to those they crushed and exploited, the intractable fact remains that their accomplishment was extraordinary. One might as well reproach Cesare Borgia or Lorenzo de' Medici for not having been St. Francis. And unlike the media billionaires of today, the Otises and the Huntingtons produced something more than fat bank balances for themselves and their cronies when they were through. They invented a city where none should have been able to exist.

There was no usable port in Los Angeles? Otis and the *Times* prodded and pushed. Soon, the ocean bottom was dredged, and the port was *created.* There was no water? The city, which is to say Otis, again, fought those water wars, probably the best-known of the skeletons in L.A.'s closet. That story was eventually transformed, in a process that is the purest Americana, from a dirty secret to a major motion picture—*Chinatown,* a vehicle for Jack Nicholson. No municipality better illustrates Walter Benjamin's observation that all history is victor's history and all documents of civilization also documents of barbarism better than Los Angeles in its early, buccaneering period—the Mexicans expelled across the Los Angeles River; the buildings built where the profits would be greatest; the water of the Owens River, a couple hundred miles north in the Sierra Nevadas, under the rigid dominion of what Mary Austin, one of America's greatest nature writers, once called the "greedy, vulgarizing hand" of the Los Angeles Water and Power Department.

From time to time the defeated have their say. These days, Chicano nationalists delight in describing the new Mexican immigration to Los Angeles as a kind of historical payback for the Anglo usurpations of the past. The fact that the new immigrants come from parts of Mexico, and, of course, from further south in the ruined, unfinished nations of Central America, is glossed over. What will happen to L.A.? "We're just going to reinstate the original composition of the city—like it was before the [Anglos] showed up," crowed the Mexican-American film producer Moctesuma Esparza. Unlike the myths so beloved of Chicano activists, history is rarely either so static or so just. The Seventh Day Adventist who, in 1965, greeted John Gregory Dunne as he stopped in the Owens

Valley with a single stark, accusing sentence was probably closer to the
mark. "You're from Los Angeles," the old man said. "You stole our
water."

Inevitably, perhaps, the downtown businessmen did not long content
themselves with profit close to home. In the wake of the Spanish-American War that they, almost as ardently as Hearst, had so unflaggingly
supported, when the United States became an imperial power outside
the American continent for the first time, their ambitions for Los Angeles
far outstripped the necessarily circumscribed pleasures of domestic development. D. H. Lawrence, who fancied he knew something about
history, might have jeered, in the wake of a visit in 1920, that "Los A. is
silly—much motoring, me rather tired and vague with it. California is a
queer place—in a way, it has turned its back on the world and looks
into the void Pacific," but the Huntingtons and the Chandlers knew
better.

Of course, intellectual visitors from the East Coast and Europe have
almost invariably misunderstood California. When they did not find it
simply barbarous, as Rudyard Kipling did, noting with horror the "un-
limited exercise of private judgment," they found it, as Lawrence did,
engagingly moronic. They were drawn to what Robert Louis Stevenson
called "the great epic of self-help," where "vast cities . . . grow up as by
enchantment," but they did not take the region seriously. But while
they sneered and joked, these businessmen pursued their undroll enterprise of city-building, and today it is hard not to feel that, whatever
California's problems or its fate, it is capital that has had the last word.

In a small park near the UCLA campus in Westwood, I happened one
day on a somewhat forlorn monument, one that had gone unmentioned
in all the architectural guides I had read. It was easy to miss, and most
people who drive by, whether peering through their windshields at all
the new office towers, or just trying to find the entrance to the freeway,
probably have no idea it's there. The statue honors the American soldiers who died in the Spanish-American War, "defending the freedom,"
so the inscription reads, "of alien peoples." All in all, a modest affair—
standard-issue "dulce et decorum est pro patria mori" stuff, pabulum
erected for the civilians back home in the immediate wake of the campaign and soon forgotten. But if civic statuary were sized according to
the importance of the event it commemorates, then Los Angeles would
have a far grander memorial to the Spanish-American War, for it marked
a turning point. For though it may have escaped D. H. Lawrence, it did
not escape the Los Angeles Chamber of Commerce that victory over
Spain in the Pacific had carried the United States not into the void but
into an empire.

The war first solidified what would persist as the resolutely Pacific-oriented world view of California capitalism. It was an attitude that would, for most of the twentieth century, distinguish Los Angeles businessmen from their colleagues on Wall Street or in the Chicago Mercantile Exchange, who remained resolutely Atlanticist until well into the 1970s, when, at last, the East Asian challenge could not be ignored any longer. And the economic lesson of the Spanish-American War was underscored by the subsequent success of the Panama Canal—a project which, when you thought about it, was crazy in exactly the same way that the invention of Los Angeles had been crazy; by any rational calculation, after all, both should have been located elsewhere. It was the opening of the Canal that assured the success of the Port of L.A., and it is in this context that Huntington's otherwise inexplicably prescient remark about the Pacific being the ocean of the future must be understood. The Pacific was Los Angeles's ocean of the future, all right, courtesy, that is, of Teddy Roosevelt and Admiral Dewey, hero of Manila Bay. It still is.

With these kinds of economic forces set in motion, people soon no longer had to be lured to Southern California with racist come-ons like Lummis's promise of a "new Eden for the Saxon homemaker," or the bogus assertions of the Chamber of Commerce's tame doctors that children would grow up healthier in the Southland. The incoming tide was soon so great that L.A., far from welcoming residents fleeing poverty or disaster elsewhere, made every effort to repel them. Mexicans were regularly deported, and, in the late thirties, California mounted a fierce campaign, complete with border checks, to discourage the migration of hundreds of thousands of farmers from Oklahoma, Arkansas, and Texas who had been thrown off their land due to soil exhaustion in the Cotton Belt and drought and mechanization on the Great Plains.

Los Angeles's success was the only drawing card it needed. Increasingly, the civic creed under which all but a few hapless malcontents and Reds were content to live was that L.A. was the city of the future, the coming attraction for America, just as surely as America was the coming attraction for the world. Not only did Los Angeles tout itself as the perfect place to live, its officials were, by the 1920s, contemplating the still largely uninhabited expanse from the San Bernardino Mountains to Santa Monica, and confidently assuring anyone who would listen that, as Clarence H. Matson of the Chamber of Commerce put it in 1924, four million people would "fill up most of the space 'from the mountains to the sea.' " By 1946, even a skeptic like Carey McWilliams felt obliged to remind his readers that "utopias are often only premature truths."

As the decades passed, the periods of economic boom seemed to last longer and longer, while the busts became harder and harder to discern. There was, it appeared, no limit to the number of people the Los Angeles

basin could absorb. Between 1920 and 1930, L.A.'s population tripled
to almost a million and a half people. This was nothing compared to the
development the city underwent during World War II. From 1940 to
1944, as L.A. became one of the great foundries of the American war
effort—producing, in three shifts a day, tanks and rubber, ships, planes,
and munitions—three quarters of a million more people arrived, many
blacks from the South among them, lured by the promise of decent jobs.
Throughout the fifties, millions more arrived. Los Angeles stretched and
sprawled, the city and its suburbs expanding in every direction.

It was as if time had been waiting to catch up with Los Angeles. What
was already, by the twenties, a city where people assumed they would
get around by car, became in the car-obsessed America of the fifties the
autotopic standard against which all other cities were judged. The industries that would really matter in Cold War America—defense, aerospace, petroleum, and automobiles—were precisely those that had been
drawn to the region, as often as not thanks either to generous federal
subsidies or else to lucrative federal contracts. The automobile industry
faltered during the sixties and all but collapsed during the seventies in
much the same way it did elsewhere in the country, but until the unexpected decision of Mikhail Gorbachev to, in effect, call off the Cold War,
Southern California could always depend on far more than its fair share
of defense appropriations, between 10 and 20 percent, all told, of all the
prime contracts let since 1945. With this cushion (and it is aerospace,
accounting for 20 percent of regional GNP, far more than the better-
publicized entertainment business, which is only half as large, that has
been the dependable engine of growth in the Southland), Angelenos
could be forgiven for imagining their part of the world was all but
recession-proof and for boasting that, were California an independent
country, it would have the tenth-largest economy in the world.

In short, L.A. had become what General Otis had said it would, and
more. Even on the culture front, things were by no means as parched as
easterners imagined. The stereotype of the writer lured to Hollywood
and destroyed is by no means the hoary cliché people in the movie
business like to pretend it is, but then America has never been a country
where high art has counted for all that much. Museums were another
story. No area that can boast the Getty in Malibu, the Norton Simon in
Pasadena, and the County Museum hard by the La Brea Tar Pits can
exactly be called underserved. Beyond that, the effect of all these high-
tech industries clustered together was to foster a level of scientific
productivity unmatched in the rest of the country. Not only does the
Los Angeles basin have more engineers than any other metropolitan
area, but the work done in biology labs and physics departments from
Berkeley to San Diego has been so important that it is hard to see how

the contest between the East and West coasts, if in reality one can be said to exist at all anymore, can be viewed as anything other than a draw.

Moreover, while it is obviously important not to exaggerate the importance of the motion picture, television, and record industries which are so often and so erroneously identified as synonymous with Los Angeles, it would be simply perverse to deny the deep effect they have had. In a country besotted by images, a place where, as Joseph Heller once said, "no one governs, everyone performs," Los Angeles is the image factory. Those images come from television now, rather than principally from the movies, and, like the country they both mirror and distort, they are far more fragmented than they used to be. Still, beginning in the 1950s, the representation of America that people, both in the United States and abroad, saw on their television screens was America or, at least, the American dream. And, when all is said and done, what was being portrayed was actually a very specific place, the suburban America that the L.A. Chamber of Commerce had virtually conjured up, decades before the invention of television.

The irony was that while Chandler, Otis, Huntington, and the rest could not and did not predict any of the particulars that would fuel the growth of Los Angeles, whether it was the Cold War or the cathode tube, and, for a long time remained oblivious to some of it (the downtown establishment to this day treats the film industry as an exotic—read Jewish—foreign country), it was as if each new development that spurred the growth of L.A. was an elaboration of their original plan for the city. How else, as Kevin Starr has pointed out wonderingly, could the Los Angeles of 1924 have "subdivided itself into a city of 7 million people nearly half a century before such a population would become fact?" In circumstances like these, even the most self-promoting hype begins to sound an awful lot like prophecy. For not only has the lie (to paraphrase William Jennings Bryan's wisecrack about Miami) that Los Angeles's boosters began circulating at the turn of the century come true, but by now what seriously taxes the imagination is any convincing scenario for its *not* having been realized, one way or another.

The real point, of course, is not that history is bunk, that view which still inspires people in greater Los Angeles today almost as fervently as it did the businessmen and speculators who founded the place, but that, in fact, the dominant historical and economic developments of the twentieth century so favored (and, many believe, still favor) Los Angeles that its rise was almost the exact opposite of a miracle. All those stories of Huntington putting markers on barren land and conjuring up in his mind's eye not orange groves but the city of Van Nuys are impressive in their way. But a simple counterfactual argument reduces them to their proper size. For to imagine a world without cars, urban sprawl, the oil industry and the aerospace business, Hollywood, Burbank, consumer loans, installment credit, twenty- and thirty-year mortgages is not only to conjure up the vision of a world without Los Angeles but of a twentieth century without the dominating presence of the United States of America.

And whatever had happened in the rest of the country, this ethos of growth, sprawl, and possibility was continuing unchecked, or so it appeared, in the Southland. The subdivisions snaked south, down the coast to northern San Diego County. They had moved north, past the Ventura County line, until they were licking at the edges of suburban Santa Barbara County, eighty miles away. Even the San Fernando Valley, the centerpiece of Otis's and Huntington's expansion plans, now had suburbs of its own, across the San Gabriel Mountains, once thought to be at the absolute outer limit of L.A.'s civic reach, in the Santa Clarita Valley, and, still further, forty miles up Highway 14, in the Antelope Valley, an area 2,000 feet up in the high desert plateau, boiling in the summer and bitterly cold in the winter, that was once thought to be all but uninhabitable except by the hardiest of rural people.

In a region where developers think they can manipulate even the environment, was it really any wonder that so many of the people whom I met in Los Angeles were embarked on their projects of self-improvement and self-transformation? Greater L.A. itself was sufficient proof, if any was required, that such projects could succeed. Look around, people said. The material prosperity was anything but an illusion. Even if the real estate market had stalled, the downturn wouldn't last forever. It never had before, had it? (Angelenos, though no believers in history, were great followers of what they called "trends.") And the natural beauty of the area was certainly no illusion, they said, even though they were perfectly well aware that most of the local flora was in fact imported from elsewhere. What they were really saying, I began to think, had more to do with Zen paradoxes than with an argument, and could be summed up as "This illusion is no illusion."

In her more sophisticated way, Allegra too was a great one for saying, "Just look around you." In our daily drives from paradisiacal restaurant to ambrosial shopping mall to cornucopial garden, it was hard to deny her argument. Nonetheless, I kept looking for the guide wires that kept this complicated, seemingly delightful machine called greater Los Angeles in good operating condition. There had to be a catch, I thought, perhaps a touch ungraciously. Even in paradise certain fruit-bearing trees have a quite different meaning than the one the people who sup at them first want to tell you about.

II *Below, the Sonoran Desert was pitch black except for very occasional speckles of light. I calculated that we were just north of the border towns of Yuma, Arizona, and Mexicali, Baja California Norte. It was still Sunday night, a good time for crossing. The emptiness was illusory: There were people down there, walking.*

—Ted Conover, *Coyotes: A Journey Through the Secret World of America's Illegal Aliens*

· ·

5. The Stoicism of Maids

· · · · · · · · · · · · · · · · ·

The two women sit sprawled on the bunchy white couch in Allegra's sunlit living room, and, as they talk, I stand at the window, looking out at the oleanders and the evergreens, fretting about maids and language. The stereo all but drowns out their voices. For the last hour, at least, Allegra has been replaying the sound track album to the movie *The Big Chill.* Both she and her friend Karin seem to grow giddier with each cut. In this era of rap and heavy metal, the songs sound so tame and sweet, as they undoubtedly did not when they were recorded in the sixties. What a complicated business it really is, nostalgia.

A few hours before, Allegra and Karin had driven over to Beverly Hills, where they had made a great show of hand-delivering to their agent the revised version of the script they have been working on for months now. Napoleon is reported to have said that every soldier in his grand army carried a marshal's baton in his rucksack. The incidence of would-be scriptwriters in West Los Angeles must be nearly as statistically impressive. How could it not be, in a place where people commonly speak about the most private events in their lives as "scenarios"? Example: "I don't like this scenario, the way it's playing out." Translation: "I hate the way he treats me."

Allegra and Karin have been working on their script in Allegra's Deco floor-through in mid-Wilshire. When they felt edgy there, stymied enough to crave a change of scene, they would sometimes drive down to the Coronado Hotel, just off San Diego, where they would tap into their laptops to a medley of sounds, benign as white noise, of low-flying Navy helicopters and the chop of the Pacific surf pounding onto the beach below their window. At other times, Allegra would go off alone to the resort town of Ojai, where her agent has a house. In the mornings, she says, she would revise ruthlessly, while in the afternoons she would swim endless lengths in the gray slate lap pool, or else go for long walks in the nearby Topa Topa mountains.

Karin draws on a small cigar—an exceptional indulgence, she insists —and sits with her head thrown back, blowing smoke rings into the air through lips parted in an exaggerated, *faux*-starlet oval. For her part, Allegra can barely sit still. She strides to the window, does a *plié* with a nervous shrug of her shoulders, lights a cigarette, and then returns to the couch. She repeats this sequence several times until Karin, exasperated, calls out, "Allegra!"

"I'm so excited," Allegra sings out.

The old clichés again. As I watched, I kept thinking that the whole scene was too much like some downmarket miniseries about life in L.A. to be actually taking place. It had that same overemphatic narrative line that a good film script needs to have, and, of course, it had its own sound track. It was also not quite lifelike (or did I mean more than lifelike?), and it was certainly somewhat oppressive. The words "too much" did not always mean "great" in the American language. When Thomas Mann moved to the Los Angeles community of Pacific Palisades, he wrote to a friend that "here everything blooms in violet and grape colors that look rather made of paper. The oleander . . . blooms very beautifully. Only I have the suspicion that it may do so all year round."

The Temptations come on—for the third time—and I walk into the kitchen where Rosa, Allegra's Salvadoran maid, stands at the sink as solidly as if she had been planted there. She is only a touch over five feet tall, and wears her hair in one thick black braid, so long that it falls almost to her waist. Rosa is opulently pregnant, her distended belly barely covered by the sky-blue, extra-large man's T-shirt with a logo that reads, "Sea World," which she keeps fingering and readjusting as she scrubs away at the breakfast dishes. By now, the lower half of the shirt is damp and soapy. "Do you want something, mister?" she asks, looking up. "I am in one minute done."

There was no room in Allegra and Karin's scripts for the Rosas of the world, and yet their daily lives had become all but inconceivable without their help. People talked a good deal about their maids and gardeners in L.A., of course, but almost invariably with respect to the difficulty of keeping them, or when one had been picked up—they were almost all in the United States illegally—by the immigration authorities, or simply to note when one of them was due to arrive. "Excuse me for a few minutes," Allegra had said only that morning at breakfast, "I've got to run"—she meant drive, of course—"down to the bus stop on Wilshire to collect Rosa." Most maids in L.A. not only do not own their own cars, they do not drive at all. They are to be seen riding the RTD, L.A.'s tortoiselike public bus system, or they must find rides with relatives, and arrive and depart like benign apparitions, both there and not there at the same time.

Most remarkable of all was the fact that almost everyone in West Los Angeles seemed to have one of these maids, cleaning up for them at least once and more often twice a week. "Rosa comes in on Tuesdays and Thursdays," Allegra had told me the day I arrived. "She speaks very little English, so if you want her to do something extra, either tell her in Spanish or else let me know." As Allegra dropped two fluffy towels and a monogrammed washcloth on the shelf in the guest bathroom, she called out, "Chances are that Rosa will take care of everything anyway. She's just great."

And how Rosa's presence did indeed turn out to make daily life easy at Allegra's. She would collect the laundry without being prompted, and when I would return at the end of the day there it would be, neatly folded away in the dresser. The towels, too, were invariably whisked away dirty, only to reappear, scented from the wash and warm from the dryer, a few hours later. It was a pure case of "He does not know the sweetness of life who has not lived before the revolution." But what was most peculiar was not how nice it was to have someone cleaning up after you, but that Los Angeles, of all places, with its belief in itself as the most democratic of American cities, would turn out to pullulate with servants. Indeed, L.A. was proving to resemble a Third World country like Rosa's El Salvador in this respect, a place where, after all, the American commonplace was that you could live cheaply *and* have what was all too euphemistically referred to as "help," a good deal more closely than it did its image of itself.

This help was everywhere. You wanted a gardener? Just take a drive down Sawtelle Boulevard early on any morning—seven days a week, it was said emphatically—and you would see groups of Mexican men clustered on every street corner for the better part of two miles. When I went there, I discovered that some even carried the tools of their trade, a rusty hand trowel, say, or a small hoe, and that when you slowed down they would wave these sad implements at you. To stop meant being immediately surrounded by men ranging in age from their late teens to their early fifties, all clamoring in English as faulty as a busted pipe for any work you could give them.

"I'm the best, mister," was the favorite line, with "I work cheap" coming in a close second. If you spoke to these men in Spanish, they seemed to become cagier, as if being addressed in their own language by an Anglo excited their suspicions. Whether in English or Spanish, however, the wages they expected were astonishingly low. Angelenos could get work done on their properties, and well done at that, by men who knew their way around tools and the soil, for under half the U.S. minimum wage. And if they were hard-hearted enough to barter with the laborers in these impromptu, outdoor hiring halls, it was no great achievement to hire men for far less.

This was bad news for established small businesses. A painting contractor named Richard Urquidez spoke for many when he told a reporter from the *Times* that "you have to work harder out here [in L.A.]. There's so many people. Competition is bringing the price down." He meant the immigrants, of course, and his defensive tone suggested that he did not expect things to get better. Why should it? Los Angeles had taken to cheap labor in much the way American consumers had taken to cut-rate appliance stores or the clothing outlets where one could buy what are picturesquely called "name brands" at wholesale prices. There seemed no reason to go back to paying the "retail" rates that men like Urquidez had to charge. In any case, this kind of dependence on the cheaper man had always been a feature of doing business in Los Angeles, from the days when the downtown capitalists had broken the backs of the newspaper and garment unions in the labor wars of the twenties and thirties.

For more squeamish types, there were any number of agencies ready to serve as intermediaries. This was obviously essential for maids, who, although some were hired through word of mouth, could hardly be expected to congregate on, say, the *other* side of Sawtelle Boulevard, dishcloth and mop in hand. Sometimes, it was the immigrants themselves who did the brokering. A Mexican who was in the United States legally might, for example, open a gardening business with money scraped together from family and friends, both in Los Angeles and back home. He in turn would hire a group of illegal aliens, ferrying them around in his truck from job to job, and paying them in cash at the end of each day's work. The freeways are full of these entrepreneurs and their indentured laborers. Usually, the boss and, perhaps, his foreman ride in the cab of a pickup truck or the front seat of a station wagon. On the bed behind, there are usually at least two copper-skinned young men who sit, sometimes quietly, sometimes shouting to make themselves heard in the hot, dry wind; more often than not, they have neither any precise idea of where they are nor much information about where they are headed on this or most other working days in that glitzy Oz called Los Angeles. What they were was at your disposal.

The entire city worked this way. You wanted a maid, a nanny, a cook? "No problem, mister." There were half a million brown women in East L.A., sometimes with but usually without green cards or work permits, and almost never with much English, willing to do whatever you needed them for. Glossy magazines like *L.A. Style, Los Angeles,* or the magazine of the *Los Angeles Times* itself might run the occasional feature about the purported maid shortage, and as they detailed the ruthless poaching going on between various Beverly Hills matrons for the services of some particularly well-regarded maid, it was possible to get the impression that it was these Hispanic women rather than their employers who had the upper hand. The fact, however, was that for all the "I don't know what we'd do without María" and the "I just *pray* she never leaves," the reverse was true.

Children, at least before puberty, might sometimes grow attached to these maids, but for their employers in West L.A. these illegal domestic workers were more or less interchangeable. To be sure, one met many Anglos who, at one point or another, had interested themselves in trying to regularize a maid's immigration status, or perhaps with subsidizing a trip home to Jalisco or Guatemala City, but these were part of what might, only somewhat unkindly, be called part of the "routine maintenance" of having a servant in L.A. The reality of this world of maids that existed only a few miles to the east was either too insignificant or, perhaps, too overwhelming to contemplate for most of the people I met.

It was very American, this willingness to intervene in an individual emergency but to reject any suggestion that there were general lessons to be drawn from the fact, say, that the maid, because she had no papers and thus couldn't get a car, had to ride the bus three hours every morning from Boyle Heights to Pacific Palisades to come to work. Almost ninety years ago, William James remarked that "callousness to abstract justice is the sinister feature . . . of our U.S. civilization. When the ordinary American hears of cases of injustice he begins to pooh-pooh and minimize them and tone down the thing, and breed excuses from his general fund of optimism and respect for expediency." The usual way this was expressed in Los Angeles was the remark, all but inescapable whenever the subject of how these illegal workers lived came up, that if life were not better in the United States then surely all these people would not have braved the rigors of the journey north.

"They're starving down there in Central America," a Studio City entertainment lawyer told me. "Which would you prefer? Their working here in L.A. or rotting in a slum somewhere?"

He was right, of course. It only took the most casual conversation with these domestic workers to confirm the fact. There were times, during boring dinner parties, particularly when the conversation turned, as it did so often in bourgeois America in 1989 and 1990, to the collapse of the Soviet empire, I would slip into the kitchen and talk to the maid. To the background of some Spanish-language variety show emanating from a small black-and-white TV set nestled, all but lost, among the high-tech appliances, the Rosa or María or Concepción in question would tell me stories about home. They would speak about the decision to leave, the good-byes, the buses to the border, the river crossing into Mexico, the trek north to the United States. Then they would tell of the venal Mexican Federales, shaking them down for their last few pesos, the *coyotes,* thugs paid to guide them across into the United States from Baja California. Such stories were as close to epics as the modern world has seen, the stuff of legend and myth. And yet what was clear, as these women talked, was that they had never wanted to be heroines, never wanted to venture far from home.

The conversation would eventually tail off. About life in Los Angeles, they were far less forthcoming. And after thanking them, or making a weak joke, I would say good-bye and walk back into the world—my world—of chardonnay, Mission furniture, and German reunification.

The kitchens and the parking lots were the only parts of West Los Angeles that these maids and car parkers could lay claim to. Anglo L.A. is comfortable enjoying meals *a la Mexicana,* and its kitchens, at mealtimes, are redolent of the spices of Veracruz or of the isthmus of Panama. Indeed, to smell these smells emanating somewhat improbably from the blenders, Mixmasters, Cuisinarts, and Calphalon pots and pans of well-equipped L.A. kitchens was something of a study in cognitive dissonance. The maids didn't seem to mind, though. By these Italian brick ovens, or in the night air, amid serried ranks of Jaguars, BMWs, and Mercedeses, girls from the Gulf of Fonseca could dream of their boyfriends back home, or young men from Jalisco could talk about blondes and soccer strikers, without constantly looking over their shoulders for the immigration police.

Inside the restaurant or across the hall in the dining room, what was playing out was not simply the California dream but exercises in oblivion. The two worlds coexisted—indeed, in reality, they had become interdependent—but the Anglos barely took any notice of the people from the South (that catchall phrase for the poor world that is far more intellectually respectable than the term "Third World") who had come to live in their midst. They often appeared as nothing so much as the ubiquitous background to life in West L.A., although far quieter, for the most part, than the sound of the Temptations crooning on Allegra's cassette player. Indeed, when an attempt was made, in 1990, to organize the Mexican cleaning ladies in the downtown office towers, and a march was held which was broken up violently by the Los Angeles police, even people who normally got quite upset about police brutality—something that Los Angeles, with its traditions of union-busting and right-wing politics, has never been short of—remained strangely mute. It was as if these particular demonstrators were not so much workers, with rights to be defended or contravened, as enablers, people who were never supposed to be seen in the first place.

The maids were not even included in stories about the good life in Southern California, so much was their presence there taken for granted. When *Los Angeles* magazine ran a story called "Secrets of the Filthy Rich" in July 1990, they included the most expensive restaurant, lawyer, golf course, health club, private school, personal trainer, dog trainer, new car, haircut, and hospital room. Neither maid nor gardener reached the list, a testimony not only to how cheap such services were but how they were so commonplace among middle-class people that to include them in an article about the genuinely wealthy would have been all but an act of *lèse-majesté*.

An even greater oddity was that in all the movies about the young, or, more properly, the youngish people, that were being churned out at the time with such depressing regularity on L.A. soundstages, there was never the slightest sign of these enabling people of color. A film like *The Big Chill*, or even such television shows as "thirtysomething" or "L.A. Law"—and these were productions that were regularly applauded, and not only by network publicists and TV critics, for their realism, what was usually described, as in an ad for a soft drink, as their "refreshing" honesty—could only be taken seriously until that inevitable, credibility-busting sequence when one of the characters strayed into the kitchen or the laundry room.

At least the makers of *The Big Chill* tried to sidestep the problem entirely by setting the action in a country house during a reunion of friends from college, although even in that film the absence of domestic help for all these successful folks who have undoubtedly not done a load of laundry in years is a little hard to credit. In the urban settings of socially conscious TV dramas, the idea is as ludicrous as it is corrupt, a direct segue from fiction to fraud. There the characters go, doing their own dishes (the way the men are always so willing to help—except, that is, when their refusal to do their share is a part of the plot—is also a bit hard to swallow, but that's another story) and folding their own sheets. As if all these people who have been presented as being prosperous lawyers, doctors, architects, scriptwriters, private eyes, and randy housewives *did not have maids*! As if—and in West Los Angeles of all places—there were, in actual fact, not just at least one car in every garage, but, in every kitchen from Hancock Park to Pacific Palisades, a Rosa, a Teresa, an Encarnita, a Mercedes (throw in the car and you had two Mercedeses), an Eulalia, a Paula, and, for every one of them, ten Marías. As if—overlayed over white Los Angeles and expanding every year—there were not tens and tens of thousands of energetic young people who had come across the border looking for work—and damn the immigration laws! If anything, the border was the least of the daunting risks these people had taken. If you were deported, as more than one laborer told me, you could always try again the following month, whereas at home there was no work. They came from El Salvador, Honduras, Guatemala, Nicaragua ("OTMs," the Border Patrol officers called them, "other than Mexicans"), and from half the rural states of Mexico as well.

And yet to hear the way people talked in West L.A., you would have thought that the city was little more than an engorged version of Carvel, Idaho, that mythical home for Mickey Rooney in the Andy Hardy movies that Louis B. Mayer's scriptwriters had concocted as the epitome of white-picket-fence, blond-haired America. When Anglos on the Westside thought of the changes in L.A. that had taken place over the past twenty years, they thought of cappuccino, of good bakeries, of music and museums, and of supplanting New York as the American city where the real action took place. More business-oriented types talked about living in a great center of the nascent Pacific Rim, conjuring up Huntingtonesque visions of economy fueled by Japanese capital, and growing rich on endlessly expanding Asian markets. But neither these boosters nor anyone else seemed much interested in talking about the Los Angeles that was rapidly becoming the home of last resort to the poor of the Americas: El Norte, the place you went in order to survive. They could talk about the Beach Boys L.A. of the past, or throw a little Japanese samisen music in if they were feeling farsighted, but this did not change the fact that the rock and roll of Southern California was being over-dubbed with mariachis, even though few people inside that amnesiac pleasure dome known as West Los Angeles had yet taken in the fact.

And why should they have? Allegra's case was typical. She was not rich herself, although she came from a prosperous family and could, I suppose, have been said to have great expectations. Still, daily life for her remained, in her early thirties, an unsettling matter of scraping by from month to month. By the twenty-seventh or so, it was not unusual to find she had to live off her credit cards until the first finally came round. This involved going to grocery stores which, by virtue of taking cards, were usually more expensive, or of reaching for the check to pay with her card when she went out to dinner with friends and collecting cash from everyone else at the table. But however precarious her financial situation might occasionally become, there seemed to be no question, for Allegra, of not employing a maid. It was as unthinkable as, say, not having a car, or a telephone, in a city where, for prosperous people, having a telephone in one's car was less and less of a remarkable occurrence.

In West Los Angeles, maids were part of the basic "kit" of middle-class life. One might do without them as a student, or, perhaps, after retirement, but otherwise, except in the most exceptional lives or straitened of circumstances, they were more or less a cradle-to-grave entitlement. This is not the way people live in parts of the country less touched by the new immigration from the South, nor is it the way people lived in Southern California twenty-five or thirty years ago.

Whenever Allegra attempted to reduce her expenses she would stop buying clothes, or eating out so much, or even resolve, fierce cigarette smoker that she was, to give the cancer sticks up once and for all. But neither Allegra nor her friends, some of whom really did live on the financial edge, ever seemed to consider getting rid of their cleaning ladies. This decision was at once deliberate and inadvertent, just as the maids themselves could appear at some moments to be what they actually were—facilitators of the lives of a privileged class of people—and at others peculiarly like the flower beds and mountains, that is to say, almost like topographical or botanical features of the environment of greater L.A. One lived in their shadows almost as literally as one lived in the shadow of the Hollywood sign, that emblem of the city high in the hills above Sunset Boulevard. Moreover, the sense of the maids of L.A. forming part of some natural order of things even found its echo in the way people talked about their comings and goings.

"Don't bother with the dishes," Allegra would say, at the end of a long and boozy dinner, "it's Rosa's day tomorrow." The knowledge that it was Rosa's *day* connoted that the rest of us had the day off, a gleeful realization with a decided family resemblance to the careless pleasure of children when they say, "It's Friday, we don't have to get up for school tomorrow morning."

Metaphorically, at least, that was exactly what many people in West Los Angeles were doing—sleeping in. Increasingly, they found themselves sucked into the promotional hype of upscale consumption, whether they liked it or not. The disappearance of household chores only left more time, it seemed, for shopping, body sculpting, and therapy, an outcome that the utopian generation of futurists like Marshall McLuhan and Buckminster Fuller, whose ideas had been commandeered so successfully by advertising copywriters and television executives, never quite foresaw. Angelenos now lived in the image of an image, the California dream of a California dream. It was a world of lists: where to go, who was hot, and what to buy. The glossy magazines that began proliferating in L.A. in the 1980s, magazines with names like *L.A. Style, Los Angeles,* and *Buzz,* all read like glorified consumer guides, the more serious stories that they occasionally ran lost in the opulent foliage of their advertising pages. One read them for the "private school and camp guide," for "top chef's dining predictions," for the "Westside infant erudition frenzy," and for "how to buy a pet."

In this world, people and their things were almost as hard to tell apart as that more vaunted distinction that Los Angeles had done so much to explode, dreams and realities. The premiere issue of *Buzz* contained several epigraphs. The first, from Jane Austen, read, "One half of the world cannot understand the pleasures of the other"; the last, from the actress Tracey Ullman, read, "Everything is entertainment in America eventually." The gesture was vintage West L.A., a magazine based on the idea that everything in life is a performance. The *Buzz* editors wrote that what they had in mind for their magazine was not "merely the buzz of gossip—though there will certainly be some of that ... [but] more the buzz of a good dinner party—of a good *Los Angeles* dinner party— the kind where you find yourself surrounded by an exciting mix of distinctive voices and provocative sensibilities." And one wanted to add, "Yes, and served by little brown women from El Salvador."

But it was not only the presence of maids, or the force of consumerism, that had contributed to this extraordinary sense of both ease and entitlement. Above all else, the construction of the city itself, the way in which one never had to encounter more than glancingly anyone in materially different circumstances from one's own, because one was always in a private space or a commercial space—a house, a car, an office building, a shopping mall—meant that large numbers of people could actually read a magazine like *Buzz* or *L.A. Style* and imagine that the image of life that they were hawking actually corresponded to reality. To be sure, no one with any sense in West L.A. identified completely with what they read in these magazines or saw on television, but it would be equally naive to underestimate the effect they have had, if only by dint of constant repetition, not to speak of the alluring wrapping in which this vision of the world was presented.

L.A. Style, which is the most graphically sophisticated of the glossy papers, is an interesting case study. It is published monthly and uses the registered trademark of a corporation called L.A. Style, Inc. The start-up money for the paper is said to have come originally from the actor and producer Michael Douglas, Kirk Douglas's son, and from some of his friends, who have now been bought out by American Express. *L.A. Style* has a New York office, and its style is largely derivative of *Interview* magazine, which Andy Warhol created in New York twenty years ago and where the previously absolute separation between editorial and advertising pages was first blurred in an interesting and original way. *L.A. Style* runs ads for such enterprises as a Mercedes dealership in Santa Monica, an upscale shopping center in Redondo Beach, and an impressive array of L.A.'s trendier restaurants, hotels, and specialty stores, as well as the usual menu of national advertising and department store promotions. In other words, the magazine presents the familiar cliché of Los Angeles, complete with profiles of stars, directors, fashion people, consumer guides, restaurant and car reviews, and, not incidentally, an excellent gossip column that used to be called "Dish" and is now called "Social Studies. Out With the In Crowd."

It comes as no surprise that, in most issues of *L.A. Style,* there are more names of visiting Spanish and Latin American celebrities in the gossip columns than there are, except when the magazine is plugging a hot new band or restaurant, names of anyone from the Chicano, illegal Mexican, or Central American communities that now make up over 35 percent of the population of greater Los Angeles and whose children constitute over 50 percent of the enrollment in the L.A. Unified School District. *L.A. Style* did once run a special issue called "Latin L.A.: Beyond the Barrio." It was, in fact, impeccably done, and had one taken the editor's prefatory note to it at face value there might have been reason to predict a break in the Westside's implacable indifference to its neighbors across the Los Angeles River. "We live in a city well on its way to becoming half Latino," wrote Joie Davidow, "a city where not being able to speak Spanish is sometimes embarrassing and often inconvenient, and which is often mysteriously segregated. Many Westside Anglos' only involvement with the great wealth of Latino culture that surrounds them takes place when they order haltingly from a Mexican menu. Throughout this issue we celebrate the spirit of Latin Los Angeles."

But as it had done before, and continues to do, the Westside, if it celebrated at all, celebrated and forgot for reasons probably not so very unlike those that underpin the "segregation" Ms. Davidow found so mysterious and is, in reality, the most fundamental thing one needs to know about the city once one has learned that it is, botanically, a desert. The next issue of *L.A. Style* was called "Art in the City of Angels," and Latino artists were noticeable by their absence. "Most serious artists working here," wrote Garrett White in his prefatory piece, "L.A. Art, 1990," [are] in Los Angeles, after all, for conventional reasons: It's where they were born or went to school, or they like the climate."

In fairness, when something both important *and* fashionable was taking place, like the opera director Peter Sellars's 1990 Los Angeles Festival, which was conceived as, precisely, a showcase for the performing groups of Latin American and East Asian L.A., all the glossies were perfectly capable of snapping to attention. But this, too, fell under the rubric of trends. Why shouldn't demography, as Tracey Ullman had said, become entertainment? The editors of *Buzz* had decreed as much when they had written that L.A. was now "a confident and cosmopolitan center, not just of movies and mass entertainment, but also of art and theater, business and finance, technology and *social change*" (the italics, for once, are mine). But since this kind of pop insouciance, in which everything is more or less interchangeable, finds its own anchors in celebrity and money, it was a foregone conclusion that Mexican L.A., which had little of either, would not come often into the limelight. The special issue of *L.A. Style* had been an anomaly of sorts, a walk on the wild side—rather like titling that month's car column "Nuevo Lowriding."

A bit of slumming was all very well, as was a bit of social responsibility, but both, as they say in L.A. these days, got "old" if they were repeated too often. The gossip, the buzz with a lower-case *b,* was another matter entirely. That never got old; that was always user-friendly.

From the "Dish" column, two representative passages. One appeared in 1988 and the other in 1990, but there is no need to date them, because they are—almost by definition—at once of the moment and completely out of time. Assuming that most of the readers of these bits do not know those being described, one can only explain them as dreams of ease, two small cuttings from the complacent eclecticism of life in West Los Angeles.

We love *Earl McGrath's* art openings—plenty of food, and drink and gossip, and a guest list you can count on. And they all showed up for *Jim Ganzer's* vernissage: *Harry Dean Stanton, Howard Hesseman, Helena Kalianotes.* Writers *Joan Didion* and *John Gregory Dunne* rubbed serious jewelry with *Joan Quinn. Bob Rafelson* and *T-Bone*

Burnett hung out. Artist *Ron Cooper* was in from Santa Fe, *Winston Barrie* from Santa Monica. Earl spent most of the time trying to give calico kittens to his friends.

and,

We attended a battery of opening-night parties, the best being photographer *Greg Gorman's* annual 29th birthday bash. The usual gang showed up for the buffet dinner: *Mickey Rourke* in the company of *Carrie Otis, Gary Busey, Boy George, Lesley Ann Warren, Sarah Douglas,* mysterious look-alikes musician *Charlie Sexton* and his steady model *Mitzi Martin.* After dinner, the doors were opened to the throngs of Westside hipsters. The private VIP room is beautiful, a vision of elegant decadence.

There must be very few party lists, passenger manifests, board of elections registers, or payroll ledgers in Los Angeles that remain so reassuringly lily-white.

In that obdurate arcadia otherwise known as West L.A., people go on pretending their lives are at the cutting edge of the future, that, in due course, the rest of the country, and—who knows?—the world, will live the way people do in Santa Monica and Pacific Palisades. And why shouldn't they feel this way? Everyone they know, everyone their children go to school with, lives the way they do. And the local politicians abet the conceit, in part because even as the population grows increasingly poor and nonwhite, the electorate remains disproportionately Caucasian and middle-class, far more likely to be knowledgeable about Israel, reunited Germany, or the environment than about Watts or Boyle Heights.

For now, things are continuing to work well for these people, whatever the frustrations of traffic and overdevelopment. But they only work because of what is being glossed over, like the fact that the brown-skinned children Westsiders see through their car windows, playing in the schoolyards of an educational system most whites long ago abandoned, are the offspring of the brown-skinned women who work in their kitchens. There are consequences to this, since the sons and daughters of maids are rarely inclined toward the stoicism of their immigrant mothers.

6. Modern Times

. . . .

The labor-saving devices that transformed the country—all those vacuum cleaners, electric ranges, dishwashers, and the like—look smaller
now. To approach them with the same wonder that young couples did
in the forties and fifties is no more possible than returning as an adult to
the house one lived in as a child and not being disappointed by its
diminution. And yet these were the devices that had permitted an America victorious in the World War to create a society that, materially at
least, seemed on the cutting edge of the modern. It was a world of
homes and roads, home appliances and automobiles. And if Los Angeles
had invented neither the garden suburb nor the freeway, the fifties idea
of domestic "togetherness" nor the outlying residential shopping mall,
it was Los Angeles that took this world of things, and the world of feeling
that accompanied it, to its logical conclusion: perfecting it, in the eyes
of its boosters; creating a barren, homogenized conformity, in the opinion of its critics.

Everyone understands what the automobile did to change the United
States, but most underestimate the effect of the washing machine. It was
home appliances that made the garden ideal of the suburb different in
the fifties. Suburbs, after all, were an old American trope, and the ideas

about the caring, not to say self-absorbed, family that most people associate with the fifties were in fact much older. The fear of the dangerous
city, often peopled by aliens and nonwhites, as well as the ideal of
suburban domesticity, was well in place by 1900. The idea of life as a
species of amusement was also nothing new. A 1923 brochure offering
tract homes in the L.A. suburb of Palos Verdes advertised that this was a
town where "your home is your playground."

What was different was that there was a surfeit of things, and, as their
effects were felt, a surfeit of time. Chores that had previously required a
week of work were diminished, in the shiny postwar world, to the effort
of a single day. It was women, many of whom were entering the labor
force for the first time and whose paychecks had permitted so many
couples to acquire their dream houses, who had to find this time. That
meant evenings and weekends, mostly, since their husbands, when they
contributed at all, only mowed the lawn—increasingly on motorized
mowers—or set the sprinklers. Father knows best, indeed.

But Dad and Mom alike were increasingly coming to view life less as
a playground than as a supermarket, which, in fact, at a time when they
were few and far between in the rest of the country, had been commonplace in Southern California since the early thirties. It was the volume
of *demand* that made the fifties extraordinary and explains the hold
they still have on the imaginations of those who grew up in them. The
children in Geoffrey O'Brien's brilliant memoir of the counterculture,
Dream Time, are described as living in "a civilization that brought them
things. They could count on a new crop of toys each Christmas, always
a little more technologically advanced than last year's models: tin robots
that spoke and walked, plastic rockets with a range of up to thirty feet.
New television programs were provided each September to set the tone
for that autumn's play, whether the props were Davy Crockett hats or
Zorro capes or a rifle like Chuck Connors used."

The system that permitted both parents and children each season's
harvest of things was largely a Californian invention. Certainly, the postwar suburbanization not only of greater Los Angeles but of the entire
United States would not have taken place with such astonishing effi-
ciency had it not been for A. P. Giannini's Bank of America. Truman's
Fair Deal hinged on single-family housing. To this end, a credit system
was devised not only for returning veterans but for other would-be
homeowners as well in which substantial tax benefits were available to
anyone who wanted to take out a loan to buy a house. But already
during Franklin Roosevelt's New Deal, Giannini's bank (it had originally
been called, in honor of its founder's immigrant origins, the Bank of
Italy) had begun the expansion of consumer credit that revolutionized

(for once, the term is appropriate) the buying habits and the material dreams of a nation.

The Bank of America, which, by 1970, before its precipitous fall from grace, had become the largest lending institution in the world, all but invented the car loan, the installment plan, and the thirty-year mortgage. Giannini lent money to individuals who wanted to buy a house in a subdivision, but, more often than not, he had financed the subdivision as well, and the businesses that needed start-up money to establish themselves in its commercial spaces. The first bank cards—that is, revolving charge accounts unconnected to a particular department store —were issued by the Bank of America, which also underwrote a speculative project called Disneyland on some unpromising orange groves well south of where Los Angeles's sprawl had reached by the early fifties.

With the advent of television in nearly every suburban home (in 1947, 160,000 TV sets were manufactured each year; three years later, the figure was 7 million), demand could be stimulated almost at will. The car salesmen who had been underwritten by a Bank of America loan officer were soon appearing on advertisements all over Southern California. With what was then called a BankAmericard (later renamed Visa), the suburbanite could wander the aisles of specialty store and department store at will, confident that as long as the boom continued the new things would never be out of reach.

What was less remarked at the time, when the good life in California appeared to most people both like a wholehearted affirmation of the American family and as little more than a sprucing up, a refurbishing of the American dream, was how radical this culture of sprawl that had come into being in Los Angeles really was. On the face of it, things were going smoothly. More Americans were living better than they ever had before, and if people in out-of-the-way places like the Owens Valley or in the black slums of Watts complained, they were neither numerous enough nor influential enough to change many people's minds. The American ideal had long been of a family in a house with children, and in Southern California in the fifties the houses were going up as fast as the developers could raise what they were increasingly calling "off-the-rack" homes. The East Coast developer William Levitt is usually credited with inventing the postwar residential suburb. But his efforts pale before those of Southern California developers like Louis Boyar and Fritz Burns.

In Lakewood Park, a suburb in the San Fernando Valley that Boyar began to put up in 1950, most of the residents were either parents themselves or children under the age of ten. It was the prototypical suburban L.A. subdivision, a town of 17,000 homes and a population of 70,000 carved out of agricultural land on which, it need hardly be added, there had never, since the end of the Ice Age, been either lake or woods. To look at aerial photographs taken of the San Fernando Valley at the time is to see these buildings sprouting like mushrooms among the dusty fields. Look at pictures of the same site taken a decade later and the panorama is completely suburban, with visibility vastly curtailed by the haze of smog. The land was expendable. By 1970, 50 percent of the surface area of Los Angeles was made up of freeways, streets, and parking lots.

As real conservatives—not the dishonest apologists for business who claim the mantle—have always understood, there is nothing more radical than capitalism. The Bank of America and the new Southern California businessmen who had risen along with it might have unseated the old Wall Street financiers, but the results would prove rather different from what they imagined to be a simple extension of the capitalist franchise based on and catering to the power of small depositors. The arguments that were made for the Bank of America's version of the California dream were made once more, astonishingly, on behalf of the Drexel Burnham Lambert junk-bond king, Michael Milken, himself a San Fernando Valley boy, who from his offices in Beverly Hills was said by some to have facilitated a similar democratizing of capital. "Instead of loaning money to the people building our economic future," Milken told interviewers from the magazine *New Perspectives Quarterly,* "the traditional financial institutions were loaning money to foreign countries and to the small group of 800 investment grade companies in this country . . . The key innovation is the creation of a financial structure that is oriented to the turbulent future, not the slow-motion past."

It is a perfectly Southern California image, informed by television and surfing. Catch the future, Milken is saying, catch the perfect wave. But what none of the boosters for the future as Los Angeles writ large ever seem to have realized is that the word "turbulent" does not have positive connotations for most people, and that opportunities for some people to make money may make a great many other people lose all sense of who they are, or what they want in life, or what to feel. The transvaluation of values that Nietzsche imagined has come to fruition, if it exists anywhere, in the nihilistic capitalism of Southern California, a capitalism that, bred of democratic intentions, untuned America as surely as the French Revolution unseated the old feudal order of Europe.

People wanted more, more things and more for themselves. The enchantment with children, which had seemed such a permanent feature during the 1950s, when all the polls showed women rating their children as the greatest satisfaction of their lives, faded. In fact, the baby boom had been an anomaly, and, plotted over the course of the entire twentieth century, the demographic arrow of white American fertility moves steadily down. The cheap buildings put up by developers like Boyar and the cheap loans offered by the Bank of America and its imitators may have lured people to the suburbs and instilled in them a limitless taste for buying, but they felt lonely in these suburbs, the men complaining of feeling hemmed in, the women, now working in increasing numbers, of being stifled. This is the world that Betty Friedan described so well in *The Feminine Mystique,* the world that Gloria Steinem believed offered only a stark choice between motherhood and selfhood. "I either gave birth to someone else," she recalled of her decision not to have children, "or I gave birth to myself."

Women doing the same jobs as men during the day were hardly—how odd it seems, in retrospect, thinking they would—going to accept for long returning not just to their homes but to sex roles based on men being the sole wage earners. Children who had grown up in the suburban autotopias were bound, imbued as they were by its promise of endless pleasures and possibilities, to rebel at the conformity it demanded of them as adults. More generally, an economy based on planned obsolescence and the steady inflation of the consumerist impulse was bound to neglect those it had left behind, like the poor and the old, and to run afoul of nature itself, which would not tolerate its depredations indefinitely. The first smog attack—dangerous pollution produced almost entirely by the sheer volume of cars combined with particularly unfavorable atmospheric conditions—struck L.A. in 1943. The fact that nobody paid much attention did not make the event any less important, at least as a harbinger of the limits of the California dream.

The solipsism of the middle class, as the social historian Barbara Ehrenreich has called it, may have permitted people not to think about the consequences of the system they had created for the longest time. By the same token, the mistaken impression in the United States—that most solipsistic of nations—that it exists not just outside history but outside geography as well (witness the country's historic indifference to Mexico, along with Canada the only country in the world with whose destiny that of the U.S. is *permanently* linked) has led it to mistake its postwar prosperity for a permanent condition, for a right. All this is understandable, of course, even America's ahistoricity the paradoxical product of its specific history. What is extraordinary is that the democratic capitalism of California, which at its core is nihilistic in the dictionary sense of believing all traditional values and systems baseless, could imagine itself and persuade others that it stood for something that could be passed on to posterity.

In bringing their vast powers to bear on the stimulation of consumer demands, the businessmen and the marketers were ensuring that an ideology of choice took hold that, though they envisaged it as a matter of purchasing decisions, became the deepest idea of all in postwar American life. One of the most naive arguments made by conservative critics is that this change in American morals was the result of the counterculture of the 1960s, a charge that the aging veterans of that moment are, on occasion, all too willing to endorse. In reality, what destroyed community and brought the family to its present "turbulence" was capitalism itself. The logic of dissolution was there from the start, even in the plywood paradises of the San Fernando Valley.

For the game to go on, for the economy to stay healthy, the sprawl had to spread. Demography alone couldn't do it; even at the time, the birthrate during the baby-boom years was viewed as at least somewhat anomalous. Besides, if people in nuclear families had shown that they would buy more things than people in extended families, why stop there? Why not, instead of selling to them as families, sell to them as individuals, and herald the necessity, say, of a car for each person? The problem is that once everyone is in a car of their own there is unlikely to be much community left, a fact that still seems to surprise people in L.A., who regularly complain of a loss of intimacy all the while relying on machines like television and automobiles that, by their very nature, corrode intimacy and enhance alienation.

By the time I arrived in L.A., of course, that summer of 1989, the earlier, heroic version of the California dream was over. The newspapers were full of dire hints about new antipollution ordinances that would be necessary to bring the Los Angeles basin into compliance with minimal federal clean air requirements. On the Westside, the talk was all of slow growth. Whenever any city project, let alone an industrial development like oil drilling off Santa Monica, was proposed it was a sure bet that a coalition of neighborhood groups would be formed to oppose it. Such groups even had a generic name, NIMBY, "not in my back yard." This did not mean, however, that consumption had slackened among the baby boomers of West L.A.; and the stores along Melrose Avenue, on Montana in Santa Monica, and on all the rest of the upscale commercial streets and malls were doing as well as if not better than ever.

There was a wrinkle. If people were to devote themselves to making money and amassing possessions, not to speak of—here, the ethos of the counterculture and that of cowboy capitalism did indeed coincide —giving birth to themselves, to use Steinem's extraordinary phrase, they were unlikely to have time to clean up after themselves as well. A life spent on the job, in the gym, between the sheets, or in the mall can only be lived with a staff. Men have always known this: that was one of the reasons so many resisted, in the sixties and seventies (before brute economic necessity—the inability of a middle-class couple to live on a single paycheck), the idea of their wives going out to work. Now, what many younger professional women were referring to as a postfeminist generation were discovering that the problem was, if anything, more acute if you were single.

A twenty-four-year-old catering director in Century City named Colleen Moore was a perfect case in point. She worked at least ten hours a day, six days a week, and affirmed that she loved every minute of it. Moore recognized that the life she had chosen had its drawbacks. She spoke of the possibility of having a family in terms that other people might have used about their hopes of winning a lottery. "I want to get married," she told a reporter from the *Los Angeles Times*, "do the whole baby thing, have a family and not work for a while. But only people who are very fortunate get to do that. Especially in L.A." Owning a house was all but out of the question. "That would probably be pushing it," Moore said.

In a Los Angeles full of Colleen Moores, maids were the obvious solution, the "Leave It to Beaver" sitcom world of a preceding generation having been replaced by a "thirtysomething" world (but a realistic one, this time) of "leave it to the maid." Life was quite literally described by many people I met as being impossible without the enabling presence of these maids, cooks, and gardeners. It was one thing to work long hours at something you cared about, or devote yourself to a sport or a hobby. But there was no way as long as they could afford it that a generation that had grown up thinking of life as, essentially, fun was going to be reconciled to mopping their own floors or cleaning their own toilets. Somebody had to, though, usually somebody whose last name ended with a *z*, an *a*, or an *o*.

Once, when Allegra wanted a week alone to bull her way through, uninterrupted, the rewrite of her script, I went to stay with friends in a beautiful house in Brentwood Park. They had an enormous dog, a Hungarian puli with hair like a catastrophe in a dust mop factory, and a sweet and clownish disposition, that I took to walking at improbable hours, as much to make my way around the unfamiliar neighborhood on foot as for any more altruistic motive. This need for a pretext was real. With fear of crime rampant—it was said that criminals from South Central L.A. referred to the Westside and the Valley as the "lands," for lands of opportunity—neighborhoods like Brentwood were a sea of barred windows and octagonal signs planted in the shrubbery or rose borders that read, "Westec Security: Armed Response."

When I would go out in the early morning, the streets would be empty, but by the time the dog and I would begin pantingly to make our way home, we would pass those telltale beat-up old station wagons and pickup trucks. Slowing to a halt, these vehicles would disgorge their cargoes of small, brown-skinned men. In silence, they would set to work, mowing the lawns, trimming the opulent hedges, seeing to the sprinkler systems, and sweeping up the natural debris—palm fronds, eucalyptus leaves, and the like—that Los Angeles discharges on even the most windless of its evenings. But if, by 8:00 A.M., the streets of Brentwood were filled with these gardeners and, as Katharine Hepburn might have said in *The Philadelphia Story,* groundskeepers, by noon they had vanished. Sometime in the interim, it appeared, the men had either walked to the bus stop on San Vicente Boulevard to begin the hours-long trek back to East Los Angeles by RTD, or else they had been collected by the same beat-up old jalopies that had delivered them to the Westside in the first place.

People who have never lived in Los Angeles tend to suppose that everything there is so green and luxuriant because the place is some kind of natural arboretum. The opposite is true, and the maintenance of West L.A.'s sparkling appearance is an extremely difficult, labor-intensive activity. The Californian natural paradise lies in the northern part of the state, not in the Los Angeles basin, a desert ringed by the Pacific, the mountains, and that much-fetishized epiphenomenon of plate tectonics known as the San Andreas Fault. A short flight over the area on a clear day is proof enough, but there is another journey, this time by car, that makes the point even more vividly. For you only have to drive two hours south to Tijuana, across the Mexican border in the province of Baja California, to get a proper sense of what Beverly Hills and Brentwood would be were they not constantly tended by armies of hired Latino help. The streets of what is, in fact, one of the most prosperous cities in Mexico are dusty and ill-kempt, having the benefit neither of gardeners (they've all gone north to work) or the stolen water of the Owens Valley to make them green, peaceful, and alluring.

Bewitched by the dryness of the climate, visitors sometimes imagine that the Los Angeles basin is such an exception to the laws of botany that all those luxurious plants they see growing in their friends' gardens would do so if left wild. As for Angelenos themselves, they too often speak as if they have forgotten the real reasons their backyards look the way they do. To be sure, people routinely fret about the water shortage, but to talk about the future in even the most apocalyptic terms is by no means the same thing as apprehending the present. The fear of fire, which every sane L.A. homeowner has in his bones, presses on even daily conversation. Except among passionate environmentalists, anxieties about the aqueducts and the drought do not. In Los Angeles, a garden is a garden, a water problem is a water problem, and connections between the two remain tenuous at best.

There is also the small matter of Hollywood. A city this long in the business of manufacturing illusions can hardly be expected to encourage its residents to peek behind the stage set. In any case, there is the stubborn hope that if a solution cannot be found, at least the moment when one has to come to grips with the problem can be deferred. In the meantime, it was best to pay the brown people whose elbow grease maintained the illusion, and enjoy the show. Still, the obliviousness could be breathtaking. "You don't have to do any work to get things to grow here," a scriptwriter friend of Allegra's told us, as we sat by his pool in the late afternoon sunlight.

Allegra, who as a Northern Californian by birth knew better, winked at me. She had seen me, earlier during lunch, as I watched the gardener gather his things and let himself out through the garden gate at the far end of the pool.

"Yeah, right," she said, spearing an endive leaf, "and I'll bet your teeth brush themselves as well." There was the usual embarrassed silence that falls over West L.A. social gatherings when people say something harsh that cannot be explained away by its connection to work.

Indeed, exceptions to this attitude were rare. When Tim Rutten, an editorial page writer at the *Los Angeles Times* (who would eventually become my closest friend in Los Angeles) told me that his mother refused to hire maids, and insisted that as long as her husband and sons sat at her table, they could do the household chores for themselves, I was not surprised when he added quickly that his mother was literally the only person he was aware of who still hewed to such an old-fashioned conception of domestic responsibilities. More common was the presumption that there would always be some unknown person to take care of the dirty bits of life. Once, as I chatted with a friend of Allegra's about her new baby, and asked her how her life was different, she replied, "Oh, it changes your life, all right." Then, pausing for a moment and shaking her head ruefully, she added, "I mean, it changes someone's life; I mean it changes some Guatemalan's life." She meant the remark as a joke, of course, but, after she had delivered it, she shifted uncomfortably, as if its truth had only then become clear to her, and swept off into the kitchen to pour herself another cup of coffee. When she returned, we talked about German reunification.

It was hard to see, however, any way that in the longer term the realities of the situation could be covered up by such jokes or the more usual bland denials. Whites on the Westside of Los Angeles had grown accustomed to delegating even some of the most important aspects of their lives to hired immigrant enablers. Every year, the degree to which the real facts of daily life were at odds with the way middle-class people understood their experience increased. To leave one's office in Century City or Beverly Hills and know that the trashcans were emptied and the floors mopped down was one thing; you didn't have to see the janitors who did that work, and, indeed, the janitors' strike in Century City in 1990 probably succeeded because the strikers, by roaming through the complex rather than picketing outside and by entering nearby yuppie watering holes at happy hour made themselves visible. But it was quite another thing to live alongside the people who were picking up after you and caring for your children.

People on the Westside do not, of course, neglect their children. Still, all of the men and most of the women I met held demanding jobs, and there was a constant tension between the demands of career and the demands of family. What resulted, more often than not, was a freeze-dried version of family life, with parents spending time with their kids when they could and trying to make up for this inevitably reduced allotment by paying more attention in the given moment, an attitude perfectly summed up by the grotesque euphemism coined in the seventies: "quality time."

The routines of daily life hardly varied. For most of each weekday, middle-class children found themselves either in the custody of their schoolteachers or of their family's maids. Only in the evenings and on weekends did their parents take over. Inevitably, most parents did their best to make these times pleasant, making up with affection the previous week's deficit of attentiveness. This dependence on professional child-care providers and consequent stripping down of the family to its "affectional core" put the social critic Christopher Lasch in mind of nothing so much as the children on Israeli kibbutzim, who, he argued, "were strongly peer-oriented ... seldom capable of deciding on their own what was true or false, what was good or bad." Lasch's prescription, in radical counterpoint to most liberal thinking which championed an expansion of day-care, after-school programs, and the like, was for a strengthening of the family itself. What he may not have seen is that the deep strains of crippling relativism and indecisiveness, the sense of being overwhelmed by choices, marked the parents of these kids (who, after all, had grown up in the heyday of the nuclear family) as much as the younger generation. A society where the quantity of every artifact of daily life, from TV channels to breakfast cereals, seemed to be doubling or tripling every decade (there were 46 cereal brands in 1970, for example, and 155 in 1989) was not one in which any choice would seem stable or, at times, even possible to make.

The maid-dependent parents of West L.A. were themselves only one version of the lives people led there. Many couples had forsworn the idea of having children entirely. And many who had not still agonized and agonized over when the appropriate time would be and under what circumstances. After the next promotion, people said, after one more vacation in Hawaii, people said, after the next script got bought. The Hollywood lyricist Marilyn Bergman, a shrewd long-time observer of the L.A. scene, summed up the difference by saying, with a resigned shrug, that in her day the moment had simply come when couples knew it was time. "Then you just took out the diaphragm," she said, adding that "the more having a child becomes a choice, the more daunting a choice it seems."

There was also the matter of the biological clock. For women on the Westside—the situation of males was more pliable—it was like being on some kind of deadline, this for people whose daily professional experience was already of schedules, due dates, and last-minute submissions. But unlike the next rewrite or the revision of a legal brief, this deadline was not infinitely extendable. And so women in their late thirties began to have children, sometimes by themselves, as the saying went (that is, without a man who accepted any responsibility for the child after it was born), and often with the sense of getting pregnant at the last possible moment, beating the clock. Style section writers were calling this a second baby boom, but demographically it had little in common with the great explosion in middle-class American fertility that had lasted from the end of the Second World War to the early sixties.

Los Angeles is a peculiarly money-conscious town, even by American standards, and in a city where most whites had long ago abandoned the public schools, the question of having children was often viewed as a financial one. And the costs that had to be factored in were not simply those of private schools, but those of domestic help as well. The former were in short supply. "We thought about Westlake, the Lycée Français, or Immaculate Heart," friends in Hancock Park told me, as if it were self-evident that in all of Los Angeles there were only three schools that their daughter would choose from. Others moved to Beverly Hills or Santa Monica, where there was little or no busing and the schools did not have to compete for funds with the rest of an overburdened county system. A friend of Allegra's told of trying to enroll her six-year-old in a public school in the largely nonwhite neighborhood of Echo Park and being greeted by the (white) teachers with incredulous smiles. Finally, an administrator had taken her aside and said, "You're not really serious about this, are you? It's all remedial work here, and your daughter already knows English."

It would be a moral solecism to look down on these attitudes. The L.A. public school system has its institutional hands full trying to educate the new immigrant population whose children make up the majority of people under eighteen in the county. In a district where instruction has to be offered in eighty-two languages, from Spanish to Hmong (an influx of rich Iranian Jews has meant that the second language of Beverly Hills High is now Farsi), the problems of middle-class kids are bound to seem secondary. Moreover, white flight is a fact of life in all urban American school districts with large nonwhite populations. Racism plays a part, of course, but so do legitimate concerns about drugs and safety. In 1989, a Long Beach high school had to erect a wall around its playground to protect its students from gang-related drive-by shootings; the case was hardly untypical.

And not only did Westside parents have reasons to fear for their kids' well-being; they were hardly in a position to give up their jobs even had they all agreed with Lasch's grim Freudian convictions about the importance of the nuclear family. It was not greed that made two-paycheck couples a fact of life in L.A., it was an ingrained attitude about what one needed to live a decent middle-class life. Still, this question of children put into quotation marks all the common assertions about the good life in Southern California. The logic of capitalism had led people to an unexpected destination there on the edge of the Pacific. For if, on the surface, L.A. seemed like the last coherent American illustration of David Hume's famous remark that the "pleasures of luxury and the profit of commerce roused men from their indolence," that great defender of what, in 1990, people were pleased to call the market economy had presumably never meant to extol a world in which people would come to believe they needed to be rich to care for their children, or, more commonly, child.

But everything had changed in a generation. Even an activity as recreational as gardening has been transformed, in L.A., into one that requires the services of a gardener. But that was no problem. Los Angeles is now a place where a middle-class person can live in a First World way for Third World prices, at least for domestic help. With illegal immigrant laborers, many of whom had worked on farms in Mexico before coming north, in abundant supply, there was no shortage of able hands willing to work for next to nothing. For the middle class of the Westside, this meant that a style of life that had been the preserve of the truly rich was now within reach. When people spoke about the work that had gone into their gardens, it was almost invariably mostly someone else's work.

When they spoke about the rigors of child-rearing, they rarely meant coping with the wash, or, after infancy, with the long, wearing afternoons only a fractious toddler can produce. All in all, such talk was eerily reminiscent of a horsebreeder at a yearling sale or puffing with pride in the winner's circle after a race. No one expects a Payson or a Whitney, no matter how proudly he may speak of "his" horse, to have mucked out the stable beforehand, or even to have ridden in the race. The speech of the rich, however, has always been riddled with the ghosts of absent servants. Now, in L.A., the speech of the middle class is as well.

On the Westside, they need staffs to perform activities that, only a generation before, their parents had taught them to perform themselves. It was neither a simple matter of complacency nor one of heedless exploitation of the new immigrants. Immigration itself was a cloudy subject, with many people on the Westside, which is heavily Jewish, under the vague impression that just as their parents and grandparents had risen from poverty so would the children and grandchildren of their maids and gardeners. In the meantime, they themselves felt as if they needed to struggle just to make ends meet. To maintain this standard of living, both members of a couple not only had to work, they had to work furiously, often to the exclusion of everything else.

Dream houses had grown too expensive to be had by any other solution, that was certain. At the end of 1989, which was, in retrospect, the height of the Southern California real estate boom, the *average* cost of a house in the better neighborhoods of West L.A.—Brentwood, Beverly Hills, Bel Air, Pacific Palisades, and Santa Monica—was a million dollars. And the quoted price, real estate agents were quick to add, represented only a mean. Anything really special would cost far more. The Los Angeles market softened the following year, and even among fervent boosters of the region it is difficult to find anyone who believes the huge appreciations of the 1980s will be seen again for a generation. This does not mean, however, that the Westside will soon become affordable. During the 1990 meetings of the California Association of Realtors, the talk was all of Bakersfield, a hundred miles northeast of L.A. "We've been getting a lot of people who can't afford to buy in Los Angeles," a realtor named Leo Worrell told the *Los Angeles Times.* Another conventioneer added ruefully, "Things had to slow down sooner or later," but the way they slowed down was with large numbers of young families priced out of the market. It was a catch-22. If the economy grew so bad that housing prices collapsed, incomes would have collapsed as well. If the economy improved so that the housing market recovered, then the same spiral of housing appreciation that had priced people out of the Westside in the first place would begin again.

With the anxiety about the future cost of things growing increasingly common in West L.A., the phenomenon Barbara Ehrenreich has referred to as the middle class's "fear of falling," stories about yuppies priced out of the greater L.A. housing market appeared to have become a preferred way for *Los Angeles Times* editors to fill up column inches on slow news days. Like restaurant reviews, such pieces could be depended on to attract the upscale readers to what a citywide ad campaign was calling "the *new* faster-format L.A. *Times*." "Home Sick," announced one particularly alarmist feature in the *Times*'s real estate section. According to the reporter, the inability to buy a house in West L.A. was producing physical symptoms in thwarted homeowners. Doctors had given the syndrome a name: "Real estate anxiety." "Sufferers," claimed Professor Mark Goulston, a psychiatrist at UCLA, "became irritable in their relationships and negative because there is a feeling of disappointment that they can't accept." Dr. Goulston, identified in the *Times*'s story as "a specialist in psychiatric problems of fast-track parents and families," pointed to physical complaints like "muscular tension, restlessness, tiredness, upset stomachs, [and] appetite and sleep problems" as the most common manifestations of "REA."

Occasionally, a note of realism would intrude. One *Times* reader reacted to the "Home Sick" story by writing indignantly:

> So our parents were the Cleavers and we want to be the Cleavers too. The implication is that the only major difference between our parents and ourselves is that they could buy a home while we, through no fault of our own, can't. But is this really the case? Compared to our parents, how often do we eat out? Have our hair done? Fly to Vegas? Do we consider dog groomers, gardeners, fitness clubs, acrylic nails, car detailing, 10 major credit cards and a trendy address as essentials?

But such responses were rare, and not only in the pages of the *Times*, whose Sunday real estate section is itself such an exercise in promiscuous boosterism that it includes a regular feature, in the upper left-hand corner of its front page, called "hot properties," which in effect is a gossip column, complete with photo of a movie or TV star, detailing the latest sales and acquisitions of the Hollywood elite.

But even the voices that dissented from the usual Westside litany of complaint ("It makes me feel like a failure," whined one Lorien Cook, a thirty-three-year-old party planner. "I feel inadequate in my earning power") shared with the whining majority a common lack of interest in the subject of children. It was one thing, it appeared, to argue about trips to Vegas or acrylic nails, but for both sides, kids were out for anyone with ambitions to own a home of their own. Moreover, the usual panaceas offered by these critics of the "wanna-be homebuyers," as the *Times*'s caption writers had called them, was a move to a place where housing was cheaper. Our parents, one writer admonished, "bought the home they could afford, in the newly developing suburbs of L.A., the equivalent of Victorville or Moreno today," these last towns being located sixty miles outside of Los Angeles, in Riverside County.

A culture that remained this subservient to the idea of mobility at any cost, and which emphasized the priority of individual advancement over family stability and of social mobility over community, was bound to find the prospect of kids, well, just a little bit of a drag. If one decided to have them at all (as a T-shirt very much in vogue on Venice beach during the summer of 1990 portraying a weeping beauty exclaiming, "Damn, I forgot to have children," suggested), the decision was less than inevitable—one had to have help. That was where those negative mirror images of yuppie success, those maids and schoolteachers remarkable precisely for being underpaid and immobile, came in.

And once people had built lives with servants, only a catastrophe would have permitted them the imaginative freedom to conceive of life without them. It was a matter of the scarcity of free time, of course, but not only of that. When I would walk my friend's dog, those mornings in Brentwood, I would pass the gardeners stooped over the green lawns of Craftsman-style bungalows, *faux*-Tudor mansions, and California-moderne ranch houses, only to emerge on San Vicente Boulevard, the area's main thoroughfare. There an equally verdant strip (also expensively maintained: L.A. County and Caltrans spend millions to keep the boulevards and freeway borders looking good) would be filled with local residents. Like their gardeners, they too were working up a sweat, but in this case by jogging. Instead of burning up the calories by prancing along in spandex outfits so bright they looked, from a distance, like strange, amphibious tropical fish, these runners could have gotten quite a decent aerobic workout in their own gardens (and a considerably better anaerobic one as well), but in West L.A. in 1990, sweat and labor had bifurcated. Jogging was universally regarded as well worth the hours one devoted to it, but, to most Angelenos with servants, yardwork was a complete waste of valuable time.

What was less clear was the question of whether, had the effects of a three-mile run been equally attainable through the proxy of a Salvadoran illegal alien, people in West L.A. would have still put on the Nikes every morning with such rigorous fidelity. Medical science not having progressed to this point, however, it seemed as if anybody in a position to do so in Southern California was alternately engaged in working themselves to death and playing themselves to death. If in doing so those over forty among them resembled their high-school- and college-aged children more than they did the middle-aged people they actually were, this too was an old Southern California trope. After all, Los Angeles has long been the city where people have employed the most heroic measures to halt time's passage, a place in which, as John Gregory Dunne once quipped, a great many people are permanently thirty-five. What was new was the extent to which all the drudgery and so much of the elementary responsibility had disappeared from people's day-to-day experience, outside of the workplace, anyway. Poof! It was gone. Just as long as the maid showed up, the gardener didn't get deported, and the day-care center wasn't shut down by the District Attorney's office for practicing Satanism during the milk-and-cookies break.

This last fear was alternately gripping and diverting middle-class L.A. the summer I arrived. In 1983, a parent at the McMartin preschool in Manhattan Beach had telephoned the local police saying that she suspected her two-and-a-half-year-old son had been raped. A few weeks later, Raymond Buckey, the twenty-nine-year-old son of the owner of the school, was arrested. The police had then circulated a letter to 200 parents at the school, implicating Buckey in "possible acts of sodomy and oral copulation." Two months later, social workers at an organization called the Children's Institute International began videotaping interviews with the preschoolers themselves. They concluded that out of the 400 kids they had seen, 369 had been molested.

The response in the South Bay area of L.A. County in which Manhattan Beach is located was immediate, and, understandably enough, panic-stricken. Parents began to come forward with other children who had attended the McMartin preschool in the past, and who now claimed that they too had been either sexually assaulted or forced to join in Satanic rituals. Buckey and his mother, who had been out on bail awaiting trial on the first charges, were rearrested. Their bail was set so high that Mrs. Buckey spent two years in jail and Raymond five before their case ever came before a jury. In the end, however, none of the charges held up. Mrs. Buckey was acquitted on all counts, while the prosecutors declined to retry Raymond on the few outstanding charges on which the jurors, who had already rejected most of them, had been unable to reach a verdict.

Whatever the other rights and wrongs of the McMartin case, what was most noteworthy to an outsider was the assumption, seemingly shared by almost everyone concerned, that it was perfectly possible for child rape and Satanism on a mass scale to go on without anyone suspecting a thing for years. The school setting was regarded as not simply one where teachers acted, in the old phrase, *in loco parentis,* but one in which the kids were on their own. It takes both an astonishing degree of fracture in a family and an astonishing faith in an institution like a preschool for parents not to notice for years what is, after all, the brutally obvious physical signs of the physical molestation of their own children. It wasn't a boarding school, a Dotheboys Hall high in the San Gabriels; it was a place where these parents took their kids in the mornings and collected them in the afternoons. Was it possible that most people looked at their cars more carefully after they took them in for servicing than at their children's bottoms when they gave them a bath?

The McMartin case may have been an example of mass hysteria, or may have had some foundation, but the larger problem remained one of responsibility and the facing of facts. The McMartin parents were, in this sense, not so very different from the wanna-be homebuyers who bitterly resented their parents' ability to buy a house. "I don't feel like any other generation had to make quite the sacrifices we do," a young woman named Lynn Powell told the *Los Angeles Times* with fine, amnesiac indignation. "Both parents work full time and that's not enough. You're doing twice what your parents did and that's not enough to get into, virtually, a hovel. . . ." As was the case in L.A. so often, it was a matter of believing that history began around 1945, of shifting the blame, and of hiring others to clean up behind. It was typical; what was probably at most a simple case of molestation was turned into a countywide emergency, just as the ordinary unhappiness at being unable to afford a house was turned into a medical syndrome, complete with its own etiology and its own subset of "caring" professionals at the ready with treatment options.

As for the maids, it would have been surprising if Hollywood's portrayal of Los Angeles *had* found room for them. The city had become a place where it was all but neurologically impossible for people to take in the fact that they were adults. They took their cues from movie stars who either boasted of being forever young, or, like Shirley MacLaine, claimed to be thirty thousand years old, which, when you thought about it, was pretty much the same thing. "When the baby comes," said the actress Amy Irving of her then husband, Steven Spielberg, "Steven will have someone to share his toys with. And he's got a lot of them." And people who could barely face the relatively no-fault tragedies of aging and death could hardly be expected to react comfortably to the news that they were not an army of harmless Beaver Cleavers and Patti Dukes but rather a class of white bosses in what was not only an increasingly nonwhite city—an increasingly Third World city, for the native black population of L.A. had slightly decreased over the past twenty-five years —but one that was situated in a nonwhite hemisphere in an increasingly nonwhite world.

During the weeks in which the *Los Angeles Times*'s real estate pages were filled with letters about the article on yuppies unable to afford a nice house, only one correspondent put the matter in proper perspective. "I translated the article for my gardener, José," wrote a certain Howard Plzak of Los Angeles, "who asked me if it was a put-on. José came here from Mexico five years ago, worked the strawberry fields in Salinas for three years, and now has his own gardening service where he puts in sixty hours a week. . . . He is twenty-three years old, just an eighth-grade education, and sends money to his mother in Mexico."

But for most white Angelenos, it wasn't a put-on. Their prosperity, at once so great and so insecure, had blinded them. As for servants, they were those starched people one saw on British television imports like "Upstairs, Downstairs" or "Brideshead Revisited," or in old American films about the staggeringly rich, Depression-era entertainments like *The Philadelphia Story.* "How can I have servants," they seemed to be saying, "when I'm not Lady Marchmain or Katharine Hepburn; they're the ones that had servants—I'm just an ordinary middle-class American."

To reply that being an ordinary, middle-class American now meant being so much richer than most people alive in the world cut little ice. That wasn't the way it felt; it was as simple as that. As for all the Rosas and Marias who came on Tuesdays and Thursdays to rescue even the most modest West L.A. *rental* apartment (she rents, people said of Allegra behind her back; imagine!) from the disorder in which their oh-so-busy occupants had left them . . . well, they belonged to some other category entirely. A generation that had grown up on television could now no longer distinguish between its fantasies and reality, and refused to recognize these stoic presences who made their lives comfortable. Sure, prewar America, that distant, hierarchical place most could only remember through the sweet dreams of the studios or the somewhat grittier evocations of Lillian Hellman, Clifford Odets, and Eugene O'Neill, had had servants galore. But postwar America? Not a chance. June Cleaver on "Leave It to Beaver" didn't have a maid, Harriet Nelson on "Ozzie and Harriet" didn't have a maid. They were just Moms with appliances. But now their daughters were downtown working as lawyers and stock analysts. Oblivious to the women who labored in their kitchens during the day, it often appeared as if they believed that what had changed was that now the appliances looked after themselves.

It struck me that the United States was beginning to look like the world as it is presented in that sublime Japanese theater form, Bunraku. Bunraku is a puppet theater. Dressed in sumptuous kimonos, the puppet characters are moved around the stage by a group of masked, black-clad handlers, while their costumes are changed by other members of the company who crouch at the back of the set, new miniature kimonos at the ready. The audience is aware that the puppets are being manipulated by these two groups of enablers (there is no attempt at concealment or darkening of the stage), but it is understood that what matters is the action of the drama. The stories are familiar, classics from the same repertoire drawn on by the Kabuki and Noh theaters. What makes Bunraku so odd and so remarkable is that it is one of the few theatrical forms in which people appear on stage, fully visible, and yet are, at most, of purely secondary interest to an audience. While we may admire the dexterity of a particular handler—they exist, they can be seen—from the spectator's standpoint, they are invisible as well (or, at least, they scarcely signify).

Something similar has taken place in Southern California. Without all the immigrants willing to do the menial work that native-born Americans (including most blacks, much as some of their leaders deny it) have forsworn, no cars would get parked at Westside restaurants, no lawns would be tended, and no infants looked after. Their employers, though, hardly acknowledge their existence, while for every Anglo child who grows attached to the maid another is confused by her presence. "I was alone all day," the five-year-old daughter of one of Allegra's friends told me boastfully. "The maid was there," her mother interjected, "but she only speaks Spanish and the child thinks she won't talk to her on purpose."

"That's right," the girl piped up, "I was alone with no one to talk to."

To Anglo L.A., nothing could be more present and yet nothing more shadowy than the lives of these servants. They are as ignored as puppet handlers, as opaque and incomprehensible as the obscurest of Stone Age hunters deep in the Brazilian rain forest. At least the aboriginal peoples of the Amazon have their backers on the Westside, people who raise money for them, give parties for them, and otherwise champion their cause. The maids have no such cachet. But then, the lives of servants never carry much weight in the minds of those who employ them. It is a natural enough conceit, rather like believing that the lives of actors, even when they are only inanimate Bunraku puppets, invariably must outshine the lives of the maids and butlers who dress and undress them, and facilitate their progress across the stage, their footsteps muffled by the background music of beautiful old songs.

A few noticed the incongruity, even if they did not quite know where to move it from there. The first time I met Tim Rutten, we had lunch at one of the fine new restaurants that have cropped up in Los Angeles during the course of the past fifteen years. City, on La Brea and Second, is a great barn of a place, looking from some angles like a converted aircraft hangar, from other vantage points like an art gallery. A video monitor over the bar showing the work in the kitchens adds to the impression of taking in a performance piece along with lunch. Toward the end of the meal I had with Tim, when the busboy, whose face could have served as the model for a Mayan sculptor in the age of Tikal or Chichén Itzá, came to clear away our plates, I found myself staring at him for longer than was civil.

"You've got it," Tim said, catching my eye. "This town runs on brown wheels." And it seemed appropriate that, as happens so often in Southern California, even the most uncomfortable act of understanding and imaginative sympathy came wrapped in the fizzy vernacular of the automobile.

7. Alien Nation

· · · · · · · · · · · · · · · · · ·

If you were to follow Wilshire Boulevard from where it begins, a few blocks away from the Santa Monica Pier in a part of town local wags have christened "Croissant Canyon," sixteen miles east to where it peters out, a nondescript street bounded by construction sites and the impassive chrome and steel towers of that far steeper canyon otherwise known as downtown L.A., you would have made your way across neighborhoods in which all the races of the world have fielded their teams. Look a little closer, and it does indeed seem as if Los Angeles has been busy fulfilling Walt Whitman's prescient remark in the preface of *Leaves of Grass* that the United States would soon become the "nation of nations . . . race of races." That drive from the edge of the Pacific to the lobby of the Security Pacific Bank building is actually a perfect storyboard version, as the locals say, this being scriptwriter country, of the ethnic present of California and, perhaps, the ethnic future of the whole country.

For the most part, the people who still decide things in Southern California—which is to say, affluent white people who vote—remain largely unaware of how much the region has changed. The 1990 gubernatorial elections, which pitted Pete Wilson, a Republican senator who had been the mayor of San Diego, against Dianne Feinstein, the former Democratic mayor of San Francisco, was a perfect case in point. Theirs was a campaign waged almost exclusively through competing television ad campaigns. "When we're on TV," Feinstein admitted candidly, "our numbers go up; when we're off, our numbers go down." Both candidates were like advertisers with an upmarket product, in this case, themselves, to sell. And like agencies handling a luxury account, campaign strategists in both camps spoke insistently of California as comprising not distinct regions, let alone interests, but ten separate media markets. If they also harped on what they delicately called California's "spread-out" electorate, it remained clear that what they meant was that the state's *white* electorate was spread out, rarely venturing outside the constricted trajectories of subdivision, mall, freeway, and office, and thus possessed of flesh that the politician could only press electronically.

As often as not during the campaign—and the 1990 political season only confirmed trends that had long been visible in California politics—a movie star or some other personality whose expertise had nothing whatever to do with politics was the entire focus of the TV spot. In an era in which the electorate has grown to distrust legislatures, California is increasingly governed through programs mandated by voter initiatives. Nineteen ninety was the year of the environment, of Proposition 103—and there was Jane Fonda (who on another day or another channel might be seen in a leotard advertising a new aerobics tape) looking seriously into the camera and, with measured folksiness, trying to rouse the voters with the phrase "Let's all get out and vote for Big Green," this being the name under which the proposed programs were universally known.

Most people in Southern California, and certainly everyone in California politics, simply assumed that this was the way things worked. When I asked Marge Tabankin, the director of the influential Left-liberal Hollywood Women's Political Committee, whether the use of stars like Warren Beatty or Barbra Streisand bothered her, she looked at me as if I were asking her if she minded that there were twenty-four hours in a day. "I want to win," she said flatly, but it seemed as if more than a reluctant surrender to reality was at stake. After all, this was a political system in which people were being invited to trust celebrities—or "artists," as the stars' political handlers, employing a term that had theretofore been the province of press agents, publicity handouts, and contract negotiations, insisted on calling them—on matters about which they had no competence whatever, except, in rare cases, some access to expert briefings and the force of their own concern. If anything, the refusal of political operatives to view criticism of the use of stars as much more than sour grapes testified to the extent that the Hollywoodization of the country had progressed. You want to sell a car? Get an eye-catching commercial. You want to sell a political position? Get a star to make the pitch.

In trying to get their message across, the political operatives were contributing to the kind of aestheticized simulation of feeling and knowledge that all image factories are in the business of manufacturing. In Hollywood, of course, no one ever had to worry about ends and means, and the true story behind the studios, or the private lives of the stars, was, even when wonderfully presented, as in Kenneth Anger's masterpiece of dish, *Hollywood Babylon,* of little importance. There were scandals that would shock the public, and these, ranging from Pola Negri's promiscuity to Rock Hudson's homosexuality, had to be covered up. But what really mattered was the industry version of Tabankin's "winning," that is, making the picture. But Hollywood was one thing. It was supposed to be in the dream business. Politics were something else, and politicians were supposed to stand for people's needs and beliefs, not their fantasies, whether manipulated or self-generated.

If both candidates in the 1990 California gubernatorial race relied on the electronic media, and had advisers telling them who their target voters were, the effect of this was unlikely to be restricted to a choice between two candidates whose views—Feinstein was a centrist Democrat, Wilson a moderate Republican—were closer than either was willing to admit. The campaign confirmed the fantasy of white Californians that they were, for all intents and purposes, living in the state by themselves. To be sure, both candidates spoke (or, as politicians now say, spoke out) from time to time about the problems of the cities and of justice for the poor. But their campaigns were so skewed (as were those of supposedly more socially responsible types like the backers of Big Green) toward a prosperous, native-born, white Californian middle class that, under the weight of all this attention, such people could hardly be expected to face the fact that they now shared their state with a non-white population that was made up largely of new immigrants who would outnumber them in a few years' time.

A full quarter of all non-native-born Americans, the overwhelming majority of whom had come from East Asia and Latin America, now lived in California. They had not been lured to Los Angeles or Silicon Valley around San Jose by high-tech jobs, as had immigrants from other parts of the United States, but rather had come, in search of a better life, or drawn by the lure of America, or fleeing war and hunger, in ever greater numbers since the 1965 revision of a previously racist immigration law had permitted the first large-scale admission of nonwhite peoples to the United States since the early part of the century. It was true, of course, that these new immigrants were often living better in L.A. than they would have back home, but not only were many of them not doing well, often they were barely surviving. But they didn't vote, and except on the six o'clock news, with its lurid assemblage of crime and arson in the precincts where the poor lived, they were as invisible to white California (except, perhaps, in its nightmares) as they were to the politicians.

Liberal activists I talked with assured me over and over again that all this would change when the "right" people were elected, another reason, it seemed to them, to use all the tricks of Hollywood to get such candidates into office. But this account was illusory and personality-driven. Logically, it implied that the only thing wrong with Ronald Reagan—who, after all, was the most successful exemplar to date of this Hollywoodization of American politics—was that he had bad views. Presumably, a progressive actor, say Robert Redford, with his devoted environmentalism and his unshakable support for the Castro regime, even after it had been discredited in most places outside the city limits of Beverly Hills, would have been just fine. There was, in short, nothing wrong with the aestheticizing, dreamy simulacrum of politics that all media-centered campaigns entailed, only with certain political outcomes.

But what the activists, and their right-wing opposite numbers, failed to realize was that, as Marshall McLuhan had forecast twenty years before, the medium was the message, or, at least, would become it soon enough. The combined force of Southern California's geographical sprawl, its infatuation with images, its rejection of history, tragedy, and difficulty meant that acceptance of news about the future that was unsettling was unlikely to sink in to middle-class California, for whom the new immigrants were invisible except as busboys, maids, gardeners, and the like, or as part of the distant mayhem of the inner city and the steady march north from the Mexican border. That much of the region's prosperity was due to these immigrants was hard to grasp, unless one actually worked in the garment business or other light industries that relied on their labor. A lawyer in Brentwood or an aerospace technician in Huntington Beach would literally never even see such people, and the fact that they figured neither on television nor in the discourse of politicians made their significance so abstract, so unconfirmed in the contexts of both daily and imaginative life, that there was really no pressing reason to come to grips with their presence.

Often, it seemed, the Angelenos who were the city's most fervent boosters also were the most blind to what was happening demographically. To hear them talk of California as the sixth-largest industrial power in the world, or revel in Los Angeles's role as the financial capital of the Pacific Rim and in its new national importance, while simultaneously acting as if the political debate embodied in the Feinstein-Wilson race still had much to do with the state's future, was to encounter wishful thinking on a truly heroic scale. A common variant was for people to talk about the city's prosperity in terms of its high-tech industries— areospace in the South Bay; software in the Valley and Orange County; banking and brokerage downtown—without ever mentioning the garment trade or light industries like paint factories, which, far from relying on a skilled, highly paid, and literate work force, required, precisely, the nonskilled, nonunionized immigrant workers, who, because they were in the country illegally, could rarely quarrel with either their salaries or the conditions in which they worked.

If Los Angeles was indeed, as its enthusiasts proclaimed, the capital of a new "United States of California"—and there was, in any case, something a little off about this talk of the California Republic as a potential if not an actual reality rather than just some words written at the bottom of the state flag, under the bear and the star—that new nation was at least as much part of the Third World as the First, and growing more so every day. A simple drive downtown would have confirmed this fact for white Angelenos, but that was the rub. There was no reason for anyone to go there, except to work or to take in an occasional show at the Music Center. And even those incursions were, by and large, a matter of interiors—cars, parking garages, auditoriums, and restaurants.

These pleasures, too, were moving west. During the time I stayed in Los Angeles, at least half a dozen of the more popular eating places people were willing to drive east (though often not very far east) to get to opened branches in Santa Monica, Beverly Hills, and Brentwood. Some of these places were located not downtown, or in East L.A., but on Melrose Avenue, which is a trendy neighborhood, shared by Orthodox Jews and young bohemians, miles away from the edges of Third World Los Angeles. Hardly a combat zone, and yet I discovered that even the area of Wilshire somewhat west around the County Museum was considered by many to be too far east. The gym that Tim Rutten belonged to was in a development called The Courtyard, diagonally across from the museum, on the other side of Fairfax Avenue. It turned out that it only remained open because the building's developers needed the extra amenity to lure tenants to such dubious precincts. And yet the Fairfax district is a middle-class Jewish area where starting prices on small Craftsman-style bungalows run around $400,000.

Tim told me that most of his friends could not understand why he and his wife, a brilliant criminal lawyer named Leslie Abramson, lived in mid-Wilshire. Leslie's colleagues all lived west of Doheny Drive, the border between West Hollywood and Beverly Hills. My own experience tended to suggest that people on the far Westside no longer even knew where mid-Wilshire was. One night, at a dinner party in Santa Monica to which, carless at the time, I had gone by cab, my hostess asked me if I needed a lift home. "It's too far," I said. "I'm staying in mid-Wilshire."

"No, no," she replied, "I don't mind driving you there. It's just around Doheny, isn't it?"

The maids who worked on the Westside were, naturally enough, better informed, even if the pronunciation of streets like Doheny often defeated them. They crossed the city regularly, but when they did so they were more or less by themselves. One saw them, sitting patiently on the big orange buses of the Los Angeles Rapid Transit Department, being ferried back and forth between their homes in East L.A. and those of their employers. Frequently the only other riders were a few old Anglos too infirm now to drive their cars, some black or Latino school kids, and the odd drunk slumped, snoring, in the rear. White Los Angeles knew nothing of these buses. Indeed, to ride one would have been an act almost as preposterous as shimmying up one of the palm trees that tower on the median strips of the boulevards. Like those bits of exogenous vegetation, the buses are a visual constant but no more—like back projection in a movie.

During the time I spent in L.A., I met no one on the Westside who had been on an RTD bus more than once or twice in their lives. One person admitted to knowing *of* someone who used the system, but this turned out to be a French student at USC who had failed the California driving test three times already and was gearing up, as we spoke, for a fourth attempt by spending every spare dollar she had at a local driving school.

Not that there was any reason for someone with a driver's license to use public transportation. The RTD buses are slow, their air-conditioning breaks down often, and even if they take you in the general vicinity of where you're going, that proximity is relative. More often than not, you still have to walk another mile or two to get to the actual street address. And there can be few experiences more disconcerting than walking along a wide L.A. street without the reassuring jangle of car keys in your pocket. Those streets are largely unshaded, their sidewalks appearing wider because they are so empty. The traffic lights, timed for vehicles rather than pedestrians, pose a menace to the scattered, largely geriatric population of pedestrians, so much so, in fact, that the impression is inescapable that the advertisements you see on benches all over the Westside for Jewish funeral chapels are really messages aimed at anyone foolish enough to expect to long survive as a walker in Los Angeles.

To move around the city on foot is like being lost in the desert that the Los Angeles basin once was, and will doubtless become again, or like floating in space. The bare concrete surfaces and the hard, flat light only underscore the sense of being adrift and at risk, even if the particular neighborhood you find yourself in is safe and its geography apparent to you. For the new immigrants, the impression must be magnified many times over. They are easy to spot, these recent arrivals from south of the border, walking along aimlessly—or is it just that they still have a long way to go?—under street signs they are far from likely to be able to decipher. Sometimes they move in complete family units, paunchy, dignified men, haggard women, and a train of children taking up the rear. Sometimes, they walk alone, in this city the size of Neptune.

Those who could afford the bus fare found themselves on territory they could make their own. I never recovered from the surprise I felt at how openly the maids on the RTD, people who were obviously illegal immigrants living in fear of deportation, would talk to each other, reminisce about sneaking across the southern border, or muse about whether some relative or friend would make it across soon. They would talk of having to go back for family emergencies, matter-of-factly comparing notes about what the *coyotes* were charging these days for the crossing from Tijuana to San Isidro or Otay Mesa, California, or about what the bus fare was from the Mexican side of the frontier to their homes in Jalisco, Guanajuato, Michoacán, and Zacatecas. The words "Los Angeles" rarely figured in their conversations. They spoke more commonly of going to the United States, of coming here, *aquí,* or of arriving in El Norte.

Perhaps they were resigned to the idea that if the immigration police wanted to capture them they would, so dissimulation was futile. It seemed to me, however, that there was something else. The women knew only Spanish, and it was as if that language itself offered them a kind of protection from the prying eyes of the Anglo world. That they assumed that the few non-Hispanic passengers on the buses would not understand what they said was clear less from the derogatory as from the flirtatious or admiring remarks they occasionally made about them. Once, absorbed in my notes, I heard a clear, middle-aged voice exclaim in Spanish, "I like him. If I were not married already . . ." I looked up to find two heavyset women staring across at me, dissolved in giggles. But when I smiled back and said something in Spanish, they froze, staring mutely and incomprehendingly into some vague middle distance. I was just not supposed to be there. Certainly, the copywriters who had mounted the RTD's 1990 poster campaign would have been almost as discomfited by my presence as the women were. They knew their target market, all right. The first of their ads was a photograph of an old man named Ulysses Lopez, pictured in the flamboyant pearl-buttoned waist jacket of a Sonora cowboy. "When I was sixteen," the caption quoted him as saying, "I rode with Pancho Villa. Now I ride the RTD."

It was a pity. The bus rides made palpable what life was like in much of this new Los Angeles. A car trip along the same route might well have produced a less enlightening effect, one's impressions dulled by the radio or tape deck, and the cosseting wind of the air-conditioning. But except by taking what could only be described as the eccentric and time-wasting (assuming, unlike me, there was someplace you had to be at a given time) decision to ride the buses, there was little reason to suppose that people on the Westside were ever going to be jarred out of their sense of living in a world that had changed little since the sixties. Chicano nationalists might warn of civil insurrection, and, more accurately, of the strong pulse of misery and discontent, particularly among the young, but predicting revolution in America, even in a place as transformed as modern Los Angeles, is unlikely to be any better a bet in the future than it has been in the past.

In any case, as things stood, the change might as well not be taking place. In a city as spread out as L.A., it has always been remarkably difficult to get one's bearings, be they geographical or sociological, even on the surface streets. As for the freeways, with their ineluctable element of travel without transit—in this, resembling what a ride on an airplane might be like if the pilot were obliged to slow down and even stop more unexpectedly and for prolonged periods of time—they were worse. And as traffic throughout the city increased, the thought of just going for a spin, the Sunday drive that was a staple of Southern California life as late as the sixties, began to seem little more than an exercise in masochism. Few people past their teens—the drag-racers in the Valley or the Chicano lowriders in East L.A. were another story—drove for pleasure. The Auto Club reported that the average mileage adult Angelenos were racking up on their odometers each year was only slightly higher than it had been at the end of World War II, which, given how much longer commuting distance had become, meant that when people finally got home from work they tended to stay home.

It was one thing for me to heed the brown faces on the streets or attend to the breathtaking mix of languages, a lower-middle-class, immigrant Babel, on the shop fronts of the mini-malls. If I learned to copy out, though not decipher, the stolid rectangles of Korean Hankul script and the florid curlicues of Thai and Armenian, that was, after all, part of what had drawn me to Los Angeles in the first place, but it was hardly the way that anybody who is not a writer (or, conceivably, a policeman or a social worker) could be expected to want to spend what—in Los Angeles, which despite its reputation, is one of the least laid back places in the world—is laughably called their "free time."

I had come alone to a city for which I felt much affection but little familiarity, eager to soak up every last picturesque drop of daily life there. But what for me was, of necessity, the center of my days and nights in L.A. seemed to most of my friends at best a strange but largely irrelevant background noise to their daily lives. The writer has no fixed hours on the road. When Tim Rutten and I would drive, as we often did, back from the *Times* building downtown to what his wife laughingly described as their home in the "slums" of Hancock Park, he was finished with his working day, whereas I might have accomplished nothing of any use to my project, only to suddenly reach for my notebook, jarred into inspiration by something glimpsed as we drove past—two Salvadoran children lunging toward a soccer ball in the front yard of a run-down housing court on Sixth and Occidental; the name of a Korean Presbyterian Church on Wilshire; or winos lined up in front of a blood bank in downtown L.A., hard under the shadow of the upscale Bunker Hill apartment complex whose construction had destroyed so much of the single room occupancy housing which, before the real estate boom, had sheltered some of them from the cruelties of the streets.

To his credit, Tim humored me, drained to the point of muteness though he often was after a day in the newsroom. It was on one such evening, as we headed away from Times-Mirror Square and turned into the tunnel under Bunker Hill, the setting of scores of American car commercials, that I learned of the existence of Los Angeles's Druze community. We had been talking about Lebanon, not L.A., and after we had got through clucking about Beirut in what I remember as being a fairly predictable way—nasty, brutish, the whole nine yards—he suddenly began to reminisce about an article he had published in 1981 supporting the American naval bombardment of Walid Jumblat's Druze forces in the Shuf mountains, who had been firing on the U.S. Marines then encamped around the Beirut airport.

"When I came into work the next day," Tim said, "there was a huge picket line set up around the building. It turned out that the demonstrators were local Druze, and that what the *Times* editorial struck them as having endorsed was the right of the guns of the USS *New Jersey* to blow the shit out of their relatives back home in the Shuf. I hadn't known that there were any Druze in Southern California, let alone that their largest community outside Lebanon itself is here in L.A. County."

If Tim Rutten, who was born in the shadow of the San Gabriels and had lived his entire life in Los Angeles as a professional journalist, did not know about the Druze, it seemed unlikely that many people on the Westside would. In any case, between their anxieties about traffic and their fears about crime, most Anglos used only a small part of the city. Both on the Westside and in the Valley, the usable space was steadily shrinking. Some neighborhoods, like Carthay Circle, just west of mid-Wilshire, had even gone to the extreme of erecting barriers to discourage through traffic. Such measures had been undertaken ostensibly to make the local streets safer for children and discourage drunk drivers from careering down local streets; of course, they were viewed as an anti-crime measure as well. Neighborhood activists tended to argue that all they meant to do was restore life to a more human scale and allow people to wrest control of their lives from both impersonal bureaucracies and the developers who had done so much to destroy L.A.'s quality of life through reckless overbuilding.

All of this was undoubtedly true. Whole neighborhoods had fallen to the wreckers' ball in the past, and there was certainly no reason to think that in a city as hostile to the idea of limits as Los Angeles had always been the builders would reform themselves. The image of the cemetery owner in Evelyn Waugh's satire of Los Angeles, *The Loved One,* murmuring to himself that "there must be some way to get these stiffs off my property" was one that every Angeleno knows to be only slightly exaggerated. "If we don't take some control of growth," Charles Rosin of the Carthay Circle Homeowners' Association told the *Los Angeles Times*'s architecture critic, Sam Hall Kaplan, "it will very shortly overwhelm us." And there is not a neighborhood in the city that does not have its examples of developers destroying beautiful houses to put up hideous apartment complexes, or chopping down stands of trees to make room for yet another parking lot.

But the paradox was that this new community-based activism, however idealistic, only further confirmed Kaplan's quip that "no one really lives in Los Angeles. They live in Silver Lake, Echo Park, downtown, Hollywood, North Hollywood, Mt. Washington, Boyle Heights, Studio City, Beverly-Fairfax, Westwood, Encino, or one of the dozens of other distinct communities scattered across the cityscape." In the context of the new immigration, that is, of the infusion into the city of millions of people who not only lived in distinct communities, but looked different from those who had lived in the city in the past, spoke different languages, ate different foods, in short could not have been more alien from the people Angelenos over thirty had grown up alongside, the retreat into community interests and parochial concerns only confirmed people's mutual incomprehension. It is one thing not to think too much about your neighbors when you can be sure that they more or less resemble you; it is quite another to make encountering them as difficult as possible when they couldn't be more unfamiliar to you in the first place.

In Los Angeles now, it was entirely possible to live not just in another part of town but in an adjoining neighborhood and be unaware that seemingly without consulting anyone but the city's Department of Transportation (whose decisions about street directions and traffic lights are hardly promulgated in any way that could make a lasting impression on anyone not directly concerned), the local community has banned parking or blocked entire streets. When Charles Rosin told Kaplan that the people of Carthay Circle had created "a small town right in the middle of Los Angeles," he spoke proudly. An outsider, though, particularly an immigrant outsider, was likely to view the matter differently, and could be forgiven for feeling that this putative small town's message was really Keep Out.

It was not surprising that people were hunkering down. With Los Angeles increasingly appearing to many who lived there as a threatening place, its law-abiding citizens at the mercy of roving street gangs, crack addicts, and aliens, the mutual impenetrability of neighborhoods was being viewed overwhelmingly as a good thing. It was often difficult to sort out people's motivations when they spoke of no growth or of banning parking in residential areas. When people complained that their streets were no longer their own, were they really complaining about traffic, or trying to repel the alien nation in their midst? Certainly, the objectives of the slow-growth advocates on the Westside had the same practical effect of those advocated by other people who were frankly fearful of being overwhelmed in the new Third World melting pot that L.A. had become. "They had taken our streets away," a planner in Westwood told me one evening as she elaborated on the plans she was about to present to the City Council for a new pedestrian mall between Wilshire Boulevard and the LeConte Avenue entrance to the UCLA campus. But her words were reminiscent of those I had heard from a secretary at the *Times* that morning who, having been told that I was writing on the new immigrants, approached me timidly and then, with increasing distress, spoke of how "they" had taken away "our" city. At the very least, the coincidence in both women's use of possessive pronouns provided food for thought.

Far from being disturbed by the fact that Los Angeles was a cognitively challenging place, most people almost reveled in it. The talk about not being able to get "there from here" was neither mere bravado nor simply a joking way of shrugging off the terrible traffic. For what many were really saying, I thought, was that you couldn't in fact get "here from there." The acronym with which the slow growthers were routinely dismissed—NIMBY—could, at its worst, be interpreted as meaning that one wanted to stave off the necessity of confronting the future in one's back yard.

Ironies abounded. When a federally subsidized subway system was proposed, running from downtown L.A. along Wilshire Boulevard to Westwood, the influential Westside congressman Henry Waxman thwarted the project by inserting an amendment in another bill prohibiting underground tunneling in areas with large deposits of natural gas. Wilshire Boulevard, which runs over the La Brea Tar Pits, is such an area, and Waxman's constituents were tremendously appreciative of his skillful and effective maneuver. But many were just as relieved by a side effect of there being no rail link between the Westside and the slums. This way, people told you over and over again, at least the young thugs couldn't just ride out to the Westside from their part of town the way they did on New York's subway or the Chicago El. And many believed that it was only this fractured quality about life in Los Angeles that was standing in the way of the city turning into New York. Indeed, so much did Manhattan stand as the model of how life would be in L.A. were things to go badly wrong that one of the most prominent slow-growth activist groups was called Not Yet New York.

What people were rebelling against, often in the name of democracy and grass-roots participation, were some of the consequences of democracy itself. This was new in a city that had always prided itself on its democratic character, so radically at odds with the rigid hierarchies of Europe or the eastern United States. L.A. was supposed to be one vast subdivision, not only undifferentiable (except in terms of relative levels of middle-class ease) from the freeway but from the surface streets as well. If the city did not have a downtown, or, indeed, had prided itself on being a city unlike all the others that had come before it, that was because people believed that they could be both a world capital and yet, paradoxically, not really a city at all. This had been the Los Angeles ideal from the beginning. The city, wrote William Smythe, an early proponent of the development of the Southland, in 1905, "will naturally spread over a vast area—the vaster the better. It should spread until they meet the country, and until beautiful forms of urban life blend almost imperceptibly into beautiful forms of rural life."

What began as a series of plush expectations, which, in any case, were when first formulated more real estate speculator's come-on than anything else—even Smythe himself, for all his good intentions, having been a long-time collaborator of Charles Fletcher Lummis on the developer-backed magazine *Land of Sunshine*—had taken on a far more apocalyptic connotation in contemporary Los Angeles. When people said L.A. had never been designed as a city "in the eastern sense of the term," as one slow-growther put it to me, it was clear enough that what was really at stake was an attempt to keep as much distance as possible between the prosperous homeowners who made up such groups and the feral youths and homeless men and women who were the new shame of America's cities. To some extent, this was more a literary than a practical solution, as if by insisting that L.A. was not a city like New York people could continue to deny it had many of the same "urban" problems. And of course it was still just barely possible, except in a few particular localities like Santa Monica, where the homeless were now camped out along the fabled beach, or in downtown L.A., with its proximity both to Skid Row around Fifth Street and to the barrio just across the river, to forget that the poor existed.

If anything, however, this exceptionalism only increased people's sense of the embattled quality of their ease. In no other region of the United States today are all the various anxieties of bourgeois life described so persistently in the militarized language of invasion. People spoke of the invasion of their bodies by environmental toxins, and all the foods—those malign fifth columnists—now believed to cause cancer, heart disease, or arteriosclerosis. There was the threat of burglary, an ever-looming invasion, and it was rare to drive along any street from mid-Wilshire to Pacific Palisades and find a single house or apartment building unburdened by either bars on every entryway or signs warning of burglar alarms, private security patrols, and "armed response." A friend even commented sardonically, as we drove along one well-guarded stretch of Brentwood, that perhaps the best of the many Japanese corporate acquisitions in greater Los Angeles would turn out to be the Westec Company, the Westside's leading private security firm.

Even nature was on the march, it seemed. According to one news report, the United States was being invaded by what was referred to as "worldwide transfers of immigrant plant species" that might well eventually crowd out "the natives." Though the story ended with a plant biologist reassuring the anxious reporter, "Don't worry. After all, our California eucalyptus actually migrated here from Australia," the play the piece got on the local six o'clock news made comparison with human immigration to the region hard to avoid. Southern Californians had, in any case, all but grown up to the background noise of reports on local efforts to combat medfly infestations. These insects, too, were foreigners, and if they weren't stopped, the state agricultural authorities insisted, they would ruin California's crops. And so every year, sections of the Southland would be sprayed by crop dusters, in an eerie recapitulation (for those who were historically minded) of other national campaigns of eradication and interdiction. Despite repeated lawsuits brought by a coalition of environmental and citizens' groups, their case buttressed by the strong suspicion among many doctors that the pesticide being used, a compound called Malathion, was unlikely to interact with human lung tissue any more leniently than it did with the paint finishes on cars all over greater Los Angeles, the spraying went on. Perhaps the authorities are right, and California agriculture would be destroyed if the medflies were allowed to gain a foothold, but at the very least the linguistic congruences between the ways people talked about the medflies and that same language of invasion and contamination used in a somewhat different context about illegal immigration was startling. As for the alarmist reports of the colonies of South American soldier ants which, by 1990, were said to have reached Baja California, there the less said the better.

It was too easy to grow accustomed to the way white Angelenos would speak of aliens "pouring" into the country, the hypertrophied rhetoric, at times grotesquely biblical in character, of "floods," "waves," and "invasions." And yet most peculiar of all, in a way, was that all this apocalyptic thinking was occurring in Los Angeles, precisely the place where people had for so long prided themselves on being beyond history, beyond ethnicity. But ready or not, all the grand and painful dramas of race, nation, and identity, dormant for almost half a century, were being resurrected. And many people were at least dimly aware that such an event could not have come at a worse time. Whatever its vices, the existence of a WASP ruling class that was so firmly in control —politically, culturally, and economically—at the turn of the century had ensured that when the great immigration from northeastern and southeastern Europe took place, there was a national culture for the new arrivals to aspire to. But precisely the Californianization of the United States over the course of the twentieth century had put paid to all that. In a country of individuals and their things, everything was up for grabs.

That was where, most of all, the new nativists who spoke of the sanctity of America's borders had got it wrong. The unsettling of the old American order had been capitalism's great work, an enterprise that had found its highest expression in the city of Los Angeles. In that system, the economy was supposed to expand indefinitely, just as the metropolis itself was destined to push its way not just to the mountains that ring the L.A. basin but across them into the desert, and north and south as well. And for the period in which growth had looked as if it would go on forever, this Los Angelesization of the country had made sense. "There is more to life than growing faster," Gandhi once said, but for a long time L.A. appeared like a living refutation of his statement.

To its detractors, Los Angeles was the city where you "got away" with everything; "reality with a substitute teacher," as the writer Ellis Weiner once quipped. Ronald Reagan's best scriptwriter, Peggy Noonan, echoed this view when, in her memoirs, she criticized her boss for reflecting "what's dangerous about California—that life is so soft there, it's like moving through a lovely haze of warm gelatin." In reality, what had been moving along so easily was not California but capitalism. The ease, the sense in which, for several generations, it provided more people with more creature comforts, was merely the by-product of its success. If people had been able to deny the harsher realities, it was because for all sorts of reasons the American economy had something of a free ride between the end of World War II and the end of the Vietnam War. Now, it turned out, that free ride was over and Americans would have to dance as fast as everyone else had been doing in the rest of the developed world.

For it turned out that the growth could not in fact go on forever, that neither the environment nor the world economy were anywhere near as elastic as had been assumed. There were limits to credit, just as there were limits to the earth's ability to withstand the defilement of man. And just as the older residents of Southern California were waking up to these limitations on what, theretofore, they had conceived of as their birthright—wasn't that the American dream? Wasn't that the promise of all those movies, and television shows, and ad campaigns?—along came the rest of the world, or, at least, a sizable chunk of it, anyway. And the irony was that in Mexico City, and Esfahan, and Seoul, in Lima, Taipei, and San Salvador, they had seen those same movies. Dubbed, of course. And now, as the California of unbridled expansion was psyching itself up to confront its own contradictions, there was the rest of the world, clamoring for admission, an alien nation before the gates of perhaps the only country in history that had genuinely believed that its dreams were unique and inviolable, and had surely never imagined the time would come when they would be unsettled by the dreary wake-up call of history and demography. The fact that, to so many Angelenos, this utopia had not been a fantasy but the daily experience of a good part of their lives made the transformation that was taking place all around them seem like the most terrible betrayal, and I found few takers for my suggestion that betrayals and reversals of fortune are, precisely, the usual currencies in which history deals. All fundamentalisms fear contamination by strangers, not least that fundamentalism called paradise. It was perhaps because he saw this that Christopher Isherwood once said that California was a tragic place, "like Palestine, like every promised land."

8. Here Comes Everybody

. . . .

What if the U.S. was Mexico?
What if 200,000 Anglosaxicans
were to cross the border each month
to work as gardeners, waiters,
3rd chair musicians, movie extras,
bouncers, babysitters, chauffeurs,
syndicated cartoons, feather-weight
boxers, fruit-pickers and anonymous poets?
What if they were called waspanos,
waspitos, wasperos or wasbacks?
What if we were top dogs?
What if literature was life, eh?

As if it weren't already? What this inspired piece of angry whimsy by
the Chicano performance artist Guillermo Gómez-Peña, failed to take
into account was that one of the premises of life in Los Angeles, from
the beginning, had been that such inversions of fantasy and reason,
dream and reality, were going to be the norm. Los Angeles, after all, was
the city that had grown up under the shadow of the motto graven on

the rotunda of its City Hall: "The city came into being to preserve life, it exists for the good life." It was also the place whose *boosters* tended to agree with the painter Ed Ruscha when he observed dotingly that L.A. was "the ultimate cardboard cutout town. It's full of illusions and allows its people to indulge in all these illusions." In such an atmosphere, small wonder that few people knew where exactly to draw the line between literature and life. They never had.

Beleaguered in the boosterist sea that was Los Angeles, the few remaining oppositional voices in the city—most of whom were either Mexican-American or black "cultural nationalists," or left-wing intellectuals with teaching jobs in the humanities departments at various local universities—were as bound by metaphoric ways of thinking about L.A. as Otis or Huntington had ever been. They described L.A. as a "narrative" and wrote academic papers studded with French phrases and epigraphs from such heroes of literary postmodernism as Jorge Luis Borges, Italo Calvino, and Michel Foucault. Their essays spoke of the need to "deconstruct" L.A., to "identify its *auteurs*" (this was politics borrowed from 1950s French film criticism), and to "rewrite" the city in the "Borgesian sense of Pierre Menard" (an allusion to a story in which a man who sets out to rewrite *Don Quixote* does so by reproducing it verbatim). And why not? Why shouldn't the radicals take their turn at willing yet another version of Los Angeles into being? Everyone else was doing it, and if it was good enough for Redondo Beach and the Chamber of Commerce, then why not the geography department of UCLA as well? After all, in a certain light the whole story of Los Angeles was a postmodernist dream, and Otis's vision only another version of the prophetic nominalism that the radicals espoused. It's not a desert, it's the city of the future, Otis had said, and there was very little space between that view and what one radical sociologist called "an imaginative ethos of remapping and renaming."

Moreover, the changes that were taking place in the city were so enormous that even in a less metaphor-besotted environment than L.A. it would have been difficult not to toy with a "literary" explanation of what otherwise was so vast as to be indecipherable. If it was going too far to imagine that the transformation of the city from a largely white city to a largely nonwhite one was best described as a literary changing of the guard—the solid bourgeois fictions of the fifties being elbowed aside by new claimants; John Cheever giving way, as it were, to Gabriel García Márquez and Carlos Fuentes—there was something undeniably strange and, if real, then magically real about what was going on. Here was the city that, only thirty years before, had been known as "Iowa's seaport" because of all the transplanted midwesterners who had settled there, now serving as the magnet, the destination of choice, for people from all over the Third World.

Accustomed to thinking in terms of destinies and pageants rather than in terms of history, Angelenos, faced with the magnitude of the change that the new immigration was bringing to their lives, clung ever more insistently to the simplifications of metaphoric thinking. It was a register as old as McGroarty writing about California's "five miracles of achievement," and as contemporary as the anonymous authors of the "L.A. 2000" report, the first word of which, set out from the ensuing text in fire-engine red type, is "imagine." "Do you believe in magic?" a celebrated pop song of the sixties had demanded, to which Angelenos, from the Chamber of Commerce to the Chicano Studies department at Cal State–Northridge, seemed to be replying, "Of course we do; haven't we always?"

As far as the new Third World immigration was concerned, the real surprise would have been if the discussion among most Angelenos, regardless of their political opinions, had concentrated on root causes or the long-term economic or social effects of an L.A. that would soon be more than 40 percent Hispanic, 12 percent Asian, 10 percent black, and less than 40 percent white. But these conversations remained largely the preserve either of specialists—federal and state bureaucrats, schoolteachers and city officials, Immigration and Naturalization Service spokesmen, and immigration rights activists and trade union organizers —or of the cranks who clotted the airwaves of AM talk radio stations with dire warnings about the foreigners who were taking over the country and threatening what was almost invariably called "the American way of life" and almost as invariably turned out to mean the 1950s.

At least the racists were actually talking about long-term consequences and had an idea, however partial or misguided, about what the American past had been. In the culture of the immediate that was Los Angeles, this was a rarer commodity than might have been expected. Most preferred to speak of the changes almost exclusively in the present tense, using a language of transformation and, occasionally, of visitation as well. If, for the radicals, this imagery was redemptive, those who dreaded the changes, or, at the very least, were made uneasy by them, took refuge in expressions Angelenos had previously reserved for mudslides, maddening Santa Ana winds, or brush fires. "They talk of nonwhite immigration," I noted in my journal, shortly after arriving in L.A., "the way the Egyptians must have spoken of the inflictions of Jehovah. All that's missing are the biblical categories for the disaster. A plague of wetbacks?"

The liberal version of this view was nicely captured in a popular television series called "Alien Nation." On the show, the aliens, or new-comers, as they were usually called, were not Mexicans who had sneaked across the border at Otay Mesa or Calexico and hoofed it to East L.A., but rather a race of extraterrestrial slaves whose spaceship lands in the Mojave Desert. The newcomers number in the millions, and in the precredit sequence there is much grousing among various representative Californians about why America should have to receive this race of hairless coneheads whose favorite tipple turns out to be sour milk, and who—most unCalifornian attribute of all—can no more survive a dip in the ocean than a human being can survive a dip in a bath of hydrochloric acid.

"Alien Nation" clearly is meant as an allegory for the ways in which America mistreats—or rather, this being television, not social criticism —misunderstands its racial minorities. The newcomers are portrayed as combining some of the traits imputed to Hispanics (they are phenomenally fertile) and of Asians (their children effortlessly outdistance all their native-born classmates in school), and of course each episode, which revolves around the adventures and private lives of a "mixed" team of L.A. detectives, ends with a plea for understanding. But if the show in some ways is one more narrow recapitulation of the old American liberal view that there is no problem that cannot be dissolved by lavish administrations of goodwill and patience, in others its success mirrors the deep uneasiness that the new immigration has produced in Southern California.

A more unvarnished version of the same trope was Ridley Scott's film *Blade Runner,* which appeared in 1982 and almost ten years later remained so resonant that it had become a part of everyday speech in Los Angeles. All someone had to do was mention it, and you immediately knew where they stood about the future of the city. It has become such a commonplace that Kevin Starr, in his epilogue to the "L.A. 2000" report, did not even feel the need to explain its origin when he warned of "the *Blade Runner* scenario: the fusion of individual cultures into a demotic polyglotism ominous with unresolved hostilities." At a dinner party in Beverly Hills, I heard a liberal actor, well known for his benefactions to various community groups in L.A., tell his dinner companions that as far as he was concerned the situation was hopeless. "You might as well face it," he said. "It will be *Blade Runner.*"

In the film, Los Angeles is portrayed as a city made up almost entirely of Asians and Mexicans. In this world of postmodern *mestizaje,* a mix not only of races but of languages is blending together. The lingua franca of the streets, themselves dark and wet from pollution and acid rain— the golden Southern California light has become, it appears, as much a memory as the golden-haired people—is a combination of Japanese, Spanish, and English, while billboards flash images of Asian beauties and advertisements for travel to the new colonies in outer space. For all intents and purposes, the Los Angeles of the film has become indistinguishable from a Third World city. One of the few white people to remain explains bitterly that he couldn't pass the physical required for those wanting to blast off to the colonies, and it is clear enough that Ridley Scott is presenting space travel not as exploration but as a version of suburbanization, or, more direly, of white flight from what one black rap group was beginning to call "a black planet."

The question remained: How had things changed so quickly? It was as if one minute everybody (or almost everybody; when pressed, white Angelenos were ready enough to concede that in black L.A. life had been anything but paradisiacal) had been minding their own idyllic business and a nanosecond later were confronting the spectacle of vast stretches of their hometown having been taken over by foreigners, either from Mexico, a proximate part of the world that Americans had always been unwilling to think about seriously, or from other, far more exotic places, so exotic indeed that, except in the context of war—after all, that was the way most Americans learned where Vietnam was—they were all but completely unknown. If the current surveys of U.S. high school students were to be believed, the eighty-two languages now being taught in the Los Angeles Unified School District represented many more nations than most American kids had ever heard of. To be sure, one did hear rueful acknowledgments of the fact that since the United States bordered on Mexico, and, by extension, on the rest of Latin America, and since people were so poor "down there," it was probably inevitable that many would have chosen to come. But this was as close as most people in white L.A. got to situating the new immigration politically or historically. For the most part, Third World Los Angeles might as well have been a demographic meteor shower as a movement of people whose presence in Southern California was by no means as mysterious as the flaccid metaphors used to account for it might have led one to believe.

The official line was no better. Nowhere in the "L.A. 2000" report, for example, did the authors attempt to explain the reasons that the city was experiencing a new wave of immigration. L.A.'s greatness is stipulated, and that, it seems, is reason enough. But it is all very well to use the metaphor of a magnet city so long as one does not find oneself trapped by the image. This was a trap L.A.'s boosters had not been able to avoid. For them, the city's appeal was as solid a fact as electromagnetism, and by 1990 that view was so firmly entrenched that it was all but useless to point out that immigration was by no means so neat or iron-clad a phenomenon. But L.A. wanted images, not facts. "Think of Los Angeles as a mosaic," the authors of the "L.A. 2000" report advised, "with every color distinct, vibrant and essential to the whole. Native American, Mexican, African-American, Japanese, Israeli, Chinese, Tongan, Indian, German, Irish, Armenian, Ethiopian, Swedish, Korean, Samoan, Guatemalan, Russian, Arab, Persian, French, Cuban, Italian, Fiji, Australian, Russian, Honduran, Scottish, Hungarian, Danish, Malaysian, Filipino, English, Turkish are only a few of the more than one hundred cultural and ethnic backgrounds that exist together in Los Angeles. Each of these groups makes its own special contribution to the rich mix that is creating a new heritage for the metropolitan area. Each brings its own ethos, arts, ideas and skills to a community that welcomes and encourages diversity and grows stronger by taking the best from it. They respect each other as mutual partners."

This was all very well as far as it went, a recapitulation of the "Alien Nation" rather than the *Blade Runner* version of Los Angeles's future, but it never posed the essential question of how this mosaic had come into being. As far as L.A.'s boosters were concerned, the logic was clear enough: L.A. was great, L.A. was now full of newcomers, therefore the newcomers must be great. To have supposed otherwise would have meant imagining a world in which things in the future were less good than they had been in the past, and this, as I soon discovered, was generally considered the view of racists and malcontents, and, perhaps, intellectuals, not fully vested Californians. For all that Southern California had changed, negativism remained one of the worst faults one middle-class person could lay at the psychic door of another.

What was breathtaking about all this was less the Pollyannaish confidence—that had always been L.A.'s stock in trade—than an adamant elision of all historical processes into whatever image the present throws up. The most the authors of the "L.A. 2000" report, for example, were willing to concede was that the new immigrants differed somewhat from their predecessors in that the melting pot conception of assimilation no longer worked in an era when the new arrivals were bringing with them "profoundly dissimilar languages, religions, folkways, and arts, and a deeply ingrained pride in maintaining their cultural identity." What was missing, of course, was any acknowledgment that these profound dissimilarities might pose any impediment at all to harmonious relations between all these disparate groups. On the face of things, this appeared puzzling. One did not have to endorse the *Blade Runner* scenario to recognize that groups whose ideas are (as the report somewhat quaintly allowed) at variance tend to go for each other's throats when they come into conflict, as—assuming their children attended the same schools and they did not close themselves off from the rest of their fellow citizens, as, notably, the Hasidic Jews of Hancock Park had been able to do—they inevitably would.

Only in a place where beliefs are viewed as a kind of seasoning or taste, like a fondness for curry or the dogtrack, could such optimism prevail, I thought. And I soon realized, as I listened to social workers and high school teachers talk about the viability of "multiculturalism," that what they usually meant was just being nice to everyone. Diversity in this generous but finally unthreatening construction meant little more than the right of immigrants to eat the foods from their native countries and have their art and culture appreciated. Certainly no one I talked to seemed to imagine diversity of this kind very differently than stockbrokers do when they refer to diversified portfolios. But if a financial manager is only reassured by assembling the widest possible variety of financial instruments, it by no means follows that a culture benefits in the same way. Stocks and bonds, it should be recalled, do not have long histories of antipathy; Koreans and Japanese, to take one obvious example, do.

It is possible that if people in Los Angeles had had a clearer idea of who the various groups arriving in their midst really were they would have been more alive to the risk. But to have done so would have run counter to a century of individualizing, anti-historical feeling and thought. Even those who disliked the new immigrants tended to dislike them on racist grounds, as nonwhites, or on xenophobic ones, as foreigners or non–English speakers, without differentiating very much between them. They were all newcomers—"Alien Nation" had got that right, at least.

As for corporate Los Angeles, it remained persuaded that as long as there was money to be made people would accommodate each other just as they always had. All that was really required was that the region's economic growth continue unperturbed and that people learn to pay a certain lip service to one another's particular folkways and habits. "What's the problem?" a securities analyst asked me querulously as I pressed him about the contradictions that the new immigration seemed to be opening up. "We learned to eat pizza—that used to be foreign— and we'll learn to eat Thai food too. People don't come here to be ethnic forever, they come here to make money. All they need is a little space for a generation or two."

And, pausing, he added, "And a little respect, I guess. That doesn't seem like too much to ask when you think about it.

"Twenty-first-century Los Angeles," he continued, "will combine the best of every culture that has come here. It will combine Asian family loyalty, Hispanic industriousness, and Anglo-Saxon respect for individual liberty. That's an entirely new package; no culture like that has ever been created before."

To create a culture. It was a dizzying thought. And yet those who were optimistic about L.A.'s future all seemed to agree that it was not only possible but would happen fast. The possibility that, if any sort of cultural synthesis were to take place, it might just as easily combine the worst rather than the best of its various constituent parts—say, Confucianism's fabled indifference to everyone outside a given family group, Latin American political intolerance, and Western European nihilism— was not a "narrative," as they would have said at UCLA, that convinced anyone. That was my East Coast cynicism talking, my acquaintance told me. In California things were different.

"You mean in California things work out," I said.

"That's right," he replied. "That's exactly right."

There were good reasons for many Angelenos, particularly those who lived on the Westside or in the Valley, to believe that this was still so, whatever they read in the newspapers or saw on the evening news. The city's horizontality went a long way toward ensuring that what in other, more crowded municipalities might have seemed like foretastes of an inevitable struggle for control, appeared, in the generous context of the Los Angeles basin, more like a harmless contest over top billing. Since it was the norm, in everyday life, for members of most groups in L.A. to successfully ignore the presence of most other groups, the occasional and circumscribed encounters that did occur continued to feel anomalous. A Salvadoran maid might buy her husband's malt drink from a Pakistani 7-Eleven owner, but usually that was the extent to which the average immigrant from the isthmus and from the subcontinent would encounter one another. What was true for the new immigrants also applied, to a surprising degree, to groups within Anglo L.A. as well. "I always like to come out here," Tom Johnson, the publisher of the *Los Angeles Times* during the 1980s, told Joan Didion at a dinner party in Brentwood. "That way I get to find out what you're all thinking out here on the Westside."

If few spoke quite so frankly, Johnson was anything but atypical in his ingrained assumption that every section of greater Los Angeles was largely illegible to every other part. Indeed, his own newspaper had contributed materially to this fracturing when it chose to divide L.A. up into zones and deliver a different edition to each of them. In no other major American city do residents of one neighborhood read different stories than their fellow citizens a couple of zip codes over. This spatial

autarchy means that when people move within L.A.—say, selling a condominium in the Valley and buying a house in Pacific Palisades—they
usually never think of returning to their old neighborhood, no matter
how nostalgic they may wax about that period of their lives. It is the old
Los Angeles time/space conflation again, with the area in which one
lived in the past coming to seem as unrecuperable as the past itself.

Over and over, I would hear residents of greater Los Angeles (particular municipal or county boundaries having become increasingly irrelevant) talk about the specific part of town they lived in being the center
of things. I was advised by residents of Orange County to forget about
the Westside and pay attention to Anaheim. In the Valley, I was told that
the real L.A. was centered somewhere around Van Nuys. As for the
Westside, Watts, or the barrio, these were worlds unto themselves. This
L.A. ideal, it turned out, was an odd amalgam of the fluid and the fixed.
It was like serial monogamy, a rolling sequence of heres and nows. As a
result, it was perfectly possible for members of any group, from a Guatemalan busboy to a Jewish garment executive, to share the same freeways and still imagine that their particular lives and acquaintances were
what defined life in Los Angeles in 1990. As for everyone else, they were
as shadowy as the neighborhoods one saw from the highway interchange, back projection and little more.

But back projection or no, the understanding that things were changing radically had, by 1990, become so inescapable that even the wealth
of buffers that L.A. provided no longer really served to conceal what
was taking place. And yet there remained something surreal about the
whole process, something startling and incongruous, like the sight in a
film about making movies of a person hurtling through a backdrop that,
theretofore, had been entirely convincing. Conversations about immigration in L.A. are all slightly unnerving this way. They seem either too
loud or too soft, too optimistic or too grim. It is as if the whole event is
both so mysterious and so compelling that there exists no clear line of
demarcation between people's perception of what is taking place and
their wonder at the experience. After a while, I grew accustomed to
even the most level-headed and well-informed people I knew prefacing
their replies to my questions about Third World L.A. with a lot of preliminary throat-clearing about the velocity with which the demographic
facts of the region had been transformed.

"When I left here in the late sixties to take over the *Times* bureau in
Sacramento," Bill Boyarsky, then the paper's L.A. City-County bureau
chief, observed, "the immigrant presence here in town seemed negligi-
ble. Sure, everyone knew that more and more Mexicans were coming
in, but what you have to remember is that there have always been

Mexicans around here. A lot of us went to high school with them. You certainly did if you attended a parochial school, even in the fifties. So to many of us local Anglos, they did not really seem like aliens in the sense that the word is thrown around today."

"What about the Asians?" I asked.

"They were another matter," Boyarsky said, "particularly groups like the Koreans and the Thais. There had always been Japanese and Chinese Californians, of course, but, probably for all the wrong reasons, Asian immigration seemed like a settled issue after World War Two. The only time it really came up was during the debate over paying reparations to all the Japanese-Americans who were put in internment camps during World War Two."

We were sitting in the bar of the New Otani Hotel, a stubby white high-rise complete with its own upscale shopping mall geared to the Japanese tourists who make up most of the hotel's guests, on the forward edge of Little Tokyo a few blocks away from Times-Mirror Square. At adjacent tables, groups of these tourists chatted amiably, sometimes pausing to rummage in shopping bags labeled Dior, Cartier, Cardin, or Mark Cross, to pull out one of the day's acquisitions, and sometimes raising a well-manicured hand to signal for a waitress and order, the English loanwords sounding all the more peculiar in the polyglot atmosphere of this Japanese-owned and -operated hotel in what had formerly been a neighborhood of poor Japanese immigrants to Los Angeles and now was the outcropping of a world in which Japan reigned supreme, another *biru* or *hoto kohee*. What would General Otis have thought, I wondered idly, had he seen the New Otani or known that it had become the favorite watering hole for *Times* reporters and their barracks on nights when senior staff needed to stay close to the newsroom? The idea, after all, had been that we would supply the needs of Asia, not the other way around.

"And when you came back to L.A.?" I asked Boyarsky.

"I returned in 'seventy-four," he replied, "and my wife and I found we had come home to a very different city than the one we had left. I suppose that even in the late sixties there must have been a certain number of Korean stores, at least on a small stretch around Olympic and Western, but they certainly weren't a big presence or a very noteworthy one. And then there were the mini-malls. It seemed as if on every major corner one had taken root—they'd never existed in L.A. proper; you associated them with the Valley, with Van Nuys Boulevard and all that. Add to that the fact that half the stores in these malls had signs not just in languages but even in alphabets I'd never seen before. I don't just mean Spanish, but Korean, Armenian, Thai, Urdu, you name it."

To Boyarsky, the mini-malls had been the biggest sign that Los Angeles was changing in completely unexpected ways. The visitor arriving in the city today would be hard-pressed even to conceive of L.A. without them, but in fact these malls are a very recent phenomenon. As late as the 1960s, the typical corner lot along a Los Angeles commercial boulevard was more likely to contain a gas station than almost any other type of business. Great fortunes had been made packaging these lots, most notably by the developer Alexander Haagen, who began buying unpromising L.A. commercial property in the early fifties and then re-selling it to the major oil companies during their great drive to expand their retail business in the years of the post–World War II boom. Even small business owners made a good living in those days. With gas prices hovering around thirty cents a gallon and supplies plentiful, owning a service station had its advantages. The result was that by 1970, gas pumps at an intersection were as much a fixture of the Los Angeles cityscape as the palm trees or the light.

The oil shock of 1973 changed all that for good. Even after the Arab oil embargo against the United States had ended, the economics of running a gas station were no longer the same. Not only had the price of gasoline nearly tripled, but the independent retailers who had made up such a substantial part of the business before the Yom Kippur War complained darkly that they were being cut off by their distributors, many of whom in turn, perhaps not coincidentally, had sold out to the major oil companies or else been driven out of the business entirely. Whether or not there actually was a conspiracy on the part of Big Oil to take advantage of the new situation in order to corner the retail market for themselves, the effects were the same, at least as far as the independents were concerned. Unable to match the prices charged by the local Shell, SoCal, or Mobil outlets, or to ensure a constant supply of gasoline, service stations began to fold in droves all over greater Los Angeles.

In a city in which suburbanization was proceeding apace, and in which, in any event, successful shopkeeping was increasingly an affair of specialized providers—the gourmet food store, the upscale boutique —or was concentrated in huge plazas rather than along the older commercial thoroughfares, it was by no means clear what could be done with all these derelict properties that were beginning to flood the L.A. real estate market. Even in a city where it was an article of faith that all real estate, no matter how ill favored, would appreciate in value, it looked like a hard sell. That was where the mini-malls came in.

For many developers had begun to realize, even if most Angelenos still had not, that in a city where the traffic jam was becoming an everyday fact of life and in which most middle-class families were now made up of two working parents, there was a market for one-stop shopping based not on price or even on quality but almost solely on convenience of both location and accessibility. To the harried white-collar worker, the new mini-malls were a godsend. Instead of fighting traffic all the way out to the mall, and then fighting for a place to park (if possible, close to the store you had come to shop in) once you got there, you could now pick up a quart of milk, or take in the dry cleaning, or get your script Xeroxed—the number of copying shops in West L.A. is compelling testimony to the persistence of the fantasy of making it in Hollywood among people who have perfectly decent jobs and might be expected to know better—by pulling into a strip mall on your way to or from work.

Most of the people I grew friendly with in L.A. practically survived on what could be bought in them. Allegra used to swear after each visit she would start shopping at a supermarket. "Well, the malls are so hideous, dear," she would say, but her resolve usually broke the minute she got involved in a new project. However much Angelenos might complain about these mini-malls, the fact remained that, just as with automatic-bank-teller machines (an innovation that dates only from the late seventies), they soon found it all but impossible to remember life in L.A. without them. True, those with more orderly lives than Allegra's still went on weekly shopping excursions to a supermarket like Von's, or, if they were feeling flush, to one of the branches of the Irvine Ranch, but a six-pack of beer or a carton of cigarettes you bought at the convenience store in the local mini-mall, even if, as you subsequently pulled out onto the boulevard, you felt dimly ashamed of yourself for having done so.

In fact, even the ugliness of the malls was less an inadvertent by-product than a conscious, and, from a business point of view, a sensible decision on the part of the developers and store owners. As one man who had built mini-malls from Westwood to Echo Park summed it up, "The success of any given property depends on two things: how likely is it that the passing motorist will see the stores from the street, and how easy is it for them to park in front of any particular store once he pulls in?" For their part, most of the shopkeepers I talked to cheerfully admitted that the luridness of their signs, the way each one clashed with every other one in a war of logo versus logo, was intentional as well. "No one notices if you don't shout," was the way one man, a Thai immigrant who had been a pharmacist in Chang Mai before emigrating to L.A. in 1980, put it. And it was worth remembering that these little stores were, with the exception of a few franchise operations like 7-Eleven, not getting any help drawing in customers from national ad campaigns, as the oil companies had done for their franchise holders. Nor were these shopkeepers able to build customer loyalty by offering particularly good service, as the independent gas station owners had been able to do, since the truth was that their prices were not competitive with the supermarket chains and any prospective customer pausing long enough to make price comparisons was more than likely to leave without buying a thing.

All the merchant could do was what merchants in bazaars had been doing for a thousand years—make as much noise as possible and hope to draw the customers in. The signs that disfigure almost every L.A. avenue are, precisely, the visual analogue to this traditional patter. "Hey, you, in the Chevy," they say, "stop here"; "Hey, you, in the Toyota, aren't you out of Kleenex?" And as West L.A. had increasingly become the home of young, single people—so unlike their parents, as members of both generations were quick to tell you—the convenience of the mini-malls became an even greater draw for people who, in any case, rarely ate at home and tended to view grocery shopping more as a matter of picking up a few cans of soda, some potato chips, a roll of toilet paper, and a banana, than as a way of seriously nourishing themselves. For that, they went to restaurants, and the rise of the mini-mall was in fact synchronous with the proliferation of good restaurants, cafés, and bars that transformed a Los Angeles that had not felt much need for them during the course of the 1970s.

Los Angeles had certainly never remotely resembled the "laid-back" place most outsiders imagined when they thought of it, but for most of its history it had been a place in which people entertained at home. Unlike Paris, New York, or Tokyo, Los Angeles, like London, was a city where even when people did go out they preferred to go to a club—or in the case of L.A., a particular restaurant that you went to so religiously it might as well have been one—rather than experimenting with a different place every week. Industries had their favorites. There were Chasen's and Morton's (this last even had an unlisted phone number that regulars could call to make reservations) for the movie industry; the Pacific Dining Car and the California Club for the downtown business and political elite; or the Newport Beach Yacht Club for the new money of Orange County. But these were places to go to either on business or as a celebration. Ordinary life was elsewhere. Now, however, an atomized middle class was making different demands, and restaurateurs and developers alike had readjusted their sights accordingly. But if there was no shortage of restaurateurs, from Pasadena to Palmdale, the mini-malls were another story.

It was not at all clear at first who was going to run these stores. After all, most white Angelenos now had other ambitions for themselves and their children than to work the minimum sixty hours a week required to make a success of running a shop in a strip mall. Had the legacy of discrimination really been as irrelevant to the American present as conservatives from Washington to the Los Angeles suburbs kept insisting, it might have been expected that black Angelenos would have stepped in to fill the vacuum. But even the most modest franchise required both capital and business experience (the turnover rate in these malls being even higher than average), neither of which were in abundant supply in places like Compton or Inglewood. By the end of the 1980s, it was clear that as had been the case for them during almost all of L.A.'s booms and boomlets, blacks had once again been unable to take advantage of the economic opportunities the mini-malls represented. Indeed even the small stores in black L.A. itself were increasingly being run by the new immigrants.

Resentment ran high. Blacks spoke grimly of Asian merchants treating them "disrespectfully," and for their part the Asians, who, while they had the advantage of arriving in the U.S. with some capital from home, were hampered by their little English and less understanding of the particular problem of black America, wondered what was going on. They hadn't come to the United States to be social workers; like the European immigrants before them they had come to make money. So when a black community group barged into a store to prevent a Korean shopkeeper in Watts from stocking blue bandanas, the "colors" of the Crips, one of the two principal black street gangs in L.A., the blacks saw themselves as trying to rescue their children, while the Asian merchants simply saw themselves as victims of a not entirely comprehensible shakedown. With each year, such misunderstandings only seemed to deepen, one more fissure in the L.A. mosaic the Chamber of Commerce was describing so ecstatically.

It would in any case have been wishful thinking to expect black L.A. to suddenly throw up a generation of entrepreneurs after many decades of economic marginalization. With traditional blue-collar industries in Los Angeles like automobile manufacturing and steel, which had at least provided many blacks with decent jobs in the forties and fifties, disappearing fast, with city jobs that had begun to offer another avenue of advancement after Mayor Bradley's election now also being claimed by L.A.'s Hispanic population, blacks in L.A., far from having shared in the city's latest round of growth, had actually seen their situation deteriorate. By now, the community was well on its way to losing a second generation of its children to the malign solace of gangs. There were between 70,000 and 90,000 gang members in greater Los Angeles, and crack cocaine was everywhere. To suggest entrepreneurship in this moment of crisis was like putting a Band-Aid on a third-degree burn. And so, predictably, the task of servicing that better-publicized Los Angeles, the pleasure dome of solitude and gleaming careers, was left to the new immigrants. Along Wilshire Boulevard and Melrose Avenue, in Brentwood Park and Los Feliz, the faces behind the counters were Han and Dravidian, Korean and Persian, Mixtec and Ethiopian—anything, it seemed, except black and white.

But no one I met in L.A. seemed at all startled by this. If opinion was divided, it was split between those who liked the mini-malls and those who did not. Those who welcomed the convenience the stores afforded (and they were more numerous than it initially appeared; like fast-food outlets, the mini-malls were something of a guilty pleasure) were no more concerned about the fact that they were being run by *truly* unfamiliar-looking people—not whites, or blacks, or even Mexicans or Indians—than they were in ascertaining the race of the guy who came to repair the telefax. Having grown used to an invisible city of Hispanic helpers, why should Anglo L.A. have blinked at buying its groceries from people from half the countries of the nonwhite world? There is a distinction in the financial markets between a technical and a fundamental trader; that is, between someone who thinks only of the current position of a stock and someone who frets over the long-term future of a company. White Los Angeles was, it appeared, a world interested only in the short-term instrumentalities. The mini-malls were a convenience, weren't they?

My questions failed to impress most people I met. The answer was so clear. There was this need, I was told, and the malls filled it. Certainly, there was nothing shocking about the fact that they had, for all intents and purposes, come into being overnight. That was the way things had always changed in Los Angeles. Why criticize an *improvement?* Why criticize an idea whose time had come? And when I replied that to try to understand something was not necessarily to criticize it, I was met with angelic California smiles that said, more clearly than argument could ever have done, that here, if ever there was one, was a distinction without a difference.

Opponents of the mini-malls echoed the stores' devotees in their "creationist" approach to the phenomenon. They just turned the story on its head. Instead of as manna suppliers from heaven, civic-minded Angelenos portrayed the mini-malls as the ultimate expression of "urban blight," and fretted relentlessly over what they called the "Van Nuysing" (a feeling of superiority over the San Fernando Valley being almost a prerequisite for residence anywhere else in middle-class L.A.) of the city. Even as informed and scrupulous a critic as the *Times*'s Sam Hall Kaplan felt obliged to entitle an intelligent piece on what might be done about them with the hyperbolic title "Mini-malls: Scenario for a Horror Film." In such accounts, the proliferation of these developments was the result of speculators' greed and of the hapless inertia of both ordinary Angelenos and their elected representatives. Beyond this, the most that opponents of the mini-malls seemed prepared to concede was that *perhaps* their development was *in part* the result of efforts to respond to the new needs of L.A. consumers, a false good idea, as the French say.

In short, Angelenos were quite willing to consider almost any explanation except the one that held the strip malls up as an inevitable by-product of the way in which prosperous people now chose to live their lives in the Southland. This question of responsibility was crucial. All the talk that one heard about self-empowerment and taking responsibility for one's own decisions did not, as it turned out, carry over from the personal life to the life of a citizen. It was one thing to declare oneself "co-dependent" with a spouse or a parent—the therapeutic flavor of the month in middle-class L.A., the phrase connoted illusory passion of addiction rather than the wholesome voluntarism of true feeling—and struggle to transcend that damaging emotion, and quite another to accept a similar degree of responsibility for the way daily existence in L.A. was now configured. Depending on what they felt about the mini-malls, Angelenos tended to describe themselves either as passive beneficiaries of the convenience they provided or else as equally passive victims of the haphazard and unsightly development they represented.

Los Angeles was full of no-fault divorces, no-fault therapies, no-fault insurance claims, and, it now appeared, no-fault citizenship as well. Certainly, no one I met and nothing I read suggested that there were many people who believed themselves personally complicit in this transformation of the city any more than they held themselves responsible for the fact that over the past twenty-five years literally millions of people from every corner of the poor world had abandoned their homes and families to travel thousands of miles, often at mortal peril, usually at great risk, to end up working sixteen hours a day pressing pants or selling six-packs of Coca-Cola, containers of sour cream, and bags of onion potato chips to the gilded residents of a foreign land called Southern California.

For the native population of greater Los Angeles, the sight of all these Thai grocery stores, Armenian travel agencies, and Salvadoran fast-food outlets had to mean next to nothing if they were not to be completely unsettling. The mini-malls were Los Angeles's self portrait of itself after its utopian moment was over, the intimation that, in the long run, the city would become a place like any other. Neither its wealth nor its will would save it from history after all. One could move further and further away from downtown L.A., take refuge at the farthest reaches of northern San Diego County to the south or southern Santa Barbara County to the north, but the handwriting was on the wall, and sooner or later the mini-malls, and the people who ran them, were bound to catch up. Ready or not, the Third World was coming to Los Angeles, coming for reasons that were as diverse in the true sense of that sadly exploited word as the "L.A. 2000" report's sunny pabulum was testimony to its misuse, coming in numbers that defied the imagination, coming fast.

If the terms of art for this event in Anglo and black L.A. were "invasion," "transplantation," and "visitation," the problem in the end was not that such terms were too metaphoric to account properly for what was actually going on, but rather that no metaphor or artistic conceit, no provocative invitations to imagine life and literature trading places, could ever suffice to encompass the magnitude of the event. Californians who had grown up with Mexicans and tended to explain the new immigration from the South as a return of a native people to Alta California confessed themselves bemused by the Asians. People who divined in the Asians a world of immigrants who would revitalize California entrepreneurship with their business acumen and their capital didn't know what to make of the great Latino barrios expanding across the Los Angeles River, east beyond the old downtown. In short, every explanation put forward to account for what Los Angeles was becoming seemed to confute every other explanation, and was thus less a "narrative" any novelist might have been attracted to than something of a study in cognitive dissonance. The Mexican story didn't fit in with the East Asian story, and neither coincided with any of the stories Los Angeles had previously been telling about itself.

All that was certain was that the city which was coming into being was now even more fragmented and various than even the great immigrant Babels of late nineteenth-century America had been. New York, Chicago, Detroit, St. Louis, those cities had been anthologies of Europe, and one did not have to be taken in by all the brave, self-serving talk about diversity to recognize that L.A. was an anthology of the world. It had boasted to itself and to the country that it was the end of the line for Americans, but now it was being filled by new Americans for whom L.A. was more jumping-off point than final destination. These people didn't see Los Angeles as being in some kind of permanent opposition to the rest of the United States, the regions that Anglo Californians tend to subsume under the rubric "back east." Rather, L.A. was the furthest east most of them had ever been, a discomfiting thought to Angelenos who had grown up with notions of geography which, however expansive, were relatively stable.

Just how discomfiting these alterations of spatial reality really were I discovered for myself during a long plane ride back to L.A. from Tokyo. My companion during the flight was a Japanese businessman who spent the first few hours of the journey entering a series of complicated calculations into his laptop computer. After some while, however, even his industry flagged, and, just past Hawaii, we struck up a conversation. I soon learned that he was a financial officer of a middle-sized electronics firm that was in the process of setting up an American plant.

"Where is the factory located?" I inquired.

"Ah," he replied, "it is in the Northeast, in a very good, number-one area."

"Massachusetts?" I said.

"No, Oregon," he answered, smiling broadly.

9. The Rise and Fall of Mexamerica

· ·

To the queasy surprise that white and black Angelenos alike were
beginning to register, the more it dawned on them that alongside the
Los Angeles they had grown up in had arisen a second, shadow city, add
a loose befuddlement at just what sort of Third World city was coming
into being before their eyes. The change made even the great political
dramas of the 1960s that had begun with the unseating of Norris Poul-
son, the downtown business establishment's handpicked man, by an
upstart demagogue from the San Fernando Valley, Sam Yorty, and ended
with Yorty's own defeat by Tom Bradley, who represented a coalition
of blacks and Westside liberals, seem all but utterly irrelevant to the
current state of the city. The future of L.A., I was assured constantly by
people who claimed to be in the know, lay neither in the hands of racist
whites nor with the "progressives" who had given L.A. its first black
mayor, but rather with Chicano politicians like County Supervisor Gloria Molina, State Senator Art Torres, or State Representative Richard
Alatorre, a group that was referred to, after the ruling party of Mexico,
as the PRI (Partido Revolucionario Institucional), and whose members,
in unguarded moments, were reported to boast that they would be the
dominant political elite in L.A. in the twenty-first century.

"Tom Bradley was not only L.A.'s first black mayor," was the way one wag put it, "he's also probably its last black mayor. Power has shifted for good here, even though most people don't realize it yet."

And while the County Board of Supervisors, which, far more than the City Council, really determined the governance of Los Angeles, had only acquired its first elected Hispanic member, Molina, in 1991, in the wake of a series of court findings of electoral discrimination, the trend, in local schoolboards and community planning groups, was indeed in the direction of a very different kind of ethnic politics. If a Richard Alatorre, or, for that matter, an ambitious young Chinese-American city council-man, Michael Woo, thought the future belonged to him, given the new demographic realities of contemporary Los Angeles, this was anything but bravado. In any case it was unlikely that the world city that L.A. was becoming—this, at least, was no mere Chamber of Commerce booster-ism—could continue to maintain the political arrangements that had arisen in a time when it was overwhelmingly composed of whites and (the word was too often thrown in as an afterthought) blacks. The point, however, was that the real nature of the change was not what even the most caustic critics on the L.A. scene had ever anticipated.

There had always been a few people who, boom in and boomlet out, had bucked the received image of the city as paradise. There had always been something febrile and, to the skeptical mind, unconvincing about both the early vision of L.A. as an Anglo-Saxon Eden and the image that succeeded it, when, in the wake of the rise of the Westside in the 1950s, the Los Angeles of myth that the Chandlers, Dohenys, Ahmansons, and Asa Calls had propagated, had to be refitted to accommodate the dreams of Westside Jews and lower-middle-class white Protestants (WASP, a term of caste rather than ethnicity, being inappropriate to describe them). But no one, not even the most disenchanted observers of the Southern California pageant, had predicted the Tower of Babel that Los Angeles increasingly resembled. At least the Chamber of Commerce was trying to be inclusive when it pronounced that L.A. was a mosaic. In contrast, the critics had only one group in mind when they hymned the Southland's new diversity, Hispanics.

There were good reasons for this. Los Angeles, founded as a Mexican *pueblo,* looked to be on the verge of returning to those colonial origins. Each day, as more and more Mexicans moved into the city, transforming neighborhoods, even poor neighborhoods like Watts, into barrios of Jalisco, *colonias* of Sonora, Spanish-speaking and even Nahuatl-speaking cities-within-cities (the immigrants now came from the remote quarters of the Indian highlands as well as from urban slums and the mixed-blood villages and towns of the Mexican lowlands), more and more Angelenos felt themselves under siege. "Fear and Loathing in the Los Angeles Melt-ing Pot" was the way one *Los Angeles Times* Sunday magazine article summed up the situation, and the headline was more than just a copy-writer's fancy. It was as if the new immigration signified far more than an influx of new people. Old ghosts were being reawakened as L.A.'s Mexican past, thought to be dormant for so long—*The Sleeping Giant* was the title of one sixties-era book on Mexican-Americans—had reared up like a monster in a horror film, spiriting the heroine away to its lair.

To be sure, there was a more generalized fear of aliens at play as well. Depending on where you lived in the L.A. basin, if you were Anglo or black your particular *bête noire* (or rather *brune, jaune,* or some variety of *rouge*) might be, variously, the local Korean merchant in Watts, Salvadoran refugees camped out in the brush in the canyons of Beverly Hills, Pakistani men playing cricket in Balboa Park in the Valley, or Chinese shopping mall owners in Alhambra, whose signs none of the Anglo residents could make heads or tails of. "If we wanted to live in China, we'd live in China," was the way Frank Arcuri, himself the son of Italian immigrants, put the matter as he launched an English-only ballot initiative in the previously Anglo and now overwhelmingly Chinese suburb of Monterey Park. For all of that, however, it was Mexico that was at the heart of things.

When Howard Ezell, then the Western Regional Commissioner of the Immigration and Naturalization Service, warned in a speech that "we can't take in all the world's needy," adding that "if America doesn't want to do something to protect her borders, we will become a Third World country, with unemployment and uneducated people," it was perfectly clear that the Third World he was referring to was not that of the Hong Kong Chinese, many of whom were bringing not only their families but their money to Los Angeles, or of the Koreans, with their professional training—many of the shopkeepers, one discovered after a few minutes' conversation with them, having been teachers or pharmacists or even doctors back home—and their access to capital through their system of family-underwritten money-lending associations called *kye.* Nor was Ezell talking about the Filipino nurses, so avidly recruited by L.A.-area hospitals, the number of American-born nurses having dropped precip-itously since American women began to be admitted to medical schools in large numbers, let alone the Iranian Jews, who, Angelenos would tell you, were buying up Beverly Hills a square block at a time.

With the exception of the Asian arrivals who had come to Southern California as refugees rather than as immigrants—the Vietnamese, Cam-bodians, Lao, and Hmong, for whom the new land was one more calvary every bit as much as it was a chance for a fresh start—there was, in fact, very little unemployment and still less undereducation among these newcomers. On the contrary, Asians in greater L.A. were known, with a mixture of admiration and fear, as drones, fierce in their commercial ambitions and still fiercer in their insistence that their children excel in school. "They work so hard," a friend of Allegra's with a child in one of the overwhelmingly Asian public elementary schools told me, her tone anything but complimentary. "It's as if they're already putting their grade point average together in second grade to ensure they'll get into UCLA."

Asian families were well known among teachers in the Los Angeles Unified School District for taking a dim view of all the various "progressive" techniques that had become the standard pedagogical fare of American education over the past twenty years. They wanted as solid an academic curriculum as possible and a minimum of "self-expression." "When Asian kids become a majority in one of the district schools," a high school teacher confided in me one afternoon over lunch in a school cafeteria in the Valley, "all their parents want to hear about are their test scores."

Of course, it was easy to overstate the Asian immigrants' success, or take for granted what they had sacrificed to achieve it. During the time I spent in L.A., I do not think a week went by when I did not encounter an article trumpeting the Asians as what many were calling "the model minority," and, implicitly at least, making predictably invidious comparisons between Asian drive and black and Hispanic failure. Asian-American kids often spoke bitterly of what was expected of them. "People say we're so good, so smart, no trouble," was the way one plump, bitter Taiwanese student at, well, UCLA, summed it up for me, as a group of her friends, clustered around a table at the Ackerman Student Center on campus, nodded approvingly. "It's not like that. You try to satisfy your parents, work in the family store or restaurant maybe four hours a day plus weekends, study hard. There is no life." She paused. "Or maybe just a sad life."

The rather fierce-looking boy next to her added, "People think because we do well, we should not mind the racism here in America, or else they say it doesn't exist. But I think American people don't like Asian people. They think if we accomplish things it is because studying is easy for us."

At that moment, two blond fraternity boys plunked themselves down noisily at the table next to ours. "God, did I get ripped last night," one of them said. "I don't know when I'll be able to make it to class again." His friend nodded sympathetically.

It was an exchange not lost on the Asian boy. Smiling tightly, he said to me, "I wish they could have my life. My life. Just for one day."

To some extent, even the impressive statistics bore out this Asian sense of grievance. While it was true, to take an example L.A.'s boosters liked to cite, that the average income for Asians in Monterey Park was $30,000 as compared to $24,000 for Anglos, the fact was that this differential did not take into account the far longer hours the average Asian put in to make the extra sum. That being said, for all the complaints younger Asian-Americans voiced when pressed, the success attributed to them was real enough, and their complaints were more reminiscent of those of their successful immigrant predecessors, particularly American Jews, than of either blacks or Hispanics. A small group of Asian-American radicals, centered around the Asia-Pacific Studies Center at UCLA, claimed otherwise, but there was something hollow about their claims. In 1990, their great cause was the fight to get tenure for Don Nakanishi, a brilliant Japanese-American sociologist whose lack of senior academic standing was indeed a scandal. Unfortunately, the militant students, in the course of their successful effort to get UCLA to hire Nakanishi permanently, were given to slogans like "1941, Concentration Camps for Japanese-Americans; 1989, Nakanishi, the struggle continues," which only tended to confirm Asian-American success. "With an oppression curve running in this direction," Allegra quipped, when I showed her one of the Nakanishi leaflets, "in ten years what will they be protesting? Matsumoto's moving violation?"

The real story at UCLA, as elsewhere in the University of California system, was a new ruling that now denied Japanese- and Chinese-Americans consideration for the places set aside for disadvantaged minorities. In the faculty clubs and student unions, it was widely assumed that Vietnamese-Americans and the children of immigrants from the Indian subcontinent would soon be struck off the list as well. At the same time, most people told you that there were secret quotas *limiting* the numbers of qualified Asian students, the rationale being, apparently, that if qualified applicants were admitted on an impartial basis, a majority of the entering class at the best schools in the UC system would be Asian-American, an attitude reminiscent of the way Jews were regarded in Ivy League schools fifty years before. In any case, even as things stood, something like a quarter of the incoming freshmen were Asian-American anyway.

In short, a statement like Commissioner Ezell's, like countless others that echoed his nativist anxieties, patently concerned a Third World that began south of the border at San Diego, not the one that was to be found on the other shore of the Pacific Ocean. And to many Angelenos, most of them anything but the racist ogres that immigration rights activists liked to portray, it was as if Los Angeles were melting into Mexico, the international border itself no longer providing the country with even the most nominal integrity. According to Immigration and Natural-ization Service (INS) officials and immigrant support groups alike, the border was a sieve. "For every alien we apprehend," a Border Patrolman told me, as we stood by the international boundary fence at Otay Mesa, watching as, on the Mexican side, scores of young men assembled, waiting for night to fall to essay the crossing, "two get through."

"That doesn't mean they all stay," he added. "What people in the States sometimes forget is that the traffic here goes both ways. People come north from Mexico to work, but they also go home, at least for a while."

"But more and more illegals are staying, aren't they?" I asked.

"Oh yeah," he replied. "They come in family groups now, where you used to just see young men, and of course they don't just come from Mexico even though they all claim to be from there so they will just get sent back to Tijuana rather than being flown back to El Salvador or wherever."

"Can you always tell who's who?"

"Sure," the officer said. "All you have to do is ask a Central American what Cinco de Mayo or any other big Mexican national holiday is. They don't have any more idea than a Swedish farm couple in Minnesota would."

A few miles north of the border, near the suburban town of Ocean-side, stands the most heartbreaking traffic sign in the Americas. There is a well-staffed INS checkpoint at Oceanside, and the men who smuggle illegal aliens into the United States, the *coyotes,* know that if they are stopped their human cargo, huddled in the backseat or in the trunk, will most likely be discovered. So most *coyotes* drop off their passengers before actually getting to Oceanside, instructing the bewildered illegals to walk a couple of miles north. "Just cross the highway here, walk north along the beach, and I will be waiting for you beyond the sight of *la migra,* the Border Patrol." Most of the aliens have walked great distances already, just to get to the border, so on the face of things this should not be too hard for them, especially with their desti-nation, golden Los Angeles, only fifty miles away. The problem is that in order to go north, the illegals must cross Interstate 5, the San Diego Freeway. They can't walk along the northbound side, where they have been deposited, because that land is part of the Camp Pendleton Marine Reserve and is heavily patrolled and fenced. So the illegals must cross the sixteen lanes of freeway traffic, on a stretch of road where the average speed of the oncoming cars is seventy miles an hour, before reaching the comparative safety of the San Onofre State Beach. Over the past three years, 127 people have been killed, a similar number gravely injured.

The sign says only "Caution," and carries an image of a man, a woman, and a pigtailed child, all holding hands, all in desperate flight.

This is not the only warning along Interstate 5. Near San Clemente, where Richard Nixon spent a large portion of his presidency—the Western White House was what the press used to call his compound outside of town—on a stretch of highway that is scary enough to drive along, much less attempt to sprint across, amid markers for gas stations, exit ramps, and notices of weather and road surface conditions, there is another sign. It is studded with yellow lights; it warns, "Watch out for people crossing road." However well intended, the sign is generally agreed to be largely useless. Some well-informed local people even suggest that, far from being deterred, the aliens think these warnings, particularly the pictograph of the fleeing family, denote crosswalks. In any case, a freeway is a completely unknown quantity to them. "They don't have any concept of it," an immigration rights activist, Roberto Martinez, told a reporter. "Many of them are from rural areas, and they don't realize the speeds."

Nonetheless, hundreds of thousands continue to come north along this stretch each year. In 1990, the INS stations in the area between San Diego and the Oceanside checkpoint caught half a million illegal immigrants. Homeowners in northern San Diego County, which had been increasingly selling itself in Southern California as the ideal place to live for those who wanted to find affordable housing far enough from L.A.'s burgeoning crime and traffic problems but close enough to commute to the city to work, now found that their fine homes were in the middle of another thoroughfare, the entry route for illegal aliens. They might be taking a morning jog through one of the county's parks or idyllic canyon roads only to stumble on an encampment of migrants. On the main streets of small rich towns like Costa Mesa and Mission Viejo, one now saw clusters of Mexican men. Whether they were looking for work, or a ride north, or were simply unsure of what to do next, was unclear. What was clear is that they were everywhere.

Surprise, surprise, the United States turned out to border on the Third World after all. It was not just an abstraction, or a black hole, or the place you drove down to from Los Angeles for some cheap and dirty fun or some good fishing. It had its own dreams and they were pressing steadily closer. To many people in Southern California, it appeared harder and harder to know just where Mexico now ended and the United States began, harder to confute those exuberant Third World–loving activists who were describing L.A. to anyone who would listen not as the most quintessentially American of cities, but rather as the capital of a new country that they had taken to calling Mexamerica. "Los Angeles," wrote Lester Langley, in his book *Mexamerica: Two Countries, One Future,* "is for the American Southwest and Mexico's northern third what Mexico City is to the southern and central regions of Mexico proper."

"Mexico proper"! It was language to make a Chicano militant pinch himself with gleeful wonder. Under the circumstances, was it any surprise that even more sober Mexican-American politicians in Los Angeles increasingly were couching what were at root entirely conventional ambitions in the giddy rhetoric of return and reconquest? "The legacy of Los Angeles left by its founding fathers and mothers, Spanish, Indian, and Mexican," State Senator Art Torres declared, "is now being reclaimed by a new generation of leaders. . . . Our modern metropolis is returning to the enduring Pueblo de Los Angeles of years past." The fact that Torres's rosy evocation of eighteenth-century L.A. was not much closer to historical accuracy, let alone applicable to the contemporary city, than Helen Hunt Jackson's portrait of a colonial arcadia in *Ramona* had been was beside the point. What mattered was that, from the Mexican-American point of view, the tables were finally turning.

Many Chicanos, not only militants or politicians who naturally viewed the new immigration as demographic good news for their own chances at higher office, reveled in being able to respond to Anglo complaints concerning Hispanics who refused to learn English or more generalized fears of a Mexican "takeover" of L.A. with exultant gibes of their own. It was an understandable reaction. There are a great number of Chicanos throughout greater L.A., after all, who, if their roots in the region do not go back to the days of the Pueblo, do reach back five or six generations. Ignored for so long, they could be forgiven for wanting to get a little of their own back. As for the militants, many of them had taken to denying that Los Angeles was in any legitimate sense a part of the United States at all. Conjuring up the mythic Aztec homeland of Aztlán, they described themselves not simply as a disadvantaged group within the American polity but rather as a colonized people, whose land had been usurped when Mexico was forced to cede the Southwest to the United States in the treaty of Guadalupe Hidalgo in 1847.

"In the spirit of a new people," began the preamble to the *Plan de Santa Barbara,* the quintessential statement of late-sixties Chicano militancy, "that is conscious not only of its proud historical heritage, but also of the brutal 'Gringo' invasion of our territories, we, the Chicano inhabitants and civilizers of the northern land of Aztlán, from whence came our forefathers, reclaiming the land of their birth and consecrating the determination of our people of the sun, declare that the call of our blood is our power, our responsibility and our inevitable destiny." Most of this bluster, of course, no more defining of the Chicano community (unsurprisingly, many of the *Plan*'s principal drafters went on to careers in mainstream politics, journalism, and the arts) than the Port Huron statement of the radical Students for a Democratic Society in the same era defined an American polity that went on to elect Nixon, Carter, Reagan, and Bush. But however inflated Chicano rhetoric could be at times, the nature of Mexican-American identity was unquestionably anomalous. Mexican-Americans were not exactly an ethnic group, not exactly a race or people (for all the talk about *La Raza,* the race, the difference between a light-skinned Mexican from the northern state of Chihuahua and a copper-skinned Indian from Michoacán was as great as between a Swede and a Sicilian), not exactly an immigrant group, and yet at the same time were all those things.

In coming to America, and, more particularly, to Southern California, which less than a hundred and fifty years before had been Mexican, they were both immigrating—it was pure rhetoric to assert that a peasant from the Altos de Jalisco had any organic relation to Alta California; that peasant barely had any real sense of the lowlands of his own state—and returning. In other words, the movement had as much of the experience of an American from, say, New York moving to California as it did of a Korean coming from Seoul or Pusan. Koreanness, after all, had not been a latent possibility in the Southland since its early settlement; but Mexicanness had. And if the United States was a country perpetually up for grabs, the new arrivals from Spanish America were making their claim not only on the basis of a vision of the future but on a memory of the past, and they arrived with, psychologically at least, deeds and titles in their pockets.

The prospect was one that some Anglos at least had been conscious of for a long time. As far back as 1946, when the glorious suburban dreams of postwar Los Angeles were still in their infancy, Carey McWilliams could assert with steely prescience that the Mexican influence in Southern California, far from having been successfully exorcised, was just about as abiding and irreducible a characteristic of the region as its desert topography. "In view of the size of this Mexican colony," McWilliams concluded, at a moment when there were only 300,000 people of Mexican origin in greater L.A., that is, one-tenth the present figure, "and its proximity to the Mexican border, it is not unlikely that, in the future, some fusion of the two cultures will occur." Now, forty-five years later, Chicano militants and Valley housewives seemed united in intuiting that this fusion was at last taking place, with, if anything, its Mexican component gaining the upper hand on the simple grounds of fecundity, or what Carlos Fuentes once playfully referred to as "the chromosomatic imperialism" of the new Hispanic immigrants.

And given this demographic outlook, what other destiny was really possible for Los Angeles? In 1990, most projections pegged the Hispanic population of the United States, then thought to stand at about seventeen million people, as doubling to thirty-six million by the year 2010. This would mean, among other things, that Hispanics would outnumber blacks. In California as a whole and Southern California in particular the change would be even more dramatic. Hispanics made up 14 percent of the region's population in 1970 but would constitute 40 percent by the year 2000. In the same period, the white population was expected to decline from 75 to 40 percent of the whole. Add the likelihood that the old would be disproportionately Anglo and the young disproportionately Hispanic, and you began to see why this new immigration was so unsettling to so many people.

But more important even than the raw statistics themselves was the perception among many Angelenos that neither the new Mexican and Central American immigrants nor, increasingly, the children of the Southland's Chicano population were interested in assimilating, at least according to those myths and norms ingrained in the American imagination since the great European immigration of 1900. Everywhere in Anglo L.A., one heard jaundiced assertions about the new immigrants refusing to speak English, or become Americans. If immigration was a journey, then Hispanics, it seemed, were refusing to make the trip even as, in reality, they were crossing the frontier in ever-increasing numbers.

To many Anglos, particularly those whose ancestors had themselves made the immigrant passage, this seemed like a betrayal. The Hispanics, I was told repeatedly, in tones of wonder and incomprehension as often as of bitterness, did not love America. European immigrants had never expected the larger society to acknowledge the national holidays of Poland, Italy, or Ireland. Their festivals recalled notables of their ethnic groups who had made a contribution to America—Columbus Day for Italians, and, for the various other groups, days honoring Revolutionary War–era generals, von Steuben for the Germans, Lafayette for the French, and so on. But for Mexicans, whose ancestors had *fought* the United States, such a strategy was obviously unworkable. Indeed, scarcely a month went by without calls from the Mexican-American community in California for statues to General Kearny or Stockton or Frémont, those paladins of the Anglo victory in nineteenth-century California, to be removed from the public squares in which they had for so long occupied pride of place.

The real parallel was to the American Indians. After all, it was clear even to the most patriotic Americans that a descendant of the Cheyenne or the Sioux who had fought the U.S. Cavalry across the plains of the West had little reason to take any pleasure in American history. But the Indians had been largely exterminated—even the names of the great tribes of Southern California, the Diegueno, the Gabrieleno, and the Chumash, being unknown to most Angelenos—and the new Hispanic immigration was the first time an immigrant group could manifest a bitterness similar to that felt by both Native Americans and, of course, blacks. Even the Asians, no matter how badly their ancestors were treated in California, could not muster the same kind of rancor. Unlike the Hispanics, they were doing well economically, and money is a wonderful bandage for history's wounds. Moreover, the commercial aspirations of Asian-Americans made it impossible for them to criticize a capitalist system that was serving them well. "I'm a professional businessman, not a professional Pakistani," was the way a character in *My Beautiful Laundrette,* Stephen Frears's film about the new multiracial London, tells off a black squatter who has appealed to him on the grounds of racial solidarity, and it was a story that might just as well have been told about Los Angeles.

Predictably, liberal Anglos pointed reassuringly to statistics demonstrating that the new Hispanic arrivals were learning English just as earlier immigrant groups had done. But though that was certainly true to some extent, and, moreover, though the militants tended to drown them out, L.A. was full of Chicanos who considered themselves white (as they were; a northern Mexican is often lighter-skinned than a Southern Italian), and fuller still of people who wanted nothing better than to assimilate in the old-fashioned way, and as quickly as possible, it was not the whole story. To begin with, the Spanish language simply had another standing than Italian had had in New York in 1900, or, for that matter, Korean had in Los Angeles in 1990, no matter how many signs in Hankul one saw on Olympic Boulevard. The proximity to the Mexican border, and, by extension, to all of Spanish America, changed everything.

There was also the constant traffic across the border. To be sure, many of the Italians, Slavs, Irish, and Jews who immigrated to America eventually returned home for good—as many as 10 percent by some estimates—while even among those who accepted the bounty of Ellis Island there were a good number who made at least a trip or two to the old country at some time in their lives. But they were scarcely in a position to go back for Christmas or Easter, as many Hispanic immigrants who were in L.A. legally were wont to do, much less work for a while in L.A., then go home, then return, then go home again, as so many illegals did, turning the border into a sort of risk-laden turnstile. When the U.S. Congress in 1986 passed a revised immigration law that offered amnesty to hundreds of thousands of illegal aliens, one of the measure's first effects was, the following Christmas, to hopelessly snarl traffic at all the major border crossings into Mexico as people traveled south to see their relatives.

Mexico was so close. With the exception of Canada and the Caribbean, immigrants to America had never come from so nearby before. It was not just a matter of a Hispanic immigrant in L.A. being able to live an entire existence, albeit an economically deprived one, in Spanish. That, after all, was true in Koreatown as well. But not only was L.A. close to Mexico but it had never succeeded in ridding itself of its Hispanic nature in the first place. The centrality of the Mexican shadow world was confirmed as much by what was missing from the image L.A. presented to the world as by what was present in it. Los Angeles is a city of discrete communities, many of which had campaigned energetically to have their identities acknowledged on freeway signs and markers along the major surface streets. At last count, there were more than four hundred of these signs strewn across L.A. They inform passing motorists that they have just crossed into or out of Downtown, Carthay Circle, Echo Park, Miracle Mile, or Larchmont.

These are imaginative jurisdictions, of course, neighborhoods rather than independent towns, but like actors hungry for screen credit the acquisition of one of these signs was an important measure of success. It is a distinction by no means restricted to residential areas and a few older commercial zones like the Miracle Mile. Immigrant communities are designated as well, and you don't need to read the shop signs in Los Angeles to know when you are in Little Tokyo, Koreatown, or Chinatown. But you can drive from City of Industry in the east to the Pacific Ocean in the west in L.A. and never encounter a sign, for all the loose, jumpy talk about diversity, that announces that you have crossed into Chicanotown, Little El Salvador, or Jaliscoville. It is as if that is information at once both too unmanageable and too obvious to fit suitably on a rectangular piece of metal, stenciled alongside the shield of the city of Los Angeles.

But if no text at least a subtext, as the Method actors say. In L.A. even the most anodyne sight can awaken, to anyone sensitive to what lies beneath the city's triumphalist surface, the ghosts of Mexican Southern California. I heard people with no conceivable interest in Mexico remark absently over lunch that today was Cinco de Mayo, or even some other, far more obscure, Mexican national holiday or Hispanic Catholic festival. Then there was the cruder though almost never remarked-upon fact that something like half of L.A.'s streets have Spanish names, some-times even Spanish versions of names, like Santa Monica or Santa Barbara, that have perfectly serviceable English equivalents. And in a city where dependence on the car means one is constantly attending to road signs and highway exit information, it is impossible, even at the farthest Anglo corners of the Westside or the Valley, to move half a mile before encountering some resonant trace of the Southland's Hispanic core.

There is something problematic, after all, about living on a boulevard called La Cienega, Sepulveda, or Pico, or shopping on Rodeo, San Vicente, and Santa Monica—or even having voted for Ronald Reagan, whose country estate is called Rancho del Cielo and is located in Santa Barbara—while still believing that all this was just a lot of verbal fluff, a holdover from the region's previous incarnation. And if it was then all those nachos, jalapeño peppers, and guacamole that Anglos in the Southland had been serving their guests for generations, there in those adobe ranch houses with their Spanish red tile roofs, and a mariachi band playing somewhere in the background, had left the most unexpected aftertaste. It turned out that these dishes meant more than the new Italian restaurant in Santa Monica or the new sushi bar in Carson City, and that their endogenous force was unmitigated even now. Nor were vacations exempt. The Hollywood scriptwriter Ben Stein might note in his amusing book of journals, *Hollywood Days, Hollywood Nights,* that "in the fall of 1981 I flew to San Jose en route to my dream town Santa Cruz on the Monterey Bay" and imagine he had written a jaunty lead to another of his accounts of his amorous conquests, but those casually dropped place names had their own resonance and were just as explosive a package, at least in the long run, as sexual desire ever was.

In retrospect, it was beginning to appear that all the frenetic activity that had accompanied the immediate post–World War II boom, all those freeways, shopping malls, and subdivisions stretching out to the mountains and beyond, had distorted the true picture of what had taken place in Los Angeles since the first Anglo settlers had arrived at the beginning of the nineteenth century. Mexican Southern California may, indeed, have receded as the Anglo migrants poured in, but it no more disappeared than the shoreline does when the waves wash over it at high tide. However often its neighborhoods were razed and its population pressed to relocate—from Olvera Street and the Temple-Beaudry area to Watts, from Watts to Boyle Heights—Mexican Los Angeles never failed to reconstitute itself. Its roots ran too deep, and what is more, those roots were constantly being watered by the nourishing flow of new immigrants.

Anglo Los Angeles soon lapsed into forgetfulness, the great drama of

Anglo versus Hispano that had wracked the Southland during the nine-teenth century temporarily overshadowed by the passions of suburban-ization. But even the idyll wasn't all that idyllic. Hints of things to come came in the Zoot Suit riots of 1943, a virtual insurrection in East L.A. that erupted after brawls between Anglo sailors on shore leave and young toughs from the barrio known as Pachucos got out of hand, and in the early stirrings of the Mexican-American civil rights movement, mild by today's standards but radical enough at the time, under the leadership of an organization called LULAC (the League of United Latin American Citizens). For its part, however, Anglo L.A., that metropolis of Greta Garbos, imagined itself to be alone.

As things turned out, however, out of sight *and* out of mind was not the same thing as out of the picture. Indeed, what took place in Los Angeles in roughly the period between the early twenties and the mid- or late sixties consisted more of a spectacular occlusion of civic vision, or, it might be surmised, a collective act of wishful thinking, than any genuine diminution of the importance of Mexican L.A. In retrospect, the Chamber of Commerce version had far more in common with those football metaphors so beloved in American political and corporate life than it did with the real history of the Southland. It was a view that proffered the history of California and its supposed crowning achieve-ment, the rise of Los Angeles, as nothing so much as an irreversible linear progress, a series of arcing forward passes from ethnic group to ethnic group. It was as if the missionaries had gotten the ball from the Indians (well, the less said about that the better, *Mission Play* or no *Mission Play*), and, in turn, had thrown to the Mexicans, whereupon the Anglo team had raced out under one final perfect spiral, snagged it, and raced triumphantly across history's goal line for the winning touch-down. That was always the American role, wasn't it, to bring history to an end? Americans had been engaged in the enterprise for more than two hundred years now, as Lincoln understood when he wrote about the country as representing the last, best hope of mankind, with empha-sis presumably placed on the "last."

But what was even more interesting about this claim than its crude and distended sense of mission was the signal inability of most Anglo Californians to consider another, distressing possibility. Could it be that the gun whose report they had heard so clearly had not, in fact, signaled the end of the game at all—that is, the completion of the region's historic development, though not, God forbid, its ever-to-be-continued patterns of economic growth—but rather the conclusion of the first half of play? If so, that would have meant conceding that Los Angeles was not a metaphor or an incarnated myth after all, however elastic that metaphor had turned out to be, but a place, trapped in the continuum of its real history and the increasingly obvious limitations of its parched desert ecology. All past citizens of the city, the concluding sentence of the "L.A. 2000" report asserts, "made their Los Angeles dreams come true," so why should the present be any different? But into this reverie came Mexico, that reproachful canker, its renewed presence intimating that history was not a progress at all but a cycle. The referee had thrown a yellow flag. The touchdown was being called back.

And it was only in a place that so obdurately construed itself as a dream that the change could have seemed like such a bolt from the sky. There were precedents galore for anyone who chose to look. Conquered in stages over the course of the 1840s, and even, as the phrase "California Republic" on the state flag served to remind the most unobservant of visitors, briefly an independent country, the Americanization of California almost from the outset included the expectation that resources would be plentiful and labor cheap. In the East and Midwest of the United States, it was immigrants from Europe who provided the muscle that fueled the great economic expansion. But of all the major cities in the United States, Los Angeles was the one least affected by the immigration at the turn of the century, and while even the most cursory reading of turn-of-the-century newspapers reveals the depth of anti-immigrant feeling among whites in Southern California, an equally cursory reading of the statements of businessmen shows clearly enough that, however much they might despise the nonwhite workers beneath them, they knew that for cheap labor they would have to turn to Asia or Mexico.

Then, as now, nonwhites were simply willing to work harder, and at lower rates of pay, than even the small number of European immigrant counterparts who had made their way to Los Angeles. Indeed, the greatest opposition to the nonwhite immigrants came from native-born workers desperately aware that employers were turning elsewhere. The railroad network that ensured the development of the Southland was built by Chinese workers, whose labor was only slightly less essential to agriculture and manufacturing in nineteenth-century California. The immigration fever of today is mild compared to the vitriolic panics of the 1870s and 1880s. The Chinese were slowly pushed out of the trades they had exercised, with the ironic coda that they became laundrymen, the activity most often associated with them in the United States in the first half of the twentieth century, as an occupation of last resort.

In 1882, the U.S. Congress, prodded largely by the nativist outcry from California, passed the Chinese Exclusion Act, which barred further Chinese immigration to America even on the grounds of family reunification. In 1907, the so-called Gentlemen's Agreement was concluded between Theodore Roosevelt's administration and a Japanese government acting on behalf of its Korean protectorate. It forbade immigration from Korea. Japanese immigration had already been curtailed on orders from Tokyo, incensed at the treatment of its subjects in America. Bars on Filipino migrants soon followed. In 1924, this menu of restrictions was subsumed in a comprehensive immigration reform act that not only effectively barred nonwhite immigration but set up quotas so restrictive that, for all intents and purposes, only people from Protestant north-western Europe had any hope of being admitted.

But such is the cleverness of history that it was these restrictive, racist impediments to Asian immigration that spurred the arrival of large numbers of Mexicans in Southern California for the first time since Pio Pico, the state's last Mexican governor, left L.A. for good in 1853. With supplies of Asian labor cut off, California employers looked south, across at a Mexico that was poor, unstable, and already had more people than jobs. The completion, in 1885, of a railroad grid that linked all of Mexico with Los Angeles ensured that workers could be brought north easily and cheaply. By 1916, six trainloads a week were arriving from the border at Laredo, and it is anyone's guess how many more Mexicans simply walked across the border from Baja California and headed north, just as their descendants do today. In fact, there was not a single moment during the rise of Southern California when, somewhere in the background, there were not brown hands busily working to ensure its continuation. Any other version is literature. If, today, Los Angeles would stop functioning were the immigrants from south of the border not on hand to do the dirty work, the reality is that the same was true in 1919 and 1946 as well.

The parallel, or, more accurately, the continuity between the city's past and its present, does not stop there. In Los Angeles today, most Anglos imagine that the refugees who have arrived in the hundreds of thousands from Guatemala and El Salvador are the first such "political" migrants from Spanish America. In fact, just as events in Central America in the seventies and eighties had profound effects on the demographic makeup of Los Angeles, so the decision of Mexico's violently anticlerical president, Plutarco Calles, to rigidly enforce the ruling PRI's constitutional ban on the activities of the Catholic Church had a similar convulsive effect in the twenties and thirties. Calles's move led to an insurrection in the Mexican states of Jalisco and Sonora, the same pauperized regions from which so many of today's immigrants hail—the so-called Cristero rebellion. For five years the Cristeros—named after their battle cry of "Cristo Rey," "Christ is King"—fought the central government to a standstill. Eventually worn down by massacre and a program of systematic starvation not so very different from the tactics the Soviet government was employing in the Ukraine in roughly the same period, the Cristeros were broken. By the tens of thousands, they headed north toward Los Angeles.

At the time, the Catholic hierarchy in L.A. was anything but pro-Mexican. It was controlled by Irish priests who, though obviously disqualified from the more florid forms of American nativism, were still eager to find their place in the Anglo-Saxon version of Los Angeles that was rising up around them. But if the archbishop during that period, Timothy Cantwell, was most interested in soliciting the financial support of the Dohenys, the great Catholic family in the downtown business establishment, for everything from charity hospitals to the opulent church of St. Vincent de Paul downtown on Figueroa Street, he was also very involved with his Hispanic parishioners, particularly the Cristero refugees. In this sense, the Catholic church's internationalism—and its view of Bolshevism as its real enemy throughout the world, the PRI, in Cantwell's view, being an arm of international communism—was stronger than the personal prejudices of its officers. Cantwell might have gotten Doheny's wife the title of Papal Countess and stood staunchly by the plutocrat during his two inconclusive trials for bribing a good chunk of the federal government in order to secure from the Harding administration favorable leases on the oil reserves at Teapot Dome, but he also built scores of new churches for Mexican parishioners and smoothed the way for the Cristero refugees to settle in the Temple-Beaudry district on the rim of downtown L.A. In 1934, the Cristeros even mounted one of the largest public demonstrations Los Angeles had ever seen, forty thousand of them parading through the downtown streets calling for the overthrow of the godless commissars in Russia and in Mexico.

These days, of course, the mass rallies tend to be on the left, demonstrations against the government of El Salvador or in defiance of the immigration laws. Luis Olivares, the Claretian rector of La Placita in the Old Plaza between 1986 and 1990, declared his church grounds off-limits to INS agents, and even the new archbishop of Los Angeles, Roger Mahony, committed the diocese to working for amnesty for illegal aliens, and, in 1986, to what he called the church's Latino Aid Plan. But these were new perspectives about old concerns, and if everything seemed to be changing in Los Angeles in 1990, there was ample civic history that demonstrated, whatever lies the city had told itself, that as far as Hispanics went there was less to this change than met the eye. The new immigration from Mexico and Central America was only unprecedented in the vastness of the numbers of people involved. Mexicans had come before, and there was even something almost inevitable about the renewal of their migration north.

And as the fact of their presence sank in, Angelenos began, almost shyly, to allow that they were not surprised. When Tim Rutten said to me, over coffee with some of the other editors at the *Los Angeles Times* one morning, that he found L.A.'s Mexican component part of the norm, I was surprised, not by Tim's views—as the graduate of a parochial school he was hardly representative—but by the degree of assent they commanded among his non-Catholic colleagues. Later that day, as we drove back toward Hancock Park, taking a circuitous route through a Temple-Beaudry district which, as yet relatively untouched by the wrecker's ball that had devastated downtown L.A.'s other Mexican neighborhoods, was now the home of tens of thousands of Salvadorans, Tim returned to the subject.

"I don't look at a Mexican and think of a foreigner," he said. "They were always here, and I don't mean in the romantic sense that this town was once Mexican—that's a lot of hogwash, like saying New York was once Dutch—but in the down-to-earth sense that I knew these people as children. They're as much a part of L.A. as I am."

"But won't the new arrivals change things?" I asked, as we pulled up alongside a bus stop crowded with what looked like a cross section of Mexamerica, sturdy *campesinos,* impish youngsters in torn T-shirts, dignified girls, half of whom looked—it was a cliché, but it was also a fact —pregnant.

Tim laughed, and it was obvious that the scene he saw there on that L.A. street corner had an entirely different resonance for him.

"That's something that all my friends who come from the East or from Europe always say," he replied. "They take a drive like this, or walk downtown from, say, Pershing Square to the *Los Angeles Times* building, and seeing nothing but brown faces, hearing nothing but Spanish on the streets, they think, 'Jesus, it's fucking *Blade Runner* come to life.' What they miss is that they're thinking in the wrong categories. L.A. has always been a Mexican town. All this talk about Mexamerica may seem like news in New York, scary news too, but L.A. will get by."

Tim himself would have conceded, I think, that he was a particularly sanguine local, but even the doomsayers who dreamed of moving away from Los Angeles toward some racially purer spot like Washington State or northern San Diego County now agreed that the Mexican shadow city had been there all along. The surprise was that even this reluctant admission was being made in a Los Angeles where, for all the centrality of the Mexican presence, this old dichotomy, this either/or of Anglo versus Hispanic, no longer entirely held water. In 1946, or for that matter in 1976, it was still possible to imagine a de-Anglicized L.A., in which Spanish was at least the second language and the political result was a strong, Quebec-style separatist movement. That was what had fired the imaginations of the drafters of the *Plan de Santa Barbara,* and was still terrifying Anglos all over greater L.A.

The irony was that if the myth of the Anglo-Saxon Eden was no longer sustainable, neither was the myth of Aztlan. The arrival within the metropolis's sixty-square-mile radius of people in great numbers from practically all the nations and ethnic groupings in the world had not only subverted Anglo L.A.'s cherished self-conception—the new Hispanic immigration alone would have been sufficient to undermine that—but its long-repressed nightmare about its Mexican past as well. For their part, if Mexicans were, as some Chicano militants insisted, coming to reclaim their lost city, they were also discovering in the process peoples who, if anything, were more oblivious to their existence and more indifferent to their historical complaints than even the most purblind of Anglos. As the comedian from East L.A. Cheech Marin put it in an interview in *L.A. Style,* "The best thing about being Latino in L.A. is that everywhere you look, and everything that you see and touch and feel, tells you that you belong here. The worst thing is that everyone else feels the same way, and it's turning L.A. into a battle zone." Chicanos, too, it seemed, were not immune to *Blade Runner*–style fantasies.

But whether the eventual outcome was the war of all against all, or a peaceful confusion of tongues, cuisines, histories, and skin tones, for the present what was emerging in Los Angeles alongside the old historical dramas of the Southwest was a Babel. Instead of some traditional theatrical resolution—an ethnic equivalent of the old saw that the gun on the wall in the first act has to go off in the third—all the old categories were pathetically insufficient to encompass L.A.'s disturbing, baroque richness, its welter of conflicting claims and dueling aspirations.

What was a Korean shopkeeper to make of the myth of Aztlán, the victory of the American General Kearny over the Mexicans at the San Gabriel River outside Los Angeles in 1847, or a term like *La Raza?* Which race? In Los Angeles there were now so many. What was a Salvadoran refugee to think as he washed dishes in an Israeli Jewish restaurant in Sherman Oaks—there were said to be at least 100,000 Israeli immigrants, many of them illegal, in the Valley—and what complicated emotions were felt by an American black from South Central L.A. as he drove past the cluster of Ethiopian restaurants on one short stretch along Washington Boulevard? The ethnic noise was deafening, and if the Anglo center was not holding, which of course it wasn't, then neither was Mexamerica. In Los Angeles, every dream now crowded in on every other dream, and every claim impinged, sometimes fatally, on every other claim. Of course people had spoken of Los Angeles, practically since its inception, as having neither any real civic nor any real cultural identity. Suddenly, it was as if the city had passed from deficit to surfeit. It had too many identities, too many cultures even to be legible to itself. But if L.A. was not to be the capital of Mexamerica after all, or, at least, if that transformation was only to be part of its destiny in the twenty-first century, then what, more than a few Angelenos with the wit to understand what was enfolding all around them were asking, was its story going to be?

10. Last Hurrahs

· · · · · · · · · · · · · · · · · ·

Like love affairs, some subjects are more narcotic than others, which, on balance, probably is a far better thing for a writer than for a lover. It was not long before I realized that in Los Angeles I had acquired just such an obsessive theme. The longer I spent in the city, the more bemused I found that I had become by its parallel world of immigrants and, in almost direct proportion, the less interest I could summon up concerning just those matters that the people I had come to care for on the Westside most often talked about. There were times, west of Echo Park, when I felt as if I were on vacation—vacations with white people, vacations from the real Los Angeles. Certainly, there was none of the sharpness there, that tang which made days I spent in Asian or Hispanic L.A. so vivid, peculiar, and unsettling. The exoticism of the immigrant city, while it doubtless contributed to this impression, was only part of the story. Rather, what seemed most important was how fraught and tense with meaning even the most mundane of stories became in the context of the new immigration.

Each day was a surprise. I might drive out to an East Asian immigrant town like Alhambra or Monterey Park, sometimes stopping for lunch in a dim sum parlor, those vast Chinese restaurants where not a word of

English was to be heard either from the patrons or from the waitresses as they wheeled huge carts full of unidentifiable dishes whose names they sang out in harsh Toi Shan accents. Later, I liked to walk for hours in vast Chinese and Vietnamese supermarkets, gaping, even as I was being gaped at—I was invariably the only white in the mall—at produce shelves crammed with bok choy and taro root, and at meat counters on which whole pigs' heads abutted packets of chicken feet and duck livers. Or else I might ride downtown to the Old Plaza, that oddest of crossroads where a Disneyfied version of Old Mexico coexisted uncomfortably with the real thing, and try to strike up conversations that would not be misinterpreted as propositions by the Salvadoran teenagers to whom Father Olivares had given sanctuary, or, failing that, talk with tourists from Ohio or Holland half-hidden behind their camcorders and burdened with souvenir packages of huaraches and Mexican jumping beans.

"I had not expected to find this Mexico here in Los Angeles," a middle-aged German woman, fashionable in her Jil Sander jacket and short Stephane Kélian heels, told me cheerfully. Looking past her at the group of slightly feral-looking adolescents clustered by the gate of La Placita, I thought, "They did."

This sort of thinking has a momentum all its own. Before long, I found that I could not undertake even the most commonplace of activities without being distracted by those immigrants I was sure to encounter, L.A. being L.A., while picking up a six-pack of beer at the local 7-Eleven, going to the movies in some gleaming Westside multiplex, or even pulling in for gas somewhere along the boulevards. At night, the sensation of the exteriors of Los Angeles being entirely garrisoned by immigrant workers became even more pronounced. For not only did every restaurant have its complement of Mexican or Central American car parkers, but if you got lost, at least anywhere outside the far Westside, and drove to a gas station to get directions, the half-chilled kid from Sonora or even Uttar Pradesh one found sitting watch there behind the scarred, bulletproof Plexiglas was unlikely to have heard of, let alone know how to give directions to, that street in Los Feliz or the nearest on-ramp for the Hollywood Freeway you had spent the last half hour trying to locate.

It was perhaps natural that these workers, who, after all, rarely spent any more time in the neighborhoods where they were employed than any tourist might have done, were disoriented. More surprising to me was the degree that even less freighted contacts than the kind one has when lost—and there is almost nothing so disorienting as being lost in L.A.; it is a weightless, unnerving feeling, as on an amusement park ride that has gone on for too long—seemed oddly bewildering as well. It was as if the ostensible and the real nature of these encounters were at odds with each other. Instead of being able to concentrate on the beer I planned to drink, or the movie I had come to the mall to see, or what might happen *after* I'd gotten to the place I had been heading toward before noticing that the car was almost out of gas, I would find myself homing in on the various immigrant spectacles unfolding all around me. Before too long, I began to anticipate these experiences even before they occurred, and I remember a period in L.A. when I couldn't enter a convenience store without the title of a fifties science-fiction movie flitting unbidden to mind: *When Worlds Collide.*

And what worlds were indeed evoked by the spectacle of the Pakistani owner of a convenience store giving orders in broken Spanish to his stolid Guatemalan stockboy. Had the man ever imagined, when securing his coveted American visa at the embassy in Islamabad or the consulate in Karachi, that he would need to learn pidgin Spanish to succeed as a small businessman in Los Angeles? For that matter, had he ever even heard of Spanish? On the Indian subcontinent, Spanish is about as exotic a language as is imaginable. The nearest place to Pakistan you might hear it spoken was in the Philippines, a thousand miles to the east, or in Spain itself, several thousand miles in the opposite direction. What a surprise it must have been for him to discover this unexpected obstacle to his immigrant dream.

And what was one to make of the gaggles of well-dressed Chinese-American girls, so demure and deferential when you encountered them in a classroom or on the premises of a family business, suddenly transmogrified into near perfect copies of any run-of-the-mill group of self-absorbed, individualistic Anglo teenagers the minute they were on their own? I don't doubt for a moment that much of the emotional charge that these random sightings produced in me came from my growing conviction that everyone in present-day Los Angeles had been, somehow, mislaid. Of course, it was true that, if you could think about this bouillabaisse of cultures, these constantly shifting arrangements and rearrangements of languages and roles, with a certain glacial dispassion, there was no reason why Chinese adolescents shouldn't favor the single black glove they had seen Madonna wear on the music videos or use expressions like "tubular" and "awesome" for the same brief, intense moment they were in vogue as did their Anglo sisters. This was America, after all, the country where the whole point was change. Anything went in America, not least the need for subcontinental merchants to learn to count to one hundred in the language of Cervantes and Pio Pico.

It was just that this outcome was, well, so unlikely. The generations of condescending observers of L.A. who had agreed that L.A. was, for better or worse, a place outside of time had been as wrong as the boosters who had prophesied its limitless growth. How hollow Nathanael West's gibes about the "half world" or, sixty years later, the French structuralist critic Jean Baudrillard's rapturous assertion that "it is Disneyland that is authentic here" now seemed. For Los Angeles was less and less the epitome of American contextlessness or meaninglessness. Rather, what had happened in the city was that, virtually overnight, it had acquired too many meanings. And there was nothing simulated about the congestion of peoples who now had to learn to coexist in the Southland. This was no Disney view of the more picturesque parts of the globe; this was the real thing. A city with the second-largest concentration in the world of Mexicans, Salvadorans, Koreans, and Armenians is no theme park, and that is its fascination, rather than any of the Southland's older imperatives like utopianism, boosterism, or halcyon moments of dreamlike ease.

But on the Westside, where I spent most of my nights, little of this had sunk in. You could sit at a dinner party in Brentwood or Pacific Palisades and hear your companions assure you that "everyone in L.A. is writing a script." There was even a joke about a man getting on a bus and complaining loudly that he has just had a project turned down at a particular studio, whereupon everyone on the bus from the driver to the little old retiree in the back assures him that they too have had trouble at the studio in question. It was a decent joke in its way. The only problem was that no one in Los Angeles who might have had such an experience was likely ever to have ridden the RTD. The premise on which the joke depended was thus both essential and impossible, essential because one cannot have people engaging in this kind of collective gripe session without putting them in some public situation, but impossible because in reality they would be alone in their cars.

It was perfectly clear, however, that when people on the Westside said "everyone" they meant everyone on the Westside. Just as "everyone" was writing a script, "everyone" was worrying about how much the recession would drive down the price of real estate, "everyone" had to think about cholesterol, and "everyone" had given up smoking. The cumulative effect of all this was to remind you of just how parochial life really was within the pleasure dome. There were more sophisticated spins, of course. People who considered themselves above this common, garden-variety Westside talk would confide gruffly that real estate and aerospace, rather than Hollywood, were the real animating forces of the city. And, in fairness, why should such people have thought more expansively? They did not live in Los Angeles so much as they did in particular zip codes. In less euphemistic times, they might even have called themselves 90049ers (for Brentwood) or 90265ers (for Malibu) rather than Angelenos. And, in fact, the cover story of the September 1990 issue of *Los Angeles* magazine had been titled "We've got your number: Who you are, how you live, what you buy, zip code by zip code." Ten Los Angeles neighborhoods were anatomized to the smallest demographic detail. Needless to say, there were no surprises as to which ones were selected.

The self-absorption inherent in a magazine that, while claiming to speak for the whole of Los Angeles, in fact was concerned with only that area from Santa Monica ("middle class, racially mixed [*sic*], college educated, politically liberal. Singles and couples, many without children. Older, smaller homes") to downtown ("Affluent, white [*sic*], college educated, politically liberal to moderate. Urban high-rise condos") only mirrored the tenor of most dinner party conversation in white L.A. There was almost as little point in bringing up the subject of the rest of the city as there was in growing indignant over a survey that could conceive of overwhelmingly white Santa Monica as being racially mixed, or of the overwhelmingly Hispanic downtown as being characterized by the fortresslike Bunker Hill development which had indeed drawn many white Angelenos back downtown, but nonetheless housed only a fraction of the neighborhood's residents.

Still, there was something altogether spectacular about returning from a day spent in a paint factory in City of Commerce (a day that had begun, on my arrival, with most of the work force mistaking me for an INS inspector and bolting for the exits) only to sit down at a dinner in which the hostess bombinated through three courses about her experiences at a self-help seminar in Northern California, where she had at last succeeded in getting in touch with the "inner child" in herself. "The inner child in me needs a drink," Allegra whispered to me, as she got up and strolled out onto the patio to smoke the cigarette that she had been forbidden—politely, adamantly, and by telephone the morning before —to consume anywhere inside the house itself.

This self-referential quality to life on the Westside extended far beyond the domestic rituals then in vogue there. More basically, there was an enduring conviction, particularly among liberal Angelenos, a disproportionate number of whom were Jews, that, despite the evidence of their own eyes, the new immigration simply recapitulated the immigration of 1900; in other words, the experiences of their own grandparents and great-grandparents. From Pacific Palisades to Brentwood Park, Sherman Oaks to Pasadena, at cocktail parties, offices, and the well-upholstered Connolly leather front seats of Jaguars and Lexuses, successful, appealing men and women assured me that everything would work out. More often than not, they proceeded by the same simple analogy. The Hispanics, they said, with their lack of financial resources, their high crime rates, and their low levels of educational accomplishment, were the latter-day Italians. Meanwhile, the Asians, with their access to capital, their reverence for study, and their entrepreneurial zest, were the latter-day Jews.

"Did you know," an indignant garment executive said to me one night, having listened, with ill-concealed displeasure, to my account of an afternoon I had just spent in the streets around La Placita, "that Italians only became truly middle-class in the 1970s and that the Jews had to face the exact same quotas they now use on the Asians?"

He spoke with passion, a worldly man, used to being listened to, but anything but a blowhard. There was nothing facile about his will to believe that nothing had changed, that the Hispanic youths he employed in his factory loft on Los Angeles Street were not so very different from the Jewish boys with whom he had worked on New York's Lower East Side fifty years before.

"So you think things will work out here?" I asked.

"Of course they will," he answered. "These things just take time, that's all. You're too young to remember when Italians were known as dagos, too young to know that a lot of Jews of my generation called WASPs white people. That's just what Mexicans get today. And nobody much liked the Italians in those days; they were naturally lazy, prone to crime and alcoholism. Now look. You've got Lee Iacocca at Chrysler. You had Giannini, who just about built this state and the country along with it. You had John Roscia over at Rockwell International. And there are more Italian CEOs today than I could name."

He continued. "The country's changed. Look at that guy Erburu over at Times-Mirror. He's a Basque or something. What do you think Otis would have thought of that? The people who founded the L.A. *Times* wouldn't have known the difference between a Basque and a Mexican on the best day of their lives. And what about Dianne Feinstein?" He drew out the syllables, emphasizing the alien quality of the name. "Fei-ein . . . stei-ein" was the way he pronounced it. "She nearly made governor," he said. "So sure I'm betting that the Asians have nearly made it already, and that the Hispanics will get there too. Just a little more slowly, that's all, like the Italians. What's happening now is part of a continuum, part of the story of America."

That morning, before driving out to East L.A., I had been watching the morning news and been startled, during one of the commercial breaks, by an ad for Fidelity mutual funds that made much the same point. The pitch had been for a U.S. Treasury fund, and the gimmick was an elementary school classroom. "Why did people come to America?" the teacher asks. A bright-eyed kid is quick with the answer. "They came here because they knew they would be safe and that they could work hard, make money, and buy lots of great things."

There it was in a nutshell, the folk memory of immigration. For there was nothing extreme about the claim. The possibility of prosperity was, indeed, the engine that had propelled the immigrants to America, and a proven record of success, of immigrants who had made good, was what still lingered in the American psyche. As Ronald Reagan, by no means the worst guide to the country's self-image, had put it, the United States was the place where people from all over the world could "finally see their dreams come true and their kids educated and become the next generation of doctors and lawyers and builders and soldiers and sailors."

To think otherwise was to give up a great deal, perhaps too much. The garment manufacturer was not alone in his faith that the country which had done right by him would do right by the new arrivals. I had heard other versions of the same credo. One afternoon in Malibu, a scriptwriter friend of Allegra's ran sandy-footed and perturbed back up the wooden steps that separated his house from the beach after having been unable to persuade me that, at its root, there was nothing very novel about the new immigration. He emerged a few minutes later, joining me down at the shoreline below, holding a well-worn paperback book that he promptly handed to me. It was Henry James's *The American Scene,* which James had written in 1906 after returning to England from the first protracted visit he had made to his birthplace in some twenty years.

On the Lower East Side of Manhattan, as he stared with horror-struck wonder at the noisy, foul-smelling streets crowded with incomprehensible Jewish immigrants, James thought he discerned the end of the America he loved and for which he had imagined he spoke as a writer. Of the Jews, he wrote that while they, in the fullness of their alien swarms, were establishing "their note of settled possession," the result for native-born Americans was the exact opposite. "*Un*settled possession," he observed bitterly, "is what we, on our side, seem reduced to." But what Allegra's friend was saying was that events had not turned out at all as James had predicted. The children and grandchildren of the immigrants who had troubled James's imagination had, in point of fact, so ardently identified with their adoptive country, the more cultivated among them with James himself—"In my twenties," wrote Cynthia Ozick, one of the best of contemporary Jewish-American writers, "I thought I *was* Henry James"—that not only their accomplishments but the very content of their characters seemed to refute the master's dire forebodings.

"Read it again," my host said seriously, "and when you do, think about the day we're spending together—Allegra, you, and me, the great-grand-children of the people James was so traumatized by. We didn't turn out so badly—I mean for the country as well as for ourselves—and I'm willing to bet you a hundred bucks against a moldy bagel that the Hispanics and the Asians will have exactly the same experience as we did."

Given that the immigrant experience of 1900 still loomed so large in the imagination of most Americans—"I know we're crowded," Ronald Reagan had said in his Christmas address to the country in 1982, "and we have unemployment and we have real problems with refugees, but I honestly hope and pray we can always find room"—such sanguine pre-dictions were hardly surprising. But there was a softness, nonetheless, at the core of all this cheery and rigid parallelism, something that went beyond the tendency ordinary people share with military leaders of always standing prepared to fight the last war to a successful conclusion. The premise itself seemed wrong to me. Was it really true that the successful assimilation of the European immigrants of 1900 had been the only possible result, as so many people I met appeared to believe? And if another outcome had been possible even then, wasn't it some-what willful to assume that the current immigration had to have a happy outcome? Even in the City on the Hill, that still seemed to be stretching things. But, in the most benign and generous sense of the term, the idea that immigration was, at best, a volatile and perilous event in which a number of outcomes were possible came across to most people I met in Los Angeles as deeply un-American. The United States, they seemed to agree, was a country as blessed in its outcomes as in everything else.

But was it true? On the face of things, the implosion of the idea of the melting pot in both the educational and the political establishment, if not yet in the popular imagination—and its replacement by the idea of a mosaic—suggested that it was not. To be sure, the newspapers in Los Angeles liked to publish immigrant success stories, Horatio Alger–like tales of diligence or raw ability. There was the eleven-year-old Chinese-American prodigy, Jimmy Hsu, of Laguna Beach in Orange County, studying for his college entrance exams along with a class of Anglo high school juniors; his exploits were often cited, the week the story ap-peared, by people on the Westside anxious to ram home the Jewish-Asian analogy. On a less anecdotal level, it was also clear that as various immigrant groups became more prosperous, they followed the traditional American political trajectory of left to right, and that even the deep allegiance Chicanos had historically given to the Democratic party did not always survive the move from working-class Boyle Heights to the more affluent precincts of Orange County or the Valley.

This did not mean that the new immigrants' idea of what becoming an American involved was necessarily the same as that of their predecessors. The move from the demands of the melting pot to the more deferential, permissive conception of the mosaic represented a decisive break. No longer would the act of coming to America involve the same losses that, willingly or not, an earlier generation of immigrants had accepted as part of the conditions of entry. Instead, there was to be an attempt to encourage immigrants to preserve as much of their cultures as possible. To be sure, much of this multiculturalist piety was window dressing. Immigrants still had to learn English, to cite only the most basic example, if they wanted to advance economically—a reality that was not lost on language schools, whose advertisements on the Spanish-language television stations in L.A. portrayed a menial worker who, having gone to their school, is then shown sitting at a desk in jacket and tie, telephone in hand, as a disembodied voice says, "I need that report by Friday." Nevertheless, the rules of engagement had so altered that it was sheer wishful thinking to believe that the situation the country faced in 1991 was the same as the one that had obtained a century earlier. The country in which Buddhist temples and Islamic mosques were sprouting in the most unlikely neighborhoods was a very different place indeed from the country where many immigrants had aspired to nothing more than to change their names and pass for white Protestants.

That it was hardly possible for a Kim to be mistaken for a Kincaid or an Abdelkassem to pass for an Anderson should have provided a challenge to the sanguine accounts that were such common coin in West L.A., but it did not. Nor was there nearly as much evidence of xenophobia—for all the lurid accounts one read in the local press of racist skinheads attacking immigrants—as might have been expected. After all, xenophobia, however odious it is, is a species of territoriality, and, as such, a natural reaction. Indeed, one of the more perplexing aspects of conversation in ecologically minded West L.A. was to hear people who worried over the slightest disturbance to the ecosystem assert that, as far as human boundaries were concerned, there should be virtually no constraints at all, let alone prosecution of those who were found to be in the country illegally. So sensitive were liberal Angelenos to the possibility of appearing xenophobic that they almost invariably used the term "undocumented worker" rather than "illegal alien," which made contravention of the immigration law sound like some trivial problem of paperwork rather than, for better or worse, a breach of the laws of the United States.

But then immigration, if it had been—along with slavery, the Indians, and the frontier—the great, defining experience of American history, had also been a subject to which much romance, much fear, but precious little clarity had adhered. To read, for example, the transcripts of the official debates over immigration reform in the early 1960s, when, under pressure first from the Kennedy administration and then from Lyndon Johnson, the U.S. Congress finally repealed the racist immigration statutes its predecessors had enacted between 1882 and 1924, is to enter the most sublime of never-never lands. For what these Solons were discusssing and what actually resulted from their reforms could not have had less in common. One can never predict all the effects of a given law, but it is rare that a law has such a diametrically opposite effect than the one its framers intended.

The 1965 Immigration Reform Act passed into law virtually unnoticed by most Americans. Unlike the major pieces of civil rights legislation enacted during the same period—the Civil Rights Act of 1964; the Voting Rights Act of 1965—or the Tonkin Gulf Resolution that, in 1965, had authorized the Johnson administration to wage a virtual presidential war in Vietnam, measures whose importance was clear from the outset, immigration reform was presented not as something pressing so much as a rather abstract matter of equity. The bill would not, its supporters repeated over and over again, when pressed by colleagues who harbored the same nativist anxieties that had afflicted their predecessors in 1924, lead to any profound changes in the racial or ethnic makeup of the United States. True, the new law eliminated restrictive nation-by-nation quotas and removed bars to immigration from Asia, but in passing it the American Congress was, in the words of the sociologist Nathan Glazer, "giving itself the moral satisfaction of passing a non-discriminatory immigration act that it expected would in no substantial way change the sources or volume of American immigration."

Robert Kennedy, then the Attorney General, was speaking for most well-informed Americans when, testifying before a House subcommittee on behalf of the proposed reform in 1964, he asserted confidently that the number of immigrants "to be expected from the Asia-Pacific triangle would be approximately 5,000." His elder brother, Jack, before he became President, had written a book on the subject, *A Nation of Immigrants.* It repays rereading, both as an example of the kinds of accomplishments past Presidents liked to claim for themselves and as a document of a time whose ignorance and optimism are scarcely credible today. Immigration, John Kennedy asserted, was "one of the dra-

matic success stories of world history." The imputation was clear
enough that this was a story which Americans could safely take pride in
without fearing that it would come back to haunt them. In 1965, when
the bill was about to come to the floor for a vote, one senator did raise
the issue of Mexico and the Caribbean. To this, Nicholas Katzenbach,
Robert Kennedy's successor as Attorney General, replied that there was
nothing to worry about. "If you look at the present immigration figures
for the Western hemisphere countries," he said, "there is not much
pressure to come to the United States from these countries. There are
in a relative sense not many people who want to come."

To people in Washington in those days, people who prided themselves on being players, on knowing how the world worked, the Third
World was a place to which one sent missionaries, and aid, and, when
necessary, the United States Marines. But the same people who so confidently dispatched troops to the Dominican Republic to quell a leftist
insurgency there in 1965 never imagined that Dominicans might aspire
to move the other way, not as an invading soldiery but as striving immigrants. One wonders now, as he recedes, ever more discreetly, into
the documentary footage of the period, what John F. Kennedy would
have thought of his "nation of immigrants" made up precisely of ever-
increasing numbers of those people from the Third World he never
imagined would show up. And what would Bobby Kennedy, that great
champion of Mexican-American rights, have made of the Los Angeles of
1991? He died in the city, gunned down at the Ambassador Hotel by a
Palestinian immigrant with a grievance that, at the time, was completely
unfamiliar to most Americans. The Ambassador has since been torn
down, and the neighborhood surrounding it is now made up mostly of
Central American and Asian immigrants and a few native-born blacks.

In retrospect, what is surprising is that the profound experience California had with immigration between 1916 and 1965 did not make
more of an impression on all those officials who told such irenic stories
to themselves in Washington during 1964 and 1965. Californians had
always known somewhere that Mexicans wanted to come north, even if
the southern border was something of an abstraction to policy-makers
in the capital. In the late 1940s, there had even been a series of mass
deportations during a federal campaign with the hateful title Operation
Wetback. Almost a million Mexicans were transported back to Jalisco
and Sonora. But perhaps by 1965, 1950 already seemed like ancient
history in an America that thought itself the leader of the capitalist
world. With everyone's attention seemingly focused on the ever-increasing levels of prosperity the country was experiencing in the postwar boom, and the ever-increasing levels of anxiety it was feeling as the

Cold War deepened, the Third World seemed less and less relevant, except, perhaps, as a battleground, a market, or a tourist destination. It might, at concessionary prices, export its raw materials to the United States. But its people? As a character in Mary McCarthy's novel *The Group* liked to say, "Who'd a thunk it?"

And yet, had Americans been paying attention, they would have noticed that 1965 was just about the time when the Third World, too, began to move into a kind of fast forward. The early 1960s were the period in which populations began to increase vertiginously. At the same time, the Green Revolution in agriculture was transforming the way farming was done. As harvests were increased, the need for farm laborers decreased, and in Mexico hundreds of thousands of farm workers suddenly found themselves without jobs. The pattern was repeated all over the Third World. At the same time, the period marked the first great postwar expansion of investment into developing countries. New patterns of employment and mobility shattered the traditional order in country after country. People who had never been out of their villages found themselves living in shantytowns at the edges of great cities, performing work which none of their ancestors had ever imagined, let alone undertaken. The European pattern was repeating itself, and, for the first time since the Stone Age, the peasantry was beginning to disappear from large parts of the earth.

It was also at this moment that the great cities of the Third World began to grow so dramatically, an increase that, in the case of Mexico City, has meant a rise in total population from about three million in 1940 to about twenty million today. People from all over the republic were lured to the capital, fired by unemployment on the land, the prospect of jobs in the metropolis, and even a romance of urban life that was powerfully encouraged by advertising campaigns portraying the pleasures of the capital. For several decades, almost every Mexican village could boast a poster for Superior-brand beer, with its image of a sexy blonde lolling against the backdrop of Mexico City's Zocalo square. The legend read *una rubia de calidad,* "a high-class blonde," a play on words, on the fact that *rubia* means both "blonde girl" and "light beer" in Spanish.

The message could not have been clearer. A farm boy knew he was never going to run into that blonde at home in his village, but in the city, who could tell? And the farm boys flocked to Mexico City, and, in steadily increasing numbers, to that greatest blonde of them all, Los Angeles, California. Never mind that life there bore no relation to the fantasy. At least you could have a fantasy, which was more than you could say for life in the Altos de Jalisco or the dry arroyos of Chihuahua.

And Los Angeles was familiar, from the films that were increasingly supplanting the homegrown movie industry and from television shows that were now a staple even in remote areas of the country. All over the world, as Hollywood became the world standard for entertainment, for fantasy itself, the dream of coming to this mythical place intensified as well.

What the 1965 law did was to make the United States in general, and Los Angeles and New York in particular, accessible to people who, a few years before, were probably all but unaware of America's existence. In 1961 a group of African diplomats were roughed up and racially abused by some white cops on a highway in northern Virginia. Hearing of this, President Kennedy invited the most senior of them to the White House, where he proffered a handsome apology. "I hope this will not tarnish America's image in the eyes of your countrymen," he added. "Mr. President," replied the African dignitary, in a most undiplomatic spasm of frankness, "most people in my country have never even heard of the United States."

Ten years later, such a response would have been inconceivable. Indeed, the legislators who debated immigration reform in 1965 probably did so in the last moments before the eyes of the world's poor turned toward the United States. It was not that the Robert Kennedys and the Nicholas Katzenbachs were being disingenuous. Rather, they were simply hopelessly behind the times, the prospect of nonwhite immigration on a vast scale no more real to them than the prospect that the population explosion, then in its infancy, would drastically alter the racial makeup of the world as a whole. The minority status that whites suddenly found themselves confronted with in California, and which, if the demographers were right, the country as a whole would face sometime in the twenty-first century, was only one reflection of this larger global transformation. But none of this was clear in the 1960s, which, in retrospect, now look like the white world's demographic last hurrah. As for homogeneity, it soon turned out that it was a privilege reserved only for the poorest or remotest of nations; that is, places no one wanted to go to or no one could find.

In this sense, Los Angeles has been only the most advanced example of what is taking place not only all over the United States, but, to a greater or lesser degree, all over the developed world. Even Japan, with its fantasies of racial purity, has immigrants nowadays. As for Europe, there no one with any sense imagines a future that is not at least somewhat multiracial. The only real question, for all the talk of a fortress Europe, is how many immigrants will come from Turkey and the Maghreb, Central Africa, the subcontinent, and the Caribbean. Today, the

Paris metro riders do not look so very different in their ethnic composition from those of the New York subway system. Even Italy, for two
hundred years a world-class exporter of people, now plays host to at
least two million African immigrants.

One Sunday morning in L.A., I was surprised to read in the *Los Angeles
Times* that one of the effects of the civil war then going on in Somalia
had been to drive hundreds of refugees into Finland. Finland? It seemed
improbable. But the article went on to explain that Somalis could still
go to the Soviet Union on transit visas and that, from there, they were
making their way across the border into Finnish Karelia. In fact, I should
not have been surprised. For both the Somalis in Helsinki and the signs
in Hankul along Olympic Boulevard were part of the same phenomenon.
They represented a world both smaller and, at the same time, far more
interconnected than anything that could have been conceived of thirty
years ago. I stared out the window of Tim Rutten's den at the shedding
ginkgo tree across the street (yet another immigrant!) and wondered at
this world on the move. Compared to what these Somali must have
gone through on their way from Mogadishu to Helsinki, the well-worn
path north from Central America or the Korean Air flights from Seoul
that delivered the new immigrants into the cacophony of LAX almost
seemed like a tamer journey. At least a Salvadoran freshly arrived in L.A.
would see signs in Spanish and not find the climate all that disconcerting.

It was another matter entirely for native Angelenos. For them, the
news was bound to create such anxiety, such weightlessness, that it was
hardly to their discredit that they preferred to believe that the new
immigration was just a rerun of what had happened before, or else to
hunker down into the privileged folds of their careers and private lives
and insist that nothing was happening at all. For the moment, at least,
the strategy could work, so long as they did not venture far out of their
familiar orbits. But this did not mean that Los Angeles was not being
transformed all around them, or that, however insistently they might hit
the mute button as history raced along in fast forward, they could wall
out their new neighbors, otherwise known as the rest of the world,
indefinitely.

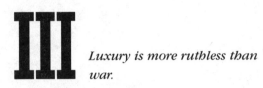

III

Luxury is more ruthless than war.

—Juvenal

11. Lest the Future Pass Them By

· ·

There was, in Los Angeles in 1990, another school of thought entirely, one that had pronounced itself completely sanguine about the city's transformation. Far from contemplating the arrival of all these new immigrants with alarm or rue, its adherents were, if anything, mostly eager to see the process accelerate. If the world really were moving en masse to the Southland, they insisted proudly, this only underscored the region's enduring vitality. The United States might be falling apart, but Southern California was not, not if despite all the smog, traffic jams, crime, and high cost of living the region not only could still attract as many people as ever from the rest of the country, but, in addition, had become the destination of choice for would-be migrants from the length and breadth of the Third World.

Of course, this formidable new group of boosters was prepared to admit that L.A. faced vast problems of acculturation, jobs creation, and, more basically if less quantifiably, the forging of some measure of civic unity out of this immigrant Babel. Though they did so perfunctorily, they even conceded that the *Blade Runner* scenario remained a distant possibility. But this gloomy prospect appeared like a tiny cloud on an otherwise sunny afternoon. The prevailing tone was, as always in L.A., one of wonder: wonder that the city continued to grow; wonder that so many immigrants continued to come; even wonder at the civic elite's own ability to interrogate itself about how it all would turn out. "How marvelous a question!" wrote Kevin Starr of the project of the L.A. 2000 Committee. "How courageous! Few world cities, if any at all, would have such courage and humility to ask such simple yet profound questions of itself."

Yeah, yeah. It was sobering to realize that the hyperbole of the most stereotypical Hollywood agent was as nothing compared to the everyday rhetoric of an L.A. booster. In reality, there was far less to this vaunted self-interrogation than met the eye. For although various pessimistic outcomes were mentioned from time to time, they were not seriously envisaged. All they amounted to were a few lonesome caveats, drowning in a sea of self-praise. The proportion of assertion to qualification in the "L.A. 2000" report was typical. Time and again, a section of it would begin with some sweeping claim for what the future held for L.A. in the twenty-first century—"THE city," "international marketplace," "vibrant mosaic," and "leading hub of world trade" being only some of the glorious titles L.A. was busily conferring on itself—while the unwelcome detailing of what would occur if Los Angeles did not immediately solve the series of pressing problems that confronted it was relegated to a perfunctory paragraph or two at the end.

The boosters' dedication to awakening Angelenos to the future that awaited them did not extend to any plurality of destinies. Just as the local enthusiasm for channeling, the New Age cult version of reincarnation in which one got in touch with one's past selves, did not extend to the possibility that one had been a scullery maid or a serf rather than a princess or a warrior, so the L.A. version of the future only envisaged glamorous improvements on what had already taken place in the region. There could be nothing mortal about L.A.'s splendor at the close of the twentieth century any more than there had been in the mind of the Chamber of Commerce flack who, in 1923, had written a pamphlet entitled "Why Los Angeles Will Become the World's Greatest City."

Because that, in the eyes of the boosters, was what had happened before, why on earth should it not happen again? The task that had faced General Otis and William Mulholland had been far harder, after all. "Do you really believe," a City Council staffer told me one afternoon, "that it will be tougher for us to learn to adapt to the new immigration, and start inventing a few better paradigms than the ones we've had, than it was for L.A. to get the water that fueled our growth in the first place? That *was* a miracle; this will just take a lot of hard work."

And as for the doubts of outsiders, Angelenos like this politician were frankly contemptuous. There was something flinty and intractable about this self-confidence. Had it not been cast in such polite cadences, and accompanied by such attractive smiles, it would have resembled nothing so much as the way Israelis—another people whose miracles went back to irrigation and land titles—talked about their country. Of course, no Angeleno would have chosen to paraphrase Menachem Begin's assertion "It does not matter what Gentiles say, it matters what Jews do," but, absent the defiance, a similar belief infused many people in the Southland.

To view things in this obdurately self-regarding light was to find a way to see everything that was happening in Southern California, except, perhaps, traffic and the environment (even the "L.A. 2000" report was untypically muted on that subject), as unalloyed good news. Thus, the most bedraggled Mexican family, newly arrived in Los Angeles from Jalisco and walking dazedly through the downtown streets, or some middle-aged Korean couple, desperately trying to find their relatives amid the punishing crush of the international arrivals terminal at LAX, came to be seen as just as emblematic of the city's ceaseless, triumphant renewal as were those Japanese bankers, Hong Kong real estate speculators, Taiwanese venture capitalists, or other moneyed nonwhite newcomers whose investments, during the seventies and eighties, had provided such a welcome boost to the local economy.

Such interpretations almost went with the territory. Every newcomer, after all, no matter where he or she came from, represented not only prosperity but growth. And growth was at the heart of Los Angeles. The city had never aspired to be a second Geneva, a haven for people's money but for as few of their persons as possible. From the founding of modern Los Angeles, the quasi-official ethos of L.A. had favored the engine over the repository. Space was something to be conquered; a city was something that expanded. Those were the rules of the road. There should always be room in the Southland for more people, more business development, more residential expansion, and to say that the city had had enough of any of those was to compromise the very quality that had given the idea of L.A. its abiding force.

Other places in California, like Carmel or even San Francisco, might conceive of themselves as Shangri-las with modern conveniences, but the model for Los Angeles was more that of El Dorado. Shangri-las, moreover, do not want to be found out—they have had their fill of people shouting "Eureka"—while El Dorados do. But there was little point for Los Angeles to advance such a claim, if, in the next breath, it turned around and told people not to bother coming. And while it was true that few people in the city could honestly claim to be as comfortable with the new immigration as they were with the memory of the last one, it did not follow, given the choice between no one arriving at all and learning to live with those who, in fact, were now choosing to make the journey, that every Angeleno would opt for things to remain as they had been.

There were other, harder economic forces at work, of course, and even the most ardent boosters of a multiracial Los Angeles would usually admit that they were not without their own political agendas or business interests. Nonetheless, L.A.'s long-standing myths about itself had, over the course of decades, become powerful forces in their own right and were not to be underestimated. You cannot grow up in a place where, almost from infancy, it is drummed into you that you live at the cutting edge of the American dream, and that L.A., as the local saying had it, was "it, the place to be," without coming to believe it at least part of the time. Such a feeling might in the fragmented context of life in the Southland coexist with other, more pessimistic beliefs—a sense of the deterioration of life in L.A., a fear of crime, an apprehension that immigration was now out of control—without being impeached by them. That was L.A.'s beauty as well as its paradox, a manifestation, on the broadest imaginable scale, of Walt Whitman's great and quintessentially American statement, "Do I contradict myself? Very well then I contradict myself."

In any case, those who remained skeptical about the city tended to leave sooner or later. They went east to New York, always an agreeable home for the congenital malcontent, or north to the more humane precincts of San Francisco, Portland, or Seattle. Meanwhile, even those Angelenos whose racial antipathies to people of color remained deep-seated were more or less trapped into at least ambivalence toward the nonwhite immigrants, who after all were the contemporary expression of the mantra Angelenos had been reciting about their city for more than a century: "Wouldn't you rather be in Los Angeles?" For even if the answer came out as *sí, hai, indio, da,* or *naam,* that still added up to the same response, to that emphatic "yes" to which Angelenos had always been peculiarly susceptible.

To have responded otherwise would have meant admitting that you did not care at all for the ways in which the future was shaping up. And that idea had never come naturally to any group of Americans, let alone to those who had spent their lives in the literal as well as metaphorical shadow of the Hollywood sign. The boosters took full advantage of this predisposition, preferring, instead of confronting more pessimistic assessments on their merits, to respond that those who could not see the virtues of the new immigration were simply behind the times. "You have a group of suburban, uneducated people out here," George Ricci, the former president of the Chamber of Commerce in suburban Monterey Park, explained to a *Los Angeles Times* writer in an effort to account for why Anglo townspeople resented the new Chinese immigrants. "[They] would like to turn the clock back to 1950 and hang a Chinese from every lamppost. These people didn't do anything to market to the Chinese. They left themselves open to be replaced."

For businessmen like Ricci, anyone who resented the new arrivals were sore losers who just weren't going to make it to the future. Even Angelenos who were less sure found themselves, as they tried to sort out what they felt about an impending nonwhite L.A., trapped by what was, after all, the oldest of regional syllogisms. If L.A. was the city most open to the new, and the new was also, by definition, what was best, then the immigration, which, whatever else it was, could hardly be described as anything but unprecedented, also had to be a fundamentally good thing, however it might appear on the surface. Of course, put in this reductionist formula, it sounded absurd, but as it was lived, in this region where the abiding American sense of being part of an unfinished project was particularly deep-seated, it was mysteriously compelling.

That there was, laced through this whole attitude, the familiar element of old-fashioned, reflexive boosterism was clear from the frequency with which that cuddly noun "dynamism" popped up. There was a word that, like the virtually interchangeable "energy" and "vitality," appeared to require no further elaboration. It had usually been enough to say in ordinary conversation in Los Angeles that a person, place, or thing was dynamic, just as it was usually comment enough— unless, of course, you were alluding to nature or to some valuable heirloom or would-be heirloom—to say that something was new. In contrast, where the city's new boosters parted company from their predecessors was in insisting that L.A.'s future economic success, rather than needing to take place in spite of the existence of a growing nonwhite population, in fact depended on its presence if it were to have any hope of being realized.

It was an epochal shift. The move from Otis's time, when L.A.'s pride had been that it was the most Anglo-Saxon of major American cities, to the more inclusive fantasies of post–World War II America had been astonishing enough. But no L.A. booster in 1916, 1956, or, for that matter, 1976 could have foreseen a time when the city's most dyed-in-the-wool enthusiasts—as opposed to white supremacists prophesying its destruction—would have welcomed the eclipse of white hegemony in the Southland. That had been the province of a few radicals like Carey

McWilliams, chimeras not worth taking seriously. And yet, on the eve of America's third century, the only boosterism that still made sense was precisely the one that hymned this improbable destiny for Los Angeles. L.A., the boosters said, was going multiracial, adding, as Angelenos always did when they spoke of their own future, that if the rest of the country knew what was good for it, it would follow L.A.'s example.

This was a very different gloss on the new immigration that was being heard in other parts of the United States, where, after all, there had also been a tremendous influx of people from all over the non-European world. It was not that the new immigrants were without their defenders in cities like New York, Houston, Chicago, or Boston. But outside the West Coast, sympathy for the new arrivals tended to be based on patriotic notions of the United States as a nation of immigrants, and the sense that if immigration were curtailed it would signal, as almost no other gesture could, the end of the American experiment. There was also the sense, particularly among the descendants of the European immigrants of 1900, that this current wave of immigration deserved a degree of welcome that their ancestors had not received from the customs inspectors at Ellis Island. This was one of the reasons that so many members of these more established ethnic groups resented the unwillingness of some of the newcomers to immerse themselves in the melting pot. This time, they reasoned, assimilation would take place so much more humanely.

But what was absent from discussions in the Northeast and Midwest was precisely what was at the center of pro-immigration arguments in Southern California, this sense that the new immigration signaled good news about the future. The time was long gone when people in these older cities had taken much joy from looking forward in time. Indeed, whatever might separate, say, New Yorkers from Chicagoans, few among them would have disagreed that their respective cities' best days lay behind them. The task at hand was to make sure that things did not get any worse. Under these circumstances, the new immigration was received, even by those who welcomed it, as recapitulation rather than forward motion. In contrast, the Angelenos who had seized on the phenomenon discerned in it a means through which they could continue to believe in the plasticity of their own lives, the malleability of their personal and civic future, and the raw potentiality of exciting times ahead. "We are going to be different from anywhere," an urban planner and former Long Beach city councilman, Marc Wilder, told the writer Joel Kotkin. "And we are going to do things differently because a Cambodian, a Hispanic, and a Jew share the same space. . . . We will see new kinds of institutions made by new kinds of people."

Kotkin himself was one of the ablest promoters of this idea that the new immigration represented a radical break with everything that had come before, leading inevitably to new types of people in a new version of the United States. The fantasy that moving to Southern California itself renewed people was, of course, as old as Lummis's *Land of Sunshine.* But it was a far more original contention to insist that the new people would renew Southern California. If it resembled anything, it was the 1960s-era radical fantasies of the New Left. Che Guevara, after all, had insisted that the greatest accomplishment of the Cuban revolution would be its creation of a "new man." Now, a group of critics like Kotkin had folded these millenarian assumptions into the framework of late twentieth-century capitalist development, a fusion that, even in the fusion-friendly environment of greater Los Angeles, was breathtaking in its audacity.

Kotkin's personal trajectory was interesting. A business writer who had worked for *The Washington Post,* he had moved to Los Angeles in the mid-seventies and become a convert to its promise. In 1982, he had published a book called *California, Inc.* There he had argued that the eastern economic establishment was exhausted, having lost its faith not only in its own powers of recovery, but, more generally, in the future of the free market itself. The East and the Midwest, Kotkin and his coauthor, Paul Grabowicz, insisted, were the "aging 'have not' half" of America. The West Coast, though, was booming. Despite the crisis of will in New York and Washington, the "real free enterprise society" of California was alive and well. The authors quoted approvingly Tom Lieser, an economist at Security Pacific, who had said that the region "just can't stop growing no matter what. This is fantasy land and nothing will be able to put a stop on it."

In a sense, Kotkin and Grabowicz were only taking Carey McWilliams's insight that California was "the great exception"—and his confidence that, as he had put it prophetically in 1949, the state would occupy "a central place in world affairs"—to its logical conclusion. The fantastic economic development of East Asia, which Huntington had only imagined and McWilliams only glimpsed, had come to pass. And while the East lagged behind, California businessmen and the policy intellectuals like Kotkin with whom they surrounded themselves were ready to join in, believing themselves perfectly able to compete with anybody. "I'm not afraid of Nomura Securities," Don Harrison, of Security Pacific, had told me, alluding to his company's gigantic Japanese rival. "They're not ten feet tall. The Japanese are brilliant, no question about it, but we're not bad ourselves here in California."

To many, it boiled down to a question of not losing one's nerve. As

Kotkin had put it in his even more radical call to arms, *The Third Century: America's Resurgence in the Asian Era,* the main task that confronted Americans on the eve of the millennium was not to submit to "the great angst of the Atlantic world." Anglos, in particular, needed to understand that their future depended on identifying themselves with "the Asians, Latins and Africans who every day become more a part of America." After all, they were the representatives of the productive powerhouses of Asia and the labor-rich, youthful markets of Latin America in which the future of capitalism would be played out. And if only the United States could jettison its oppressive baggage of nostalgic Atlanticism, then it could be assured of playing a central role in that future as well. Eureka!

As for the decline of the United States that so many commentators had been predicting, it was simply not necessary, according to Kotkin and his colleagues. The main reason? Immigration. "Immigration," Kotkin wrote, "has the potential to play the most revolutionary role. . . . Due to the presence of [nonwhite immigrants], we are moving rapidly from being a 'melting pot' of Europeans, to a 'world nation' with links to virtually every inhabitable part of the globe." The economic promise of such a shift, in his view, particularly when coupled with the nation's abundant natural resources and the energetic entrepreneurial culture that remained its peculiar strength, was so enormous that it could not come a moment too soon. And why waste another minute, when, to Kotkin's way of thinking, the task at hand was really the long-overdue fulfillment of America's original promise—that Whitmanesque vision of a nation of nations rather than what the United States had wound up being for the first two hundred years of its history, an anthology of Europe?

Of course, one of the reasons writers like Kotkin had pinned their hopes on California was that the move to universalism, and away from what he bluntly called America's "white ideology," made special sense in a state whose trade was already overwhelmingly with Latin America and East Asia. Despite its history of racial antipathies, California businessmen were now, just as Kotkin claimed, so focused on what was happening in Osaka and Guadalajara, Singapore and Taiwan, that the Anglo-Saxon fantasies of its founders had become more evidently counterproductive than those of, say, the American states that bordered on the Atlantic Ocean. In this context of burgeoning trade with the countries on the other side of the Pacific, and atrophying relations with Europe, many Southern California businessmen were coming to agree with Kotkin that old-fashioned racist attitudes and what the educational multiculturalists were increasingly referring to as "Eurocentrism" were atavisms that a successful twenty-first-century American capitalism could no longer afford.

In any case, there were Third Worlds and Third Worlds. Those for whom the encounter between the settled reality of Los Angeles as it had been until the mid-seventies and the L.A. that was being born out of the new immigration was less a tragedy or a mystery and more the impetus for another cycle of prolonged business growth had every interest in portraying what was going on as another L.A. dream come true. That was the great thing about the city: you could make it up as you went along, expunging old dreams, claims, and beliefs when necessary to make way for better, more profitable ones. So Lummis's dream of the Eden of the Anglo-Saxon homemaker went the way of the dinosaurs who had once roamed the La Brea Tar Pits, where Wilshire Boulevard now stood. That was an improvement, wasn't it? And anyway, as those few boosters who still remembered Lummis would add, the racial prejudice he had exhibited was an unfortunate limitation of his time and class; what mattered was that he had understood that L.A. would be great.

Like the electric railway, the water, and the subdivisions, the immigrants were only the latest rabbit the magicians of L.A. had, against all odds, pulled out of their collective civic hat. To hear some businessmen talk, businessmen who, earlier in their careers, had probably never given a passing thought to the prospect of a multiracial Los Angeles, it was as if demography itself had suddenly reversed field. Had all those fertile Hispanics and Asians not begun to flood across the border, they said, the American population would first have stabilized, then begun to decline, as was already the case in Western Europe. And what opportunity for growth would there have been then? Who would have bought the houses, the washing machines, the Big Macs, or the Treasury bills? Instead, as a result of the immigration, the United States' demographic profile more closely resembled that of Brazil than that of Germany. And if that carried with it the inevitable condition that the country would also come to have a racial composition closer to the former's than to the latter's, then so be it.

The immigrants were coming to L.A.'s rescue. They would secure for the city its rightful place as a great entrepôt. They would usher the region into that brave new world of money divorced from nation that loomed on the horizon. And they could provide the context for answering not only the old Los Angeles question of where it fit into the nation as a whole, but where it could insert itself into that unprecedented world economic geography in which New York, Frankfurt, Tokyo, and Mexico City were just points on a financial map—a world that would be a kind of souped-up space-age version of medieval feudalism, with people owing their allegiance more to the multinationals who employed them than to the nations whose passports they carried. In the radically fragmented, heterogeneous world of the future, a world of mobility, contingency, and isolation, the radically fragmented city of Los Angeles believed it would find a comfortable—and profitable—niche. "We're a collage city," Don Harrison had told me as I left his office. "That's not a bad thing to be in a collage world."

Was it a case of any future in a storm, a kind of willful suspension of disbelief? If so, it was widespread. Across the Los Angeles basin, from office suite to think tank, and from think tank to country club, you heard a remarkable unanimity. A policeman would have found the whole thing suspicious; a priest would have nodded approvingly. L.A. would soon be the crossroads of world trade, the vital link between the United States, Asia, and Latin America. To be sure, there was a great deal more emphasis placed on Japan and the East than on impecunious old Mexico and its neighbors to the south, but this was far more than updated Huntington, garnished and modernized with some fine lip service to diversity and a reluctant surrendering to demographically rather than legally mandated fair racial hiring practices.

What the boosters of this new, multiracial Southern California had understood, as their predecessors had not, was what a radical turn capitalism had taken. In the borderless world of the global economy, the Japanese management theorist Kenichi Ohmae had written, "It is harder every day to see where national interests lie. . . . The real battle, if battle there is, lies between regions, not countries." To some extent, the idea that it was better to get on a plane to Tokyo than to New York suited deep-seated L.A. predilections, but even for a state that harbored at least fantasies of what its role might be as an independent country there were new elements as well. In Henry Huntington's day, and, for that matter, during the 1950s, when heavy industries like Kaiser Steel and General Motors provided the underpinnings of the Southland's prosperity, it would have been impossible to imagine this degree of bifurcation between the interests of area business and national political interests. Now businessmen were, as Californians liked to say, way out front. The CEO of a given corporation might be a white man, but that did not mean he put particular stock in that condition, any more than his American citizenship stopped him from transferring jobs abroad if he thought the move would be profitable.

Businessmen were perfectly capable of waving the flag when it suited them, but, for the most part, politics was regularly coming in a poor second on a local as well as a national and international level. Certainly, it did not appear that the L.A. business world and the boosters either shared or was particularly interested in the fears that many Anglos in the region were expressing about the new immigration. During the last part of the period I spent in Los Angeles, the newspapers were full of the de Klerk government's decision to move South Africa away from apartheid. There were many accounts of the opposition of Boer farmers to the reforms, and, as well, of the unswerving support the abolition of apartheid had received from the Johannesburg business elite. And while it was unfair to compare whites in L.A. with whites in South Africa, it was no exaggeration to say that capitalists in both societies seemed to have decided that a division of the world into racial groups, or, for that matter, construing the national interest in terms of preserving the privileges of whites over nonwhites (as opposed to, say, bondholders over wage earners), no longer made economic sense. That they called this power-sharing in Pretoria, and multiculturalism in Los Angeles, really made little difference in the end, however dissimilar the two societies were in other ways.

It was not a question of morality, far from it. California business had little time for that invalid category. They lived comfortably at home in a "free enterprise" society, one of whose main accomplishments was to have all but written off the poor. Even apologists like Kotkin had to interrupt their accounts of California's brilliant, unstoppable destiny to concede parenthetically that young blacks in L.A. faced, by and large, a future of hopelessness and despair, while even the white middle class, the supposed beneficiaries of Southern California's high-tech, entrepreneurial civilization, were subject to steadily increasing feelings of "alienation and anomie." As for the world outside California, local businessmen consulted only their brokers and their bottom lines. When the Chinese students were massacred in Tiananmen Square in Beijing in 1989, the only worry most California executives with interests in the Far East seemed prepared to express was whether China remained stable enough for continued investment. Those who thought it was held steady; those who did not took their business elsewhere. All the rest was window dressing.

"It will all blow over soon," an executive with a plastics firm that imported a good deal from a plant in Guangdong Province told me at the time. And it was clear that the "it" in question referred only to the Congressional and editorial outrage over Deng Xiaoping's crackdown, not the repression itself.

"The Japanese had the right idea," he remarked to me a few months later, shortly after it had been announced that major Japanese banks were again going to lend money to China. "They said nothing, even when the press was baying for blood, rode the whole situation out, and, when the time was right, got on with their jobs."

It takes a certain single-mindedness, in a conversation about the after-effects of a massacre, to describe the press as "baying for blood," or to construe American businessmen rather than Chinese students as having been the injured parties in the whole affair. But in this, as in so many other things, Southern California businessmen had learned from their Japanese counterparts. The Japanese would trade with anyone, and so should Southern California. In such situations, sentiment was a luxury.

The Japanese were at the heart of the matter. There were times when it seemed as if their success possessed the imagination of Angelenos completely. For all the talk that had come before, that too was a change. When Huntington had launched his Pacific orations, he had been doing little more than occupying the space available to him. It was not as if he would ever have been able to compete with the House of Morgan, back in New York, for the custom of the British Empire. Now, however, all of Asia, but particularly Japan, loomed not only as the most logical market for Southern California but as the greatest market in the world. Given the choice between trading with Japan, Taiwan, and the rest of resurgent, rapidly industrializing East Asia and trading with the European Community, most L.A. businessmen would tell you they would opt every time for the cornucopias of opportunity presented by the Pacific Rim.

The imaginative homeland of American bondholders at the beginning of the twentieth century had been England—an affiliation from which the American political class back in the Boston-Washington corridor had not yet emancipated itself—but the demi-paradise toward which the Southern California business elite had turned its sights, now, as the century closed, was Japan. They had even managed to convince themselves that they were in many ways closer to Asia than to the East Coast. Los Angeles, you were told, did not just trade with the Pacific Rim, it was an integral part of the Pacific Rim. All the Japanese acquisitions in the United States were but evidence of this impending fusion. "This new definition of the Pacific and of American-Japanese cooperation," wrote Jiro Tokuyama of Mitsui Bank, "is far more important than discussions of American decline or Japanese dominance," adding, in a phrase guaranteed to bring a glow to the heart of L.A.'s boosters, that this "Pacific interdependence" could not be stopped by "the emotionally charged arguments of the U.S. Eastern establishment or Midwestern manufacturing interests."

To be sure, the old racial animosities that had played so defining a role in the pre–World War II history of Southern California still lingered on. Nowadays, however, they were more likely to be encountered among those Angelenos who felt that they were losing ground—black and Anglo factory workers, for example—than among white-collar workers or businessmen. I once asked the sister of a Southern California real estate tycoon whether her brother minded doing business with people whose style, I hazarded to guess, was completely alien. "Mind?" she replied, smiling gently. "How can he mind? The only way he was able to take his company private last year was with the financial backing he raised in Tokyo."

"That's right," her husband added stonily. "He learned to eat sushi like everyone else in Los Angeles."

The Japanese seemed irresistible anyway, their success inextricably linked to that of the Southland. "The vision of Los Angeles as the U.S. capital of the Pacific Rim trade and finance," David Shulman and Sandon Goldberg stated flatly in their 1990 Salomon Brothers report on L.A. real estate, "underpins the valuation of some of the priciest real estate in America." Japanese investors, they added, had discovered that " 'L.A.'s the place in the 1980s,' " and because the city had attracted so much Japanese investment, "it has become increasingly linked to the Japanese economy." In 1990, the Japanese had even bought Pebble Beach Golf Course, said to be the best on the West Coast. If that didn't solidify their claim to being the captains of the future, what did? And certainly, if you added that acquisition to Matsushita Electric's buying MCA/Universal studios and Sony acquiring Columbia Pictures, the impression that the "Ameripan" the boosters were predicting was coming to pass was hard to resist, even among those who realized full well that Japanese investment in the United States still was less than that of Britain.

During the summer of 1990, a joke made the rounds of corporate offices in Los Angeles that seemed to sum up the prevailing mood. President Bush, it began, falls into a coma from which he only awakes a year later. The first thing he sees is Vice President Quayle sitting by his bedside. Understandably panicked, the President tries to find out what has happened in the interim. "Things are just fine, sir, don't worry," says Quayle. Disbelieving, Bush reels off the ills that afflict the United States —inflation, the deficit, the recession. "Oh, they've all been solved," says Quayle airily. Eager for details, the President asks, "Well, how much is a quart of milk?" "I don't know," Quayle replies, "I think about a hundred yen."

But leaving aside such disturbances in the zeitgeist, stories like that of the real estate executive were commonplace. Software designers on the Westside, independent movie producers whose projects were deemed too offbeat by the major studios, painters of even the most middling reputation all seemed to be almost as familiar with the afternoon Pacific Northwest flight to Tokyo's Narita Airport as they were with the freeways of Los Angeles. Among the new generation of talented Southern California fashion designers as well, it was an article of faith that practically the only place a younger talent could find financial backing nowadays was in Japan; that is, it was often whispered, if you were a woman or at least not too obviously gay, since, in this age of AIDS, Japanese moneymen were rumored to balk at risking any cash on people who very well might die before they had reaped a suitable return on their investment.

Reliably, at least two or three times a week during the entire period I spent in L.A., I could depend on hearing someone say that the future "belonged" to the Pacific Rim. The American Century was giving way to the Asian Era, that was all there was to it. After all, the Japanese, the Koreans, and the others had so convincingly demonstrated their superiority in industry after industry that had once been American domains that it was hard not to believe that the Pacific Rim was as much an improvement on the idea of America as America had been on the idea of Europe. Indeed, however overemphatic this view sometimes appeared in Los Angeles, the simple experience of counting cars on the freeway, and noticing the increasing predominance of Japanese makes, seemed to confirm its basic outlines.

Of course, it was typical of Angelenos that they could think of localities more as ideas than as places. Nevertheless, a region which had, as the critic Bill Bradley put it, been "based on the prospect of things going one's way" was also a place whose relationship to change, however discomfiting, was likely to be far more elastic and optimistic. People in the Northeast, Angelenos seemed to be saying, might be willing to fall into the trap of outmoded states of mind and unproductive allegiances, but Californians were not, nor were they obliged to be. If the future would mostly be played out on the far side of the Pacific, then the task at hand was not to resist this event, but to try to figure out a way of playing an important role in its unfolding. This was the boosters' strength.

In any case, from Otis and Huntington to the Hollywood magnates, L.A. had rarely had any patience for failure. And given the fact that every calculation of demography and economics came out so lopsidedly in East Asia's favor, was there really any reason to pay attention to either exhausted Europe or the worn-out Northeast, that region Angelenos had long regarded as a European subsidiary? Even in the best of circumstances, Southern California's boosters foresaw only genteel decline for

the "Old World"—that startlingly old-fashioned, almost Jeffersonian way
of referring to the continent that I heard spoken, for the one and only
time in my life, by an Orange County developer not otherwise given to
verbal archaisms. Its future, he had declared confidently, was simply
Britain's writ large.

"Don't get me wrong," he had insisted—it was the denial that affirmed
—as we drove out to his favorite sushi bar in Studio City, a place where
the chef was famous for infusing his preparations with the spices he had
encountered during his two years as a young Japanese hippie in the
Peruvian altiplano, "London's a great town. I was over there last Christmas, and the theater there is as wonderful as ever. And don't they just
intimidate you the minute they open up their mouths? I could just listen
to them talk all day."

But the Parthian shot was not long in coming. "London's not where
the action is today, that's the problem," he had said, before politely
steering the conversation back to the relative merits of chiso leaf and
cilantro as garnishes in the eclectic Peruvian-Japanese cuisine that we
were about to sample. "It's a nice little town, though."

How the tables had turned over the course of the past thirty years.
For not only had Los Angeles shrugged off, once and for all, its collective
sense of inferiority vis-à-vis the Northeast, but it had gone on to carry
that process to its logical conclusion. In the past, visitors from New
York or Washington could expect to be hectored with slightly defensive
questions about just why any Angeleno should still want to visit the East
Coast when he could as easily head straight on to Europe. The implication was that while New York was merely an unsatisfactory reproduc-
tion of a European capital, L.A. was a one-of-a-kind, unforgettably
American place. Now, however, people were beginning to offer their
condolences to deprived eastern visitors condemned to live at such a
great remove, both psychologically and in air miles, from Asia and the
future's action. "I don't just miss L.A. when I have to spend any time
back east," the developer had told me. "I miss the whole Pacific Rim."

I doubted that this man would have felt anything of the sort fifteen
years before. Then, his tone would have been rawer and less self-as-
sured, and his claims for Los Angeles more modest. Now, a catchphrase
like "L.A. is it" referred to the city's place in a world in which the
Northeast and Europe were paltry suburbs, not simply to the region's
long-standing ambition to be America's premier city. Such a message
even seemed to contain a fallback position. If the future did not belong
to Los Angeles, the boosters were suggesting, then at least Los Angeles
could belong to the future. And that result could scarcely be accomplished by paying too much attention to Europe. It was fine to like going

there, of course, but as the developer had implied, such a taste was more on a par with stamp collecting or white-water canoeing—perfectly defensible, particularly in L.A. where few pleasures are frowned upon, but fundamentally extracurricular. To hear Angelenos talk, Europe was rather what Ireland was to many Europeans, a charming place with great culture and fine antique shops to which one day one might conceivably even retire.

"I like Holland fine," the developer had said, and it was safe to assume that the example had been chosen more or less at random, "but you have to remember that it reached its peak in the seventeenth century." Spearing the last piece of crabmeat and avocado sushi, a dish the Japanese called a California Roll since it was invented in L.A., not Tokyo, he continued. "Now you take Thailand. It has nearly three times the Netherlands' population—and unlike the Dutch, the Thais are still adding people—and its greatest moments haven't even happened to it yet."

In the context of Los Angeles, there was nothing particularly strange about this fretful reliance on rankings, pecking orders, and destinies. Such habits of mind had long been as inextricably a part of the city's cast of mind as its more celebrated weakness for futurology. It went with the boosterism, which derived its force from a rhetoric of invidious comparisons. General Otis and his friends would hardly have gotten very far had they tried to sell L.A. to the rest of the country with only a few reasonable assertions about its likely future importance. No, L.A. had to be Oz or it was nothing, and, by the same token, the boosters knew they had to be truculent or they were through.

If the latest boosterist line—"Los Angeles: Gateway to the Pacific Rim"—had not been heard before, the sense that L.A.'s success would only be assured if the rest of the world accepted whatever view of itself it was putting forward at the moment was entirely familiar. An Angeleno who told you he hated New York was not so much imparting information as trying to recruit you to his way of thinking, into an admission that living in L.A. was better, just as an Angeleno going on about the Asian future was inviting you to agree that his future was better. But in fact, long before New York had declined or Japan had become the economic standard against which America unhappily judged itself, L.A.'s boosters had busily preened and flexed in front of any audience they could attract, while periodically peering surreptitiously over at the competition, like naked men in a health club locker room eyeing each other's endowments. What made things different, though, this time around, was that the rest of the country had started to cover itself up modestly, while more and more Angelenos, for all their anxieties, had become convinced that, in American terms at least, almost any comparison was bound to come out to their advantage.

What had been set in motion by Otis had been institutionalized by Hollywood. Of course, it had never been true that the Southland's prosperity owed all that much to the contributions of the motion picture business. That said, it was undeniable that Hollywood's mannerisms, its fondness for self-promoting talk, and its monocular attention to the criterion of the bottom line—to who and what was bankable and who and what was not—had increasingly become the norm even in circles in which the Westside was unloved terra incognita. That the entire country was going that way was obvious, but nowhere were there fewer firebreaks between the values of the entertainment world and what had existed of a more independent-minded America than in Los Angeles, where the whole thing had originated. Pick up a business magazine and you discovered that it was almost as personality-ridden as the lowliest movie fanzine. Flee to the real estate pages of the *Los Angeles Times,* and what did not concern the latest property acquisition of some minor star seemed to concentrate on the personality of some successful realtor. It was a world aspiring to the condition of *People* magazine.

There were moments when it appeared that fame, rather than money, had become the dominant ambition of a plurality of middle-class Angelenos. Life might be a beach, as the most famous of all L.A. T-shirts declared, but the more exclusive a beach, it seemed, the better. How could it have been otherwise? Fame winked at you from the magazine rack at the supermarket checkout line. It stared down at you from the billboards along Sunset Boulevard in West Hollywood that shilled the latest movie or album releases. It beckoned on interview shows with celebrities you'd never heard of, and from AM talk radio that you listened to in traffic jams on the way to and from work. It teased you in the persons of the local TV reporters—acting more like soap-opera stars than journalists—you watched on the evening news when you got home. Fame was what you had grown up with, what surrounded you. Your own "real" life paled by comparison to your existence in the viewing-area version of Los Angeles. To compete, it would have needed a sound track, popcorn, an ad budget, velocity.

Small wonder, then, that even level-headed Angelenos saw nothing strange about the idea that it made just as much sense to rank cities, and countries, and futures, as it did to compare the batting averages of baseball players or the bankability of movie directors. In the end, what was the difference between having it in your head that Robert Redford was no longer a surefire box-office draw but that Sylvester Stallone, for the moment, still was, and of conceiving of Holland and Thailand as existing on a similarly sliding scale? That was the lesson of Hollywood, this state of mind that had always been as obsessed with hierarchies as people are in an army, or in the Catholic church, or, of course, in Japan.

There was another lesson as well. These were entities which, almost above all else, were practiced in ensuring their own survival. That was also the objective of L.A.'s boosters, who, beneath all their blustery talk, had never lost sight of the fact that survival was the whole object of the exercise.

But they were a good fit, Japan and Los Angeles, and the taste for ranking was not the least point of affinity. As Angelenos had learned, quite a bit before the word had spread to the rest of the United States, these Japanese were world-champion classifiers. Let an Angeleno spend an evening at a sushi bar, whether it was located in downtown Osaka or down the freeway in Studio City, with any average group of Japanese businessmen, and the odds were against his making it to the third round of sakes before finding himself bombarded by impassioned questions about what was best. Who now made the best sports car under $30,000? What was the best area in Orange County in which to buy a house? Where was the best golf course in the Valley? And these were less conversations about money (a subject which the Japanese, unlike Angelenos, tend to refer to rather prudishly) than status—in which both groups shared such an exuberant interest.

It could be a giddy experience, in its implacable way. Along with the creamy belly tuna, the gooey sea urchin with its topping of quail egg yolk, and the bilgelike raw shrimp would come this second binge in which the diners set about organizing the world into those things that were *ichiban,* or "number one" in Japanese, and those that most decidedly were not. This was followed by sighs of appreciation, giggly toasts. But beneath it all, these reactions were no more expressions of merriment on the part of these new Japanese lords of the earth than those wide, toothy grins and fresh-faced courtesies of the Angelenos (which had, for generations, punctuated even the most trivial of their interactions) were signs of a frivolous approach to the world. Both were forms of concealment. It does not take long, after all, whether in Tokyo or in Los Angeles, to discover that the salaryman's after-hours silliness and the Angeleno's naive smile are inane masks behind which hard heads and harder ambitions go about their business.

Actually, these questions of precedence and standing have always been a prime concern of the newly rich. Only old money is socially secure enough to prize the shabby over the gleaming or, with full confidence, assert that it is capital, not income or ornament, that gives a person substance. And for all their arrogance and success, both Japan and Los Angeles remained parvenus, both possessed of a provincial past —Japan with regard to China, and Los Angeles with regard to both San Francisco and New York—and a chip on their collective shoulder. Even the games that Japanese businessmen liked to play were not so very different, in the end, than that question, as old as the L.A. freeways and upon which so many kinds of success—sexual, professional, social—in the city partly derived: "What do you drive?"

On the deeper question, "Where are we going?," however, Los Angeles and Japan could not have diverged more radically. What Japan desired was a borderless world for its product and absolute ethnic homogeneity at home, and for the twenty-first century to resemble the last decade of the twentieth as closely as possible. In contrast, Los Angeles—having shed such impulses toward racial purity and in any case having no such options (the immigrants were coming anyway)—was looking for a new paradigm. That was where the boosters came in, with their great vision of an entrepôt joined to the nonwhite world.

For all their audacity, they really had very little choice. Throughout most of the United States, both the man and woman in the street and the professors and pundits who wrote books with titles like *The Rise and Fall of the Great Powers, The Closing of the American Mind, Selling America,* or *Japan as Number One* seemed to believe in the country's inexorable decline. Each new story of some Japanese corporate acquisition was being greeted as further proof, as if any were needed, of the inability of American capitalism to hold its own. And the boosters of Los Angeles agreed to some extent. It was just that they had come up with an idea of how the region could avoid sharing the same fate as the rest of the country, how it could remain Carey McWilliams's "Great Exception."

Their idea, brilliant in its simplicity, was to psychologically secede from most of the country. That was why the books the boosters wrote had titles like *The Borderless World, Material Dreams,* and *The United States of California.* They proposed pluralism with a vengeance, as only a city that had never believed in history could have conceived of it. Of course, such a notion depended on the idea that this great mixture of races and peoples would forever be bound together by the desire to make money and the opportunity, whether it devolved on oneself or on one's children, to live an ever more comfortable life. The doomsayers kept insisting that there were limits to growth, and pointed to California's deepening water crisis as a sign of things to come. But the boosters' optimism reigned unchecked. They were sure that things would be all right, assuming, that is, that they could get a fix on where the future lay, and, of course, on just who held the deed to it.

If that involved joining the Japanese in a Pacific Rim condominium, an enterprise that often seemed to resemble nothing so much as the updated, renamed version of Japan's World War II–era "Greater East

Asia Co-Prosperity Sphere," then so be it. Any other version of the future was simply too bleak and demanding to be imagined. Perhaps that, as much as long-established habits of feeling, was why so many Angelenos had taken to the boosters' vision, so godlike, so Californian. The alternative, after all, was that long-delayed moment of reckoning, not with Los Angeles's triumphant future, but rather with the complicated present that, so unexpectedly, it found itself having to confront.

12. The Way They Live Now

· ·

At least superficially, the boosters' fervent obeisances to the idea that L.A.'s future would be assured only when the importance of the new, nonwhite city was accepted, and its corollary, that native Angelenos could either throw in their lot with this multiracial metropolis or else find themselves relegated to the world-historical sidelines, did seem to echo what a narrow band of radical activists in the region had been predicting since at least Carey McWilliams's time. But then, Los Angeles had always been a city awash in hopes for the future, and so it was hardly surprising that what remained of the local Left, knowing to its cost how resistant the white Protestant city of yore had been to both the labor movement and the Left, chose to discern in a Third World L.A. a more promising future of political mobilization. Like practically everyone else in the city, be they boosters, leftists, or, for that matter, survivalists and apocalyptists, the radicals believed firmly that whatever happened to be going on in Los Angeles at a given moment would set the pace for the rest of the country before too long. If the example of Los Angeles meant anything, they said, it was as a harbinger of a time when not only Southern California but the country and indeed the entire world would be overwhelmingly nonwhite.

It was true already. By the year 2000, most demographers agreed, whites would represent no more than 11 percent of the total population of the earth. And if Los Angeles and New York would still be among the ten largest cities in the world, this at a time when the European capitals had dropped off the list, it would only be because of the huge influx of nonwhite peoples. With these brute facts of demographic change, however, most similarities ended. It was true that the new partisans of the L.A. that was to be a multiracial, global business center, and the radicals with their evocations of the city as a thuggish, racist dystopia, often used the same sheafs of economic statistics and cited the same population projections to buttress their arguments. And both shared, albeit for their very different reasons, a conviction that the old slogan of the *Los Angeles Times,* "It all comes together in the *Times,*" was, indeed, finally coming true in the city as a whole, though not, of course, in the way Harry Chandler might have anticipated. But this was by no means the whole story, and, if anything, the initial surprise one felt at routinely hearing businessmen and militant trade-union organizers speak in almost identical tones of pained condescension about the mixture of fear and amnesia with which the Westside and the Valley were responding to the new immigration, proved, on closer examination, to be a red herring.

After pausing to contemplate the wonder of the changes that immigration was wreaking on the established order in Los Angeles, the boosters would quickly go on to add that Anglos should thank their lucky stars for the Asians' arrival. "These immigrants hold the key to the Pacific Rim," one businessman told me. "Their own success is phenomenal enough, but the next generation just makes you salivate. Think of it: L.A. will have tens of thousands of highly educated people, completely comfortable in both the U.S. and on the other side of the Pacific. Without them—their language skills, knowledge of both cultures, family contacts—we'd be sure to lose out to the Japanese. But this way we've got a shot."

After pausing to contemplate the wonder of the changes that immigration was wreaking on the established order in Los Angeles, the radicals were quick to heap scorn on the boosters' claims. "Don't even talk to me about Asian entrepreneurs," a left-wing labor organizer in Orange County exclaimed bitterly, after I had suggested that things in L.A. might not turn out so badly if the Asian success was even a quarter of what the boosters claimed. "I know all those downtown types love to take you on the guided tour of some software company that was started by a boat person, or down to Chinatown to meet a guy who arrived ten years ago from Hong Kong without a penny to his name but has done so well that he now has a beach house in Trancas and two kids at Cal Tech."

"Such people exist," I said.

"Sure," he replied. "I've met them. But what all these consultants never tell you is that they're exceptions."

For this man, who had spent half a lifetime in the sweatshops and light industrial plants of the Los Angeles basin, the boosters' hopes were mere rationalizations, designed to make white Angelenos feel that the city didn't have to turn into *Blade Runner* after all. In the larger scheme of things, even the most florid immigrant success stories were petty events. "Most immigrants," he insisted, particularly the Latinos, but more of the Asians than some people in L.A. like to admit, "are in survival mode at the very most."

What was peculiar about these clashing views was how little their opposition was based on facts and how much on interpretation. Context was all in the politicized corners of Los Angeles. A phrase like "the globalization of capital and labor" or a notion like the "Californiazation" of American corporate life had a critical, bitterly indignant connotation when it was expressed by the UCLA economic geographer Edward Soja. But when advanced by a banker at Wells Fargo, or a trader on the Pacific Stock Exchange, such catchphrases had all the exultant implication of a soon-to-be-realized best of all possible worlds. Still, though boosters and radicals might agree on the substance of the evidence, it was pretty much impossible to find evidence of any common ground.

For me, one of the more immediate results of hearing so much of the same basic material put to these diametrically opposing uses was to heighten my impression of cognitive dissonance that, in any case, seemed to punctuate so much of daily experience in Los Angeles. One man's oppressed immigrant was another woman's enterprising guarantor of the region's future. Far from moving along a more or less legible continuum, whether of space or of ideas, the discontinuities that kept cropping up in L.A. between information and meaning could seem so great that, just as looking at the city from the freeway did not, even though it was the vantage point from which more was visible, show you anything very revealing, listening to the information that should have led to a conclusion about L.A.'s future in fact required a context to make any sort of sense. Often, after spending a day shuttling between radicals and boosters, I thought of McWilliams's description of Southern California as an archipelago, since to move between their offices and their arguments had something of the feeling of paddling despondently between widely separated islands, recording the songs and beliefs of the autarchic tribes that dwelt upon them.

I could spend the morning at UCLA, or else drive down to USC and hear in detail just how cruel and exploitative a "world city" Los Angeles had become, only to then drive downtown to some resplendent corporate suite, or out to one of the gaggle of international art galleries that had lately proliferated in Santa Monica, and listen to the same familiar figures on cross-border displacement or worldwide capital flows adduced as definitive proof that the region's greatest boom years lay well in its future. And my discomfiture would only be heightened by my sense of there having been little if any continuity between the contradictory accounts that I had heard. During the long car trips that were required in order to get from radical point A to capitalist point B, the point of whatever I had just been told with such authority would grow steadily harder to hold on to. And there was the old L.A. story: to drive was immediately to free yourself from the press of responsibility, including, it often seemed, the responsibility to think critically. Before too long, the celebrated narcosis of the road had set in.

Theory and the freeway—now there was an odd couple. No wonder the radicals so often seemed most noteworthy for their embittered tone and apocalyptic rhetoric, when they had spent their lives trying to transform their analysis, much of it doubtless right, into action in a setting where the notion of the collective seems like the greatest abstraction of all. In a traffic jam, it was possible to think in terms of social groups and grim futures, but when the traffic was moving? Fat chance. Anyway, who even cared about the future when you could move along at seventy or seventy-five under a bright L.A. sun, with the radio on and the whole city laid out in front of your windshield? Life, then, did not seem like the result of forces over which you had no control. One was alone, and free; at least that was the way it felt.

And if the conditions of life as it was lived in contemporary Los Angeles militated against political activism, the events of the preceding twenty years had only made the radicals' job that much more daunting. They knew it, too. For all their brave talk about grass-roots organizing and insurgent coalitions of intellectuals and the disenfranchised, the leftists were anything but confident about how much they could really hope to accomplish, at least in the short term. The labor organizer Mike Davis, whose glum book on Los Angeles, *City of Quartz,* is far and away the best writing on the city from the Left, was reported as having remarked sadly that the full extent of achievable change in L.A. for the foreseeable future would probably entail no more than the restoration of the same social guarantees Franklin D. Roosevelt had promised the poor of America during his 1932 presidential campaign. And while it was doubtless more than a bit hyperbolic to compare contemporary L.A. to the United States at the height of the Depression, such a concession testified to the real political relations of force in Southern California. As the radicals understood perfectly well, the outcomes that the business establishment desired were the outcomes Angelenos would get.

To which any remotely sardonic observer of the L.A. scene would surely have inquired, "What else is new?" However much the Marxists might identify with the oppressed, the oppressed themselves tended to identify with the business establishment. That had been true in the United States since the nineteenth century. The German sociologist Werner Sombart had even written a book on the subject, as far back as 1906, with the title *Why Is There No Socialism in the United States?* "When the matter is considered objectively," Sombart wrote, "the worker in the United States is more exploited by capitalism than in any other country in the world ... [but] it is one of the most brilliant feats of diplomatic artifice that the American employer has realized how to keep the worker in a good mood despite all the actual exploitation."

Among American-born workers, such a good mood was wearing thin. The son of an L.A. steelworker, if he had not moved on to white-collar employment, was likely to live less well than his father had. And sky-rocketing housing prices meant that the possibility of owning a home, a common expectation in the great days of the Bank of America in the forties and fifties, was more and more remote in 1990. If you drove to old industrial towns like Fontana or Vernon, the mood was grim. That was where the immigrants came in to rescue the classless dream of America. The immigrants, said the boosters, proved once more that L.A. was a city where anyone could rise as high as their dreams propelled them. The fact that it was unquestionably also a place where you could fall without the slightest hope of society doing anything for you was not so much left unsaid as understood. That was the point of America; for better and worse, you were free.

The radicals might insist that the immigrant belief in Los Angeles and L.A.'s belief in the immigrants were prime examples of the Marxist category of "false consciousness." In fact, Sombart had pointed out the same thing almost ninety years before. It hadn't made much difference; the immigrants had kept on coming. And if, in the early years of the twentieth century, plutocrats like the Carnegies and the Mellons had enticed the poor with what Sombart called "miraculous stories about people like themselves who began as newsboys and finished as multi-millionaires," Los Angeles was telling the same stories to the immigrants today and holding up those who had indeed succeeded as examples of what was still possible in the Southland. It was powerful myth. Where once it had inflamed the poor of Europe, it now inflamed the poor of the entire world. El Salvador today was just as closed and hopeless a society as Austrian Galicia or the West of Ireland had been a century before, and Sombart could have been speaking of the new immigrant when he said that "the mere knowledge that he *could* become a free farmer" (today we would say shopkeeper, or, on a grander level, entrepreneur) "could not but make the American worker feel secure and content, a condition that is unknown to his European counterpart. One tolerates any oppressive situation more easily if one lives under the illusion of being able to withdraw from it if really forced to."

That the immigrants chose to come served one purpose. Why the illegals were allowed to stay was more complicated. Even the activists who were dedicated to securing the rights of foreigners to cross the border into the United States, regardless of their legal status, were quick to acknowledge that the deep reason these workers were being permitted to remain in the region was that few local employers wanted to see them go. After all, the U.S.–Mexican border, however long and porous, *could* have been made more secure, and even if East L.A. had grown so enormously in recent years, a great deal more effort could have been expended on tracking down the illegals and expelling them. That was what had happened in the 1940s, during Operation Wetback, and the resources the authorities could command had scarcely diminished since then.

Instead, little was being done. As any Border Patrol officer would tell you, the resources of that department had not only not been expanded to cope with rising levels of immigration, but had if anything diminished over the past decade. Appropriations had been cut, and those officers that remained, no matter how cleverly they deployed themselves, were in no position to deflect more than a fraction of the traffic across the border. In Los Angeles itself, the efforts of immigration rights activists, Mexican-American political groups, and certain judges had played a role in the immigrants' having been able to remain, but the real forces at play were the inertia of so many Californians, who, when they did not actually encounter an immigrant, rarely gave the matter a second thought, the belief that the immigrants testified to the region's strength, and, most importantly, the desires, both practical and ideological, of the business community.

That those wishes were intimately bound up in the new business paradigm for the Southland was part of the story—the radicals were themselves indulging in a good bit of wishful thinking when they claimed that it was a smokescreen—but not all of it. For where the radicals were right was in their assumption that businessmen think not only in terms of the future but in terms of the present. And it was the precise conditions under which the immigrants lived, and, more significantly, worked, that were viewed with such unabashed favor by the employers in the Los Angeles basin.

Had the truth been elsewhere, it would have been possible to imagine a moment in L.A. when the situation of the illegal aliens would have started to be regularized, when they could stop living like criminals on the run, cheated by everyone they encountered, from used-car salesmen and landlords to their employers and the neighborhood toughs. Instead, most Americans whose voices mattered seemed quite content to allow them to subsist in their juridical limbo, collectively cowed by the pervasive threat of deportation, but, in the case of any individual immigrant, unlikely actually to be subjected to it. This was a situation that, though they had not instigated it—L.A. employers did not foment immigration so much as benefit from it—businessmen now found suited them perfectly. After all, who else but an illegal alien would be willing to work for a pittance in a plastics factory, or hunker down on shop floors where the decibel level was so high that an eight-hour shift resembled nothing so much as sitting right up against the speaker bank at a rap music concert? And, for all that, who else but an illegal immigrant would think such conditions not only an improvement on life back home, but a stepping stone to a better life in the future?

The boosters might couch the new immigration in metaphoric terms, and invoke Whitman and "Ameripan," but it was clear that there were more down-to-earth considerations at play as well. Predictably, the Left discerned what, in those halcyon days before such images were judged "politically incorrect," used to be called a darker purpose. Speaking at a conference on L.A. sponsored by the radical magazine *L.A. Weekly* in the spring of 1990, Edward Soja described a twenty-year-long economic cycle in the region that had resulted in the destruction of organized labor and a new reliance on immigrant workers. Where the boosters preferred to describe the L.A. economy in terms of emblematic immigrant success stories—Hong Kong meets Horatio Alger—and described the fundamental shift as being toward an entrepreneurial, free-market system, Soja stressed the breaking of the unions and the closing of heavy industry after heavy industry. Once this had been accomplished, he argued, there had followed a "reindustrialization" of Los Angeles based on a bifurcated economy of high-tech, high-skilled industries on one end and low-tech businesses on the other that required little more from their poorly paid workers than strong backs and stamina.

Even the boosters were hard-pressed to deny that, for the moment, anyway, Los Angeles had become a city in which most people were either well off or poor, and that the vaunted American middle class, like the vaunted American nuclear family, was increasingly more the stuff of advertisements than of reality. Of course, they were quick to insist that things would soon improve, that out of these sweatshops and light industrial plants would develop a new, immigrant middle class. The steel

mills, auto factories, and refineries that the leftists mourned were economic anachronisms anyway, they said, doomed to fail whatever steps
the employers might have taken to preserve them. What Los Angeles
needed was managers, not a proletariat, and it was in their self-interest
to see that the immigrants succeeded. After all, white males would
account for only 20 percent of the new workers in Southern California
by the second decade of the twenty-first century: there would simply
not be enough of them, whatever the businessmen might have preferred, to go around, and so the upward mobility of the immigrants was
not only desirable but an economic necessity.

But what the boosters were less comfortable discussing, as they
sketched their vision of a Los Angeles in which the manufacturing base
had remained strong, high-tech industries had proliferated, and the
American entrepreneurial ethic had been reinforced by fertile Hispanics
and both Asian capital and Asian capitalists, was just how well the current situation suited a large number of local employers. You did not
have to believe everything the leftists said to see that the illegal status
of so many of the new immigrant workers had effectively "privatized"
relations between workers and managers. For all L.A.'s tradition as an
anti-union town, nothing quite like it had been seen in the city, or
anywhere else in the United States, since the rise of the trade union
movement more than a century earlier. This was the employer-
employee relationship as the late nineteenth-century plutocrats had envisaged it in their most extravagant moments, a throwback to the last
American gilded age—the one that Ronald Reagan's two terms in office
seemed to so many to have recapitulated—when Jay Gould boasted that
he could buy one half of the American working class to kill the other
half.

There was nothing fanciful about the comparison. Like nonunionized
workers of a century earlier, the illegal immigrants had few rights, if any.
They could neither complain to a government agency about working
conditions nor go on strike, since their employers could put a stop to
almost any dispute with a twenty-five-cent phone call to the Immigration and Naturalization Service. But then, General Otis had warned prospective arrivals that L.A. wanted "no loafers," and the new boosters, for
all their insistence that the city's young, nonwhite work force of the
future was, along with location, its greatest asset, seemed to share the
magnates' fierce disdain for anything so patently unproductive as a work
stoppage. There was, it appeared, to be nothing so mundane as conflicts
between labor and management in the brave new entrepreneurial world
that the boosters were forecasting, just industrious workers, managers
with fertile brains, and venture capitalists with deep pockets and a taste
for risk.

This question of what working conditions were to be like was what was most obviously missing in all the glowing predictions about L.A.'s future. Like most utopians, the boosters had little interest in seeing that contradictions between people are often inherent in a situation rather than the product of poor management, and that, say, an employer's desire to maximize profits and an employee's desire to make as high a salary as possible might simply be irreducibly at odds. The "L.A. 2000" report was a perfect example of this kind of myopia. It bent over backwards to be multicultural in the sense of trying to solicit the opinions— "input" in the computer-besotted lingo of late twentieth-century America—of Hispanic and Asian community groups. Again and again, the report insisted on the need for Angelenos to embrace their city's growing diversity, even suggesting that not only would the immigrants have to adapt to America but America would have to adapt to the immigrants. But though it warned of the dangers of a "bi-modal city," that is, of a place divided between rich and poor, and emphasized the need for better education, improved family services, and increased job creation, no link at all was admitted between the prosperity of so many white-collar Angelenos and the almost diametrically opposing circumstances in which so many of L.A.'s poor now lived.

It appeared that the boosters had convinced themselves that prosperity and poverty simply coexisted on parallel tracks, and that there was no connection to be drawn between the multimillion-dollar houses on the Westside and the slums of South Central or East L.A. The notion that the successful "pursuit of happiness" by some—and reading documents like the "L.A. 2000" report again made one wish that Jefferson had not substituted that beautiful phrase for the original, "the pursuit of property"—resulted, whatever the intention might be, in misery for others simply had no place in a city that prided itself on being a dream made palpable. Small wonder, then, that businessmen were represented on the "L.A. 2000" board, as were politicians, academics, community organizers, lawyers, civil servants, ministers, journalists, police officials, teachers, overseas investors, and psychiatrists: everyone, in short, except anyone who might fairly be thought to speak for organized labor. And yet it was surely not unreasonable to suppose that someone from, say, the Amalgamated Clothing and Textile Workers' Union might have had at least as much to contribute to the report's "Crossroads City" section as did such sitting committee members as Takashi Maruyama of the Industrial Bank of Japan, or Joel Fishman, a partner in the law firm of Weissmann, Wolff, Bergman, Coleman & Silverman.

For worthy though these gentlemen undoubtedly were, they could hardly have been in much of a position to talk about the effects the "crossroads city" was having on people whose standard of living had declined, rather than improved, since it had come into being. What the absence of even a passing acknowledgment of these concerns suggested was that the organizers of the L.A. 2000 Goals Subcommittee had grown so accustomed to living in a world where everyone they knew was doing well, and anyone who didn't was either a failure or resided in Los Angeles illegally. Moreover, the notion that the L.A. they were trying to bring into existence would make of this oversimplification a reality, and that such an outcome might not be to the advantage of the majority of Angelenos, never even seemed to occur to them.

This was not to say that the radicals did not have their own blind spots. In their accounts of the new immigration, for example, they oscillated between an emphasis on what, in the current term of art, they called the "push" factors—that is, deepening immiseration and political stalemate or war in the countries from which most of the immigrants had come—and on a series of "pull" factors—that is, on the abundance of jobs that were known to exist in L.A., and, for Hispanic immigrants, the added advantage of being able to disappear into the enormous Spanish-speaking parallel world of the barrio. Predictably, the push factors were the sentimental favorites. It was, after all, far easier to elicit sympathy for Salvadoran refugees on the grounds that they had been forced to come north to escape a civil war that had, in any case, been partly "Made in U.S.A." than it was to suggest the colder, less guilt-inducing explanation of an L.A. that was simply too great an economic magnet for the poor of the continent to resist.

Blaming the business establishment of the Southland for their hardheartedness toward the immigrants, once they had arrived, went some way toward restoring to the newcomers the exclusive role of victims. But even that approach had its difficulties. Not only did the Los Angeles Area Chamber of Commerce make a rather less satisfying villain than, for example, the U.S. Military Advisory Group in El Salvador, or a favorite regional bogeyman—the Nicaraguan Contras, say, or Guatemala's Pentecostal strongman, General José Efraín Ríos Montt—but there was something inconsistent about insisting that people who have chosen to make a journey should, simultaneously, be regarded as having been compelled to undertake it.

The more thoughtful defenders of immigrants' rights did not, after a bit of preliminary throat-clearing, try very hard to press the point. They conceded frankly that it had indeed been the pull factors that had strongly influenced most individual decisions to come north to L.A. "You can see Mecca right across the fence from the Tijuana side," a brilliant immigration lawyer named Peter Schey told me one afternoon, as we sat in his office in a modest frame house in a Salvadoran neighborhood on the western edge of downtown. Surrounded by overstuffed files, law books, and the stack of phone messages that so often provide the backdrop to the work of the best pro bono advocates, Schey had outlined with steely passion what his clients went through both as they crossed the border and as they tried to make a start in L.A. Nonetheless, he was adamant that they would continue to come, whatever the cost. "You wouldn't have this problem," he added, making the point one last time as he ushered me to the door, "if Los Angeles were at the North Pole."

But then again, wouldn't you? The way the world of work was changing in cities like Los Angeles, and the way the population was growing in most parts of the developing world, it was by no means clear that even an L.A. that had miraculously been transported thousands of miles further north would have escaped the attention of the jobless poor of the planet for very long. Perhaps, instead of a preponderance of the immigrants coming from Mexico and Central America, more would have come from China or the Muslim republics of the Soviet Union, but the pattern would have remained the same. The world had simply grown too crowded, and its prosperous areas had become too accessible from its slums. And when you added the fact that these slum-dwellers were still willing to do jobs that most people in Japan, Europe, and North America would no longer even consider, and that their presence in the great northern metropolises was as welcome as it was fearsome, what other likely outcome could there be?

The boosters were right in a way. The world was changing. Again. If Talleyrand's great bow to the beginning of Europe's democratization, uttered two hundred years ago, had been the idea that one "has not lived who did not know the pleasures of the old regime," then Los Angeles, less epigrammatically to be sure, was making its own bow to a de-democratized future: "He has not lived who has not known the pleasures of illegal 'help.' "

And those pleasures were considerable. There were not only the private joys of having your baby minded, your car parked, and your house cleaned, but the corporate one of having a large pool of people who would work for next to nothing. The leftists even claimed that the illegal immigration was useful to employers because it helped them keep their native-born workers in line. Obviously, no member of the Chamber of Commerce was likely to confirm such a theory, but there was something unsettling, given the realities of the lives of the working poor of Los Angeles, about the way so many local businessmen praised the economic effects of the immigration. It had "loosened up" the local labor market, they said. It had made the region more "hospitable" than it might otherwise have been to corporate expansion. It had permitted failing or endangered businesses to "compete" on more equal terms with their overseas competitors. Could the radicals be right in saying that what all this really meant was that unionized workers, fearing the loss of their own jobs to the new arrivals, were much more likely to submit to the reduced wage and benefit packages employers were increasingly demanding?

The pull explanation not only made sense in terms of how the illegal immigrants were received, but also in terms of why they came in the first place. To use an obvious Los Angeles example, had those hundreds of thousands of Salvadorans only been trying to get out of the line of fire between their own government's soldiery and the equally trigger-happy guerrillas of the FMLN, they would have needed to proceed no further north than Mexico, where, as it happened, about fifty thousand of them remained. In all previous wars, people looking for safe haven alone have crossed a border, not half a continent. The Afghan refugees fleeing Soviet air strikes and armor during the 1980s went to Pakistan or Iran, not on to more prosperous Thailand or Italy. The truth was that though many of the Salvadoran immigrants were legitimate political refugees, just as their advocates so staunchly maintained and the INS just as fervently disputed, they were after more than refuge. That the Mexican government, impoverished though it was, had been honorably prepared to offer them.

But what it could not hope to provide them with was jobs. The Salvadorans were perfectly aware of this, and, faced with a Hobson's choice between the hopelessness of a refugee camp in southern Mexico and the prospect of returning to the bombs, conscription, and death squads waiting back home, they usually kept moving north. In the United States, they knew, there was not only safety but the possibility of work, another way of saying the possibility of a future. Over and over again in conversations with Salvadoran refugees, I heard talk of this future. The desire for change was so strong that many of them, like other recent arrivals from Mexico and Central America, were leaving a Catholic church that seemed to offer little more than resignation for an evangelical Protestantism that promised self-reliance and prosperity. "I have had enough of history," a waitress in a Salvadoran fish restaurant said to me, in reply to my question about where she came from. "In Los Angeles, I am only thinking of my future and of my children's future."

And there was plenty of work, of a sort, anyway. Surely it was preferable to be a live maid, earning a hundred dollars a week plus room and board in Palos Verdes or Brentwood, than a dead primary school teacher in San Salvador. It was certainly better to be one of the busboys at the

City restaurant on La Brea than a private in the elite Atlacatl regiment of the Salvadoran army. And the refugees I met were proud of the role that they played in L.A. "Americans do not want to do these jobs," a car parker at a fashionable French restaurant in Santa Monica told me one night, as we sat together on folding metal chairs, at eye level with the hood ornaments of the Mercedeses and Jaguars parked all around us.

He continued. "They think they are . . . ," then his voice trailed off for a moment as he groped for the right word, "taller than this work. But it is work we are happy to do, and, if you will give me pardon for saying this, I think we do this work much better. Look, we do not expect life to be so kind as the people do in Los Angeles."

The question of whether the refugees had arrived first and the jobs they now occupied were created in their wake, or the other way around, was one on which only the most reckless or ideological of observers dared to venture an opinion. Undeniable, however, was that every variety of L.A. employer, from the middle-class couple in need of a housekeeper to a manufacturer with a small factory to run, was at least as pleased by what had happened as the boy in the parking lot. It was a case not so much of pennies from heaven (although there were plenty of people on the Westside who were spending more on their psychiatrists than on their maids) as servants from heaven. Or Michoacán. And all this in a Los Angeles in which, well into the 1970s, few people had dreamed their own lives could be undergirded in this pleasing way and in which most industrial work was still being performed by people holding union cards, not to mention citizenship papers.

Now, even in the high-tech sector there was considerable demand for immigrant labor. If nothing else, someone had to clean up after all those aerospace engineers and computer software designers. There are few moments in the day in an L.A. office complex more arresting than the period between five and seven in the evening. At five, the white-collar workers pile out of the elevators and stride through air-conditioned lobbies, headed for parking lot, traffic jam, and home. For a time, there is silence, with only spasms of desultory banter from the security guards to punctuate the stillness. Then, with a clatter, there is the sound of Spanish and of pails of sloshing water. They call each other *mi amor* and *mi cielo,* "my love," "my sky," and talk about children who make them proud, husbands who've let them down, their aching feet, and their hopes for the future.

It is the cleaning staff arriving. Floor by floor, they make their way through the suites of offices, emptying wastebaskets full of crumpled faxes, Post-it notes, and computer printouts, sluicing down tiled bathroom floors, and vacuuming cushiony carpets, the imprint of their sensible shoes making their mark on surfaces where, during the course of the day, only Gucci loafers, Maud Frizon pumps, and the other fashionable footwear that can be had at Neiman-Marcus or the Beverly Center have gone before. The change the maids effect is more than sartorial. It is only during these hours that a cigarette is smoked in a Los Angeles office building: the practice is officially banned in L.A. County, but in the maids' L.A. County everyone smokes.

There is clarity to be found in this twilight, for it is only at such a moment that it is possible to take in just how intertwined the First and the Third Worlds, those utopian and dystopian versions of the future, have become in greater L.A. But if the attentive visitor could find this Third World even in the office towers and the high-tech industrial parks of the Westside and the suburbs, this did not mean that it was the principal place it was to be found. Whatever the boosters might claim, the Southland in 1990 was no more defined by its most forward-looking industries than it was by the entertainment industry—the importance of both looming far larger than it otherwise might have because of all the publicity that seemed to adhere to them, like algae to a pier.

For unlike northeastern cities such as New York, Boston, and Philadelphia, traditional manufacturing jobs still abounded in L.A. In 1988, for example, aerospace had accounted for only 7 percent of the jobs in Los Angeles County, while the figure for the manufacturing sector was 22 percent. And though a visitor to some state-of-the-art defense plant, with its robotics and its zeal, might be forgiven for imagining he had seen the industrial future of the United States, the country's industrial past was alive and flourishing in L.A. as well. Indeed, most of the region's factories were actually anything but modern. Some were good old-fashioned sweatshops, a vision of turn-of-the-century New York City or the nineteenth-century English Midlands, which, when you thought about it, were as long established in the Southland as the imperial palms and the eucalyptus.

Certainly, conditions varied. Some plants carefully met all the requirements that federal and state labor regulations demanded, but, particularly in the clothing and textile industries, a great number did not. Downtown on Los Angeles Street, the city's traditional garment center, and, increasingly, in Chinatown sweatshops and in Vietnamese sections of Orange County, where women and children assembled garments in private houses converted for the purpose, the work force was composed overwhelmingly either of recently arrived legal immigrants or of illegal aliens, few of whom spoke any English. If you saw a sign for *operadora,* "sewing machine operator" in Spanish, tacked on the wall of some gloomy, peeling entryway along one of the downtown Mexican immi-

grant shopping streets like Broadway or Hill, it was a safe bet that on
one of the floors above you there were people working in conditions
that would not have seemed out of place across the border in Tijuana
or across the ocean in the Philippines or Hong Kong.

Those who owned or managed such factories tended to boast that the
great thing about Southern California was that industries in the state
were still nowhere near as encumbered by what I almost invariably
heard referred to, as if if had been a single word, as "rules and regulations." This usually turned out to mean such things as fire rules and
health regulations, but such details were rarely volunteered. People
preferred to speak in reassuring generalities, and to assume a consensus
about what was good for California that did not necessarily exist. When,
for example, James Morgan, the head of a high-tech firm called Applied
Materials, warned in a 1990 *Forbes* magazine interview that the state
should think twice before imposing too many requirements on manufacturers, he was only expressing a view that had predominated in L.A. for
generations now. "If you look at New England or New York City," he
said, "you will see that if you abuse your manufacturing population and
it leaves, you will wreck your economy." Unsurprisingly, neither Morgan nor his interviewer seemed to have felt the need to specify exactly
which "population," the owners or their employees, stood in such stark
need of protection.

It was a selfishness that made sense, though, one that carried over
easily to what otherwise would have been the more vexing question of
the new immigration. Usually, one could tell where a businessman
would come down on the subject by figuring out whether he required
a literate, educated work force, or an undemanding, untrained one.
Those in need of the former tended to talk a lot about improving education and about L.A.'s diversity—a fair cross section of them had had a
hand in drafting the "L.A. 2000" report. Those whom the present situation suited to a T said little, but when they did speak out, it was usually
to assure people that things would work out, and that the laborers of
today would be the managers of tomorrow.

This last view was one that was sure to appeal to old-style California
optimism, with its emphasis on the ready accessibility of the impossible
and its assurance that the region's future was bound to be superior even
to its splendid present. Moreover, few employers spoke in terms of
large-scale trends but rather in the uplifting language of the anecdote. It
sometimes appeared that there wasn't a business in greater L.A. without
an employee who had started out in a leaky boat in the South China Sea
and was now in middle management. The problem was that, even if all
these stories were true, and the perseverance of the local work force

and the benignity of local management a bottomless well, these stories tended to mask rather than reveal what was going on—which was that the schools were unable to educate immigrant children, and that too many people in L.A. were making too much money from things the way they were now to want to do the real work required to change them.

A clever variation on this was the argument that only if Californians stopped meddling with the state's business environment would things turn out as well as hoped. In the same *Forbes* article in which James Morgan had spoken of the need not to burden California manufacturers with onerous demands, the new immigration was adduced as a further reason for civic restraint. "Anti-growth and extreme environmental measures," the authors of the piece wrote—and it was hard not to feel that their words accurately reflected the majority view in the Los Angeles Area Chamber of Commerce—"are the most regressive forms of all taxation. Three million immigrants, most of them poor Hispanics and Asians, are expected to pour into California in the next decade. They are not likely to find work selling annuities in Santa Monica, or real estate in Marin County. But none of this much bothers the state's small but vociferous legion of limousine liberals, Hollywood headline grabbers and tree huggers, people who have never seen the inside of a manufacturing plant and have very little sympathy for the blue-collar types who are hurt by their activities."

In Los Angeles, this attempt to oppose immigrant East L.A. to the liberal Westside proved a potent weapon. In the fall of 1988, the late Armand Hammer, friend of every Soviet leader from Lenin to Gorbachev, wanted to secure permission for his Occidental Petroleum Company to drill for oil along the east side of the Pacific Coast Highway near Santa Monica. Predictably, many local residents were outraged, and used their not inconsiderable influence to move, through the courts and the county authorities, to block the project. But the man who had talked the Bolshevik government into letting him buy the czar's treasures from them was not to be so easily bested. Rather than trying, as most businessmen would have done, to fulminate from the Right, Hammer tried to outflank the Westside from where it was most vulnerable—on the Left. By denying him permission to drill, he argued, the people of Santa Monica were really denying the black and Hispanic poor of L.A. the same chance for good jobs and economic mobility that Westsiders had enjoyed in the 1950s when no environmental scruples had prevented the despoliation—development was the way it was usually put—of so much of the region. Oil had fueled the first of L.A.'s booms, and who were these well-off people to stand in the way of another one?

The scheme almost worked. There were angry questions about Santa

Monica's stance in the L.A. City Council. Santa Monica was not, as a separate municipality, under its jurisdiction, and the implication that the town was a white enclave selfishly ignoring the needs of the non-white city only inflamed the debate further. What was the difference, Chicano supporters of the plan like Dan Garcia, the former head of the L.A. Planning Commission, demanded, between drilling off Santa Monica and making your money off developing parcels of land in Tarzana? And it made a persuasive argument, one to which the Westside found it difficult to reply since it cut to the heart of a liberalism that did not like to think very hard either about its own past or, for that matter, those darker corners of its own stock portfolios.

The Westside prevailed, of course, as it usually does in Los Angeles, and Occidental erected no oil derricks to befoul the beaches and sightlines of the denizens of "Croissant Canyon." Still, among Hispanics in East L.A., at least the majority whose politics consisted largely of wanting their share of the Southern California dream, a palpable bitterness persisted. "I thought the point of being a liberal was that you were more fair," the owner of a small restaurant in East L.A. complained one evening, as he and several other Chicano businessmen discoursed about what future they wanted to see in Los Angeles. "But what is fair about saying that you think more of preserving a beach than of giving work to honest people?"

I said, "So you don't think much of liberals?"

He smiled wryly. "I prefer people who are honest about who they like and who they don't like. You can deal with them. The liberals? They say a lot of fine things, but sometimes I think that even they do not know what they mean."

One of his friends cut in. "Yes, they say how sorry they feel for the poor immigrant, and then, when the poor immigrant has a chance not to be such a poor immigrant, like working on the oil, they cut off his balls."

The drilling controversy had not been the first occasion on which the Southern California business establishment had found itself in an otherwise unlikely alliance with Hispanic L.A. In 1985 and 1986, it had joined with immigration rights activists and Mexican-American political and civil rights organizations in an attempt to defeat those provisions of the impending Immigration Reform Act that mandated stiff financial sanctions against any employer found to have hired illegal aliens. Obviously, the employers were worried about curbs on their freedom of action, whereas the advocacy groups feared that any singling out of one group of Hispanics in the United States would lead to discrimination against all of them. But what at first appeared like a marriage of convenience proved, on closer examination, to be something deeper, as if the new world of investment and the new world of work were somehow twinned. "I think," Peter Schey had told me, "that if there is to be free movement of capital in the twenty-first century, then there should be the free movement of people as well."

Of course, the businessmen were rather more reluctant to accept such a corollary on the record. Many still harbored that menu of derogatory feelings and opinions about blacks and Hispanics that Anglos in Southern California had so often entertained, but, in practical terms at least, these sentiments were of secondary importance now. What really mattered was uninterrupted economic growth, and a great number of L.A. employers had once again concluded that cheap labor was the way to get it. It was almost like going back to square one in the Southland, and if there was a significant difference between Huntington's trains carrying Mexican workers north from El Paso in 1916 and the barrios of contemporary East L.A., it was that nowadays the immigrants had to make their own way across the border.

By 1990, immigration reform had come and gone, and it was clear to everybody that the much-touted, much-dreaded employer sanctions had had scant effect on the numbers of illegal aliens coming to Los Angeles. Paradoxically, the biggest change most observers could discern was that instead of the immigration being made up largely of young men looking to stay for a season's work, more and more entire families were coming up from Mexico. As one observer, Wayne Cornelius of the U.S.–Mexico Studies Center at UC–San Diego, put it sardonically, the trend seemed to be for L.A. now to be home base and for the migrants' home villages to serve as centers for "rest and recreation."

With the new law having proved largely ineffective, employers were free to concentrate on another bugbear, antipollution statutes. It was never clear how effective the most sweeping of these, a comprehensive ballot initiative nicknamed Big Green, would have been had the voters approved it in 1990. Some California initiatives (the process of determining policy at the ballot box was one of the many holdovers of that state's history of suspicion toward organized government), most famously Proposition 13 in the late seventies, which had barred the state from imposing new property taxes to boost revenue, had been immensely important. Others, like the rollback of auto insurance rates in 1988, had not. But until the business establishment organized against it, Big Green had been expected to win handily. Its defeat demonstrated, to those who had not yet gotten the news, that Californians might ooh and ah over the Hollywood stars like Jane Fonda who had campaigned so hard for the proposition, but they still tended to vote with the Chamber of Commerce.

The businessmen took their victory in stride. The most obvious effect of the initiative's failure on them was that it quieted some of the grousing about California's toughened building and health codes and the intrusive sweep of its air-quality legislation, particularly in the Southland. While there continued to be a certain seepage toward the even more employer-friendly reaches of greater Phoenix, Arizona, which, during the 1980s, had registered the highest growth rate anywhere in the United States, most L.A. manufacturers seemed likely to stay put. For the time being, there was no real reason for them to move any save the most intractably polluting of their plants out of the state, or, as it was discreetly put, "offshore." L.A. advantages were still too significant. Not only did remaining in the city cut transportation costs from factory to target market, but employers retained another, more significant edge over their Third World competitors—that of, for all intents and purposes, already operating in the Third World.

13. *La Raza Cósmica*

· ·

But just what kind of Third World place, exactly, would Los Angeles wind up becoming in the end? To understand that some variant of this once improbable destiny was now in the offing did not necessarily entail having a clearer idea about which of the several possibilities was most likely to come about. Even within the most luxurious shopping plazas in Beverly Hills, or in mansions in Bel Air—two venues where West L.A.'s pervasive reality gap was to be found at its most extravagant—it was obvious enough that in the near future the city would be as much and probably more Asian, as the boosters had been predicting, or, in the disturbing eventuality that destiny did not fully pan out, at least far more Hispanic, than it would be American, as it had been in the past, let alone be remotely construable as an extension of Europe.

And for those few who had not yet heard the news, there was always the *Los Angeles Times*. By the close of the 1980s, the *Times,* whatever the enduring inadequacies of its hiring and promotion practices, had certainly signed on to the credo that Southern California would lead the rest of the United States into the profitable splendors of a multiracial twenty-first century. Shortly after its new editor, Shelby Coffee III, arrived in L.A. from his previous job at *The Washington Post,* he showed every sign of having assimilated the local line and was heard assuring business leaders that he considered L.A. a Pacific Rim city, and wanted the paper's focus to reflect that belief. In 1990, the *Times* turned its attention toward Hispanic L.A., first by upgrading its Spanish-language magazines, supplements, and weekly editions, and then, the following year, by acquiring an interest in *La Opinión,* one of the oldest Spanish dailies in Los Angeles.

Meanwhile, the paper's soft sections, like "View," which featured what it called "lifestyles and trends," and "Calendar," which showcased the arts, began paying more and more attention to the Southland's multiracial future. A fairly typical "View" story that ran early in 1991 was entitled "Beyond the Melting Pot." The centerpiece of its argument was a quote taken from a *Time* magazine piece called "America's Changing Colors: What will the U.S. be like when whites are no longer the majority?" "By 2056," *Time* had insisted, "when someone born today will be 66 years old, the 'average' U.S. resident will trace his or her descent to Africa, Asia, the Hispanic world, the Pacific Islands, Arabia—almost anywhere but white Europe." Continuing in her own voice, the *Times*'s reporter went on to observe cheerfully that "this is already a reality in Southern California where ethnic and racial 'minorities' compose the majority."

The inflation of rhetoric seemed to go with the territory. The likelihood, for example, of the descendants of immigrants from "Arabia," wherever that might be—the writer presumably meant the Arab world, not the Saudi desert—outnumbering the descendants of white Angelenos was fairly remote, no matter how much Third World immigration took place during the next half century. That being said, the experience of reading such stories, even allowing for the exaggerations and the trend-spotting, must have been peculiar inside the pleasure dome of the Westside. These dire abstractions were so completely at variance with the cosseted realities of daily life there. "What do you mean we're not the city?" Westsiders had every right to demand indignantly. "We sure look like the city." It was all a bit like thinking about your own mortality —terrifying, and yet finally something over which you were so powerless that to brood over it meant having little life at all before it finally happened.

Nonetheless, no matter how assiduously Anglos might try to cultivate their own gardens (or, at least, supervise their cultivation by some small, brown persons), it was hard to believe that they did not at least shiver occasionally when they thought of the magnitude of the impending shift. Even the most optimistic among them, those who still believed that the new immigration simply recapitulated previous mass arrivals,

would have been hard-pressed not to wonder what L.A. would be like
when, somewhere between the year 2000 and the year 2015, the student body of the Los Angeles Unified School District had become *entirely* nonwhite. Of course, it was still possible to interpret this daunting
prospect more as evidence of the failure of public schools, or else of
white L.A.'s willful acquiescence in the resegregation of the city, rather
than as the harbinger of great demographic change. But for how much
longer? However much confusion was still overwhelming light, most
Anglos understood, if only instinctively and intermittently, that what
they were in fact witnessing was the de-Europeanization of Southern
California, and, only a little farther down the line, of the United States as
a nation as well, and that this inexorable process was proceeding far
more quickly than almost anyone had anticipated.

Early manifestations of the change, however often, as in the case of
the racial composition of the schools, these were misidentified as something else, were visible everywhere. They could be found in the bitter
debate concerning the overhaul of the academic curriculum that had
been shaking university campuses all over California for almost a decade. The current liberal arts concentration, the radical multiculturalists
and feminists were arguing, was too Eurocentric, too smugly focused on
the works and personalities of a set of figures increasingly derided as
DWEMs—"dead white European males"—to adequately reflect either
the cultural inheritance or psychological needs of the myriad non-
European races and national groups who now made up the majority of
California's secondary-school and college-age population.

What was needed instead, the reformers claimed, was the cultural
equivalent of the affirmative-action laws that had integrated the American workplace over the past twenty-five years. Europe needed to be part
of the story, of course, but the activists insisted that to permit it to hold
center stage as it had done for so long was not only undemocratic—it
was the hierarchical nature of culture, or, at least, what used to be called
high culture, that most offended the campus Left, a feeling one often
heard echoes of at the Chamber of Commerce—but destructive. It
would, they said, prevent nonwhite children from acquiring the self-
esteem they needed to succeed both in school and in later life. It might
even, in the words of James Okutsu, associate dean of the School of
Ethnic Studies at San Francisco State University, constitute a form of
what he identified as "pedagogic hegemenocide"—whatever that might
mean.

Of course, the campuses were something of a special case since there
this rhetoric of self-esteem and empowerment was frankly seen by its
proponents as part of a larger, radical agenda of social transformation.

The curriculum of inclusion, as it was sometimes called, was a means to an end. "In response to America," ran a leaflet from the UCLA Asian American Studies Center, "[the Center has] forged a commitment to research and social change. Emerging from the civil rights struggles of minorities—Blacks, Chicanos, Latinos, Asians, and Native Americans—to define their own history, education, and future, the Center was founded in 1969 as part of the movement for ethnic studies." And that movement, Karen Umamoto, one of the leaders of the UCLA group, had told me proudly, when I had visited her in her office at the center, was as much about "mass empowerment" as about any more narrowly construed academic project.

Still, however much they might imagine themselves out on an ideological limb, the radicals, with their talk of self-esteem, were only mirroring a broader discussion of the subject that had little, if anything, to do with any form of Left or racial politics. In fact, the idea of self-esteem had become so mainstream that, in 1986, the state of California had even gone so far as to establish a legislative panel on the subject, the Task Force to Promote Self-Esteem and Social Responsibility. Headed by a senior figure in the State Assembly, John Vasconcellos, its legal mandate was to establish "the causal relationship between a sense of low self-esteem and many of the state's social problems." The more that state and local governments succeeded in raising the self-esteem, both individual and collective, of all Californians, the bill's sponsors argued, the more likely it would be that the entire panoply of ills besetting late twentieth-century America, from teenage pregnancy to crime and drug addiction, would finally be brought under control.

But here, too, closer examination turned up the fact that talking about self-esteem was in many ways just another way of pondering the effects of the new immigration. "California," wrote Assemblyman Vasconcellos, in his preface to a book, *The Social Importance of Self-Esteem,* based on the task force's findings, "is experiencing a revolution of race and ethnicity. We are about to become the first state in the mainland United States with a majority of nonwhites . . . California is becoming an 'international' state, with the opportunity to create a truly multicultural democracy. Our ability to do so may depend on each of us developing a healthy sense of self-esteem so that, instead of being insecure and threatened by persons who differ from us, we can appreciate one another and be enriched by persons of different races, ethnic backgrounds, and cultures."

And then again, it might not. In reality, the task force's conclusions were anything but conclusive. A member of the commission, like one Kenneth W. Ogden, M.Div., Ed.D., might sum up his service by saying it had brought him "new insights about myself and others," and that he had learned "much about human concern, sensitivity and compassion." But the final report's language was so hedged with "mights" and "likeliests"—"self-esteem is the likeliest candidate for a social vaccine," "researchers believe high self-esteem may be an important factor in reducing teenage pregnancy," or "low self-esteem may be experienced by a member of an ethnic or cultural minority [sic] that is stereotyped in a negative way"—and, like the road to hell, so paved with good intentions, that it was hard to believe that anything very substantive had been established. The only compelling message was one of wonder at the new ethnic diversity of the state, and an insistence that, somehow, coming to terms amicably with this transformation was the most important subject on California's agenda. For all the talk of good feeling and mutual respect, there was an undercurrent in the task force's report, more evident there than in the "L.A. 2000" report that it otherwise resembled, of will we be able to cope with this new world in which we shall shortly find ourselves?

Along with the radicals on campus, the establishment in Sacramento and in the Chamber of Commerce, the Southern California avant-garde was pitching multiculturalism as well. In the fall of 1990, the director Peter Sellars, known for his daring interpretations of classical opera— he had staged Mozart's *Così fan Tutte* in a 1950s-era diner; Handel's *Julius Caesar* in the Middle East at the time of the Lebanese Civil War —took over the Los Angeles Festival. Founded in the mid-eighties as part of the vast cultural expansion the city had bankrolled out of the profits from the successful staging of the 1984 Olympic Games, the festival had played it fairly safe up until then, preferring to invite legendary directors like Peter Brook and Ingmar Bergman rather than book anything too exotic, or, for that matter, too local. And however desultory their attendance at its offerings, most Westsiders preferred the festival that way. There was something reassuring about driving down to the Dorothy Chandler Pavilion at the Music Center and seeing the same stars whom you had read about in *The New York Times.*

Sellars had a completely different festival in mind. There would be no European works on the 1990 program at all, he announced. Instead, he planned to celebrate the indigenous cultures of Los Angeles, "with particular focus on the Pacific, Asia, Latin America, Oceania and the Far North." In practice, although he did invite a commendable number of Chicano and Latin-American performance groups, Sellars meant more or less the same thing the boosters did when he talked of multiculturalism and the post-European city: the Pacific Rim. And, scattering the performances all over greater L.A., including neighborhoods most people on the Westside could barely have found on a road map, Sellars regaled the city for two weeks with gamelan music from Bali, traditional Hawaiian hula dancers, Korean-American performance artists, and Japanese experimental theater. The most noteworthy American piece he included had an Asian theme as well; it was a new production of John Adams's opera *Nixon in China.*

Not surprisingly, Sellars initially had a difficult time raising the money for such a festival. Most of the important donors in Los Angeles, he confided, perhaps unwisely, to a reporter from *L.A. Style,* were accustomed to "supporting Carnegie Hall–type culture at the Music Center." And yet, Sellars insisted briskly, this had to change if L.A. were ever to transcend its richly deserved reputation as a cultural backwater, a wealthy receiver of the cultural productions of the northeastern United States and of Europe rather than a producer. He added that this did not need to be the case. Angelenos were just looking at the wrong things. Instead of looking east, they needed to look both to the Pacific Rim and to the Asian and Hispanic performers in their own midst. "This is the cultural vocabulary of this region," Sellars said. *"You will* have to know something about Chinese opera [in Los Angeles], you just will."

As things turned out this first time around, several major Japanese corporations had to step into the breach before the 1990 festival could go on as scheduled—they at least, presumably being already familiar with Chinese opera—but this did not mean that Sellars had failed. To the contrary, he was only fractionally ahead of his time. Six months after it had ended, many Angelenos had come around to the view that Sellars had been right all along. They also found that they didn't miss the European imports nearly as much as they had imagined they would. (Now if people had tried to take their BMWs and their Jaguars away, that would have been another matter.) "The festival was the kind of cultural event we should have more of here in L.A.," one of the garment executives I had met through Allegra told me over dinner one night. "It makes you feel part of the world, makes you understand your neighbors better. I've lived here all my life, and it takes Sellars to come in and tell me about the Buddhist temple out in San Gabriel."

From across the table, a friend of his, who had only caught the tail end of the conversation, chimed in. "Personally, I didn't understand much of that Buddhist music," he said, good-humoredly, "but then I didn't understand all that Italian opera my wife used to drag me out to see in Long Beach a few years back."

"You understood the ballerinas from the New York City Ballet she took you to see at the Music Center," my companion shot back, and, in a burst of bawdy laughter, the conversation wandered elsewhere. That

Sellars's version of culture, if not so sexy, was something you could take your Japanese and Taiwanese clients to see was left unsaid. Nor was it necessary to add that if the incorrigibly peripatetic Sellars decided to remain in L.A., he would never again encounter the same kind of resistance when he tried to raise money downtown or on the Westside. The point had been made that, in his version at least, multiculturalism had not turned out to be so unpalatable after all; even if, as my companion had suggested, this last held true for more traditional offerings as well, it still seemed like something of an acquired taste.

And this question of palatability was anything but a metaphor. Indeed it was on the less controversial, albeit far more basic level of what people ate that this multiculturalization of the Southland had progressed the farthest. Ethnic restaurants and fast-food restaurants, only recently largely confined to particular neighborhoods or immigrant-owned mini-malls, seemed to be sprouting up everywhere. Thirty years before, apart from the occasional taco wolfed down at one of the drive-through Mexican chains like Jack-in-the-Box or Taco Bell, Italian food had been about as experimental as most Anglos in Southern California liked to get. Today, however, a generation of Anglo kids whose parents had been raised on steak and baked potatoes could comfortably tell the difference at a glance between Thai and Cantonese food. A previously exotic prospect like, say, a Szechuan dinner now seemed almost tame, a Mexican burrito as American as a hamburger. In other words, their bellies were growing up multicultural even if, in myriad other ways, most noticeably language acquisition, they remained just as parochial as their parents had been.

On the level of food, at least, Los Angeles needed no boosterish nudging to propel it into its post-European future. The prestige of East Asia, in combination with the thirst for novelty—what besides food could so literally satisfy the taste for new sensations—so characteristic of contemporary life in the Southland, had seen to that. Sometimes, the strongest proof of how much had changed could be found in the statements of people who thought they were making fun of what had happened. The *Los Angeles Times Magazine*'s columnist Margo Kauffman, for example, wrote a witty piece in October of 1990 sending up Angelenos perpetually searching for still more exotic cuisines. But in a closing paragraph in which she tried to distinguish herself from these faddists, Kauffman gave herself away. "Frankly," she wrote, "I've never awakened in the middle of the night with a hankering for Middle Altitude Andean food. If I have to pick a restaurant, a modern-day act of courage, I automatically head for my favorite sushi or salad bar." There it was, *sushi,* as American as apple pie.

As Kauffman's piece so perfectly, if inadvertently, demonstrated, a wide gulf still separated what Angelenos could digest, both literally and figuratively, and what they could acknowledge about the ways in which their lives were changing. After all, these transformations, however radical when considered in their totality, were mostly taking place piecemeal and under the surface. Those that either had already made or promised to make the biggest difference, like the demographic shift in the school-age population or the altered eating habits of younger Anglos, still did not so dramatically impinge on the daily experience of most people on the Westside or in the Valley (let alone in Orange County or other more remote areas of greater L.A.) that they couldn't still be ignored or explained away, or simply bypassed the way any California driver all but instinctively bypassed those routes that might lead him into a dangerous neighborhood.

This indeed, was a new twist on things changing yet remaining the same. The public schools were perfect examples. As late as the 1960s, the L.A. schools occupied a central place in neighborhood affairs. You sent your kid to the local school, attended the PTA meetings, and, often as not, used school facilities for other community events. The abandonment of these schools by Anglos (the number of white children enrolled in the Los Angeles Unified School District in all grades dropped from 252,000 in 1966 to 88,000 in 1990) in the face of integration and new immigrant populations—the celebrated phenomenon of white flight—did not, however, mean that whites abandoned their neighborhoods. Rather, they sent their kids to parochial and private schools, leaving the old buildings as the territory of interlopers, unfamiliar presences bused in and out during the course of the day. And yet all you had to do to avoid thinking about these schools was to drive a little faster as you passed by them.

The celebrated Angeleno amnesia about the past, that gift for living with extreme discontinuity, helped too. So what if Hollywood High—alma mater of countless movie stars, from Lana Turner and Mickey Rooney to James Garner and Carol Burnett—now ranked in the bottom 20 percent of all California schools and was better known for its English as a second language program than for its amateur dramatics? "No one," as they said on the Westside, lived in Hollywood anymore. As for the ubiquitous Asian restaurants, well, after a few years of seeing sushi bars in the Beverly Center or Thai restaurants on San Vicente Boulevard in Brentwood, a good number of people in L.A. would have had trouble recalling viscerally what life had been like in those Paleozoic days before these places had opened their doors, and people ate pot roast and mashed potatoes. What was to remember? The Westside had given up all kinds of pasts—cigarettes, butter, meat to an increasing degree. In that context, giving up community seemed almost like a small thing.

And when Angelenos did occasionally take a moment to think about what was going on in the city, they tended toward slogans and formulas that were all but guaranteed to inhibit thought, and ranged from the harmless bromides of self-esteem and the celebration of diversity, to rosy economic scenarios of the type the boosters were peddling, to various leftist or nativist versions of an impending class or race war collectively known as the *Blade Runner* scenario. That none of these descriptions quite conformed to what was going on in L.A. was obvious. But more remarkable was the parallelism, the fact that Angelenos seemed to be able to accept the more outlandishly cheerful prognostications of Pacific Rim–oriented entrepreneurs and their tame futurologists without abandoning their sneaking sympathy for every doom-laden prophecy about what L.A. would be like in the twenty-first century.

This dual-tracked attitude could crop up in a single conversation. One morning, I called a friend of Allegra's who was in the import-export business, in the hope that he would take me around the Port of Los Angeles, which he knew well. He was happy enough to do it, he said, and we agreed that he would collect me at Allegra's house in mid-Wilshire early that same afternoon. "You'll love the container port," he'd said just before we hung up. "It's one of the most efficient operations of its kind anywhere in the world."

By the time he turned up, both the weather and his mood had deteriorated. It was raining, a steady, listless drizzle, and as we hurried out to the curb and got in his car, I heard him muttering about the lateness of the hour and how bad the traffic was likely to be. Then, turning the key in the ignition and flipping on the windshield wipers, he added: "It's a real *Blade Runner* of a day out there."

Fortunately, just as this dystopic reflection seemed to have careened, full-blown, straight out of his unconscious (all I saw was the rain, not the metaphor), it quickly evaporated. Though the rain got worse, and the traffic was as bad as he had feared, he was soon his former cheerful self, spouting on happily about how much tonnage the port could unload in a given day, docking facilities, and, more generally, the pleasures of doing business in the Southland, particularly if your market was, as it should be, the Pacific Rim.

Cognitive dissonance and more cognitive dissonance. Was Los Angeles really becoming the twenty-fourth ward of Tokyo, the de facto capital of a region where, as Kenichi Ohmae had only half-jokingly suggested, you could not always tell where "America ends and Japan begins"? Well, yes; it certainly was beginning to look that way. But did this mean then that the Los Angeles would now be spared its alternative future as another version of Santiago de Chile or Jakarta, a nightmarish urban agglomeration of high walls, shocking extremes of poverty and wealth that, over time, would be less and less buffered by the ameliorating presence of a large middle class? Well, no, it didn't actually. Both outcomes might very well come about at the same moment. And even in L.A., a city whose inhabitants had, after all, long been predisposed to welcome change, no matter how convulsive, the prospect of *two* destinies, one triumphant, the second apocalyptic, occurring synchronously, was almost too outlandish to try to think about critically.

Of course, through thick and thin, despite a national recession that had finally struck supposedly recession-proof Southern California in 1991, a drought that was crippling the state's agriculture, post–Cold War cutbacks in the defense industry, and a fall in real estate values for the first time in living memory—harbingers, even to some people in greater Los Angeles, of leaner times to come—the boosters continued to insist that the city could go on choosing its own destiny. As if the future were a menu, or, indeed, as if Angelenos were gods. Actually, it was this continuing act of exuberant hubris that had provided the deepest motivation to the "L.A. 2000" report and countless other documents that took a similar line. For, despite the mounting evidence to the contrary, many Angelenos still firmly believed that they stood a chance of channeling the future's course almost as imperiously as William Mulholland had channeled the waters of the Owens Valley through the great aqueduct to the L.A. basin. "There it is, take it," the city's demonic master builder had said, as the first of the water began to flow.

And they had, ever since. Now, the new boosters had taken to arguing that if Los Angeles's present preeminence was due to the will and imagination of people like Mulholland, of "the vision of yesterday," as they put it, the task that faced the contemporary city was to create the new vision that would "shape the L.A. of tomorrow." Skeptics might choose to wonder if notions like multiculturalism or self-esteem, which had none of the grandeur of the earlier conceptions out of which the Los Angeles dream had been fashioned, were doomed to failure. After all, it was one thing to call, in the grandiloquent words of a popular nineteenth-century California slogan, for "men to match my mountains," and quite another to appeal for more sensitivity toward others, fortified by great doses of mandated harmony and prescribed self-respect. That seemed as likely to produce "wimps to match my anxieties" as anything else.

But was the comparison necessarily as invidious as it first appeared?

On the face of things, the old-fashioned blood, sweat, and tears approach of engineer Mulholland, like all traditional appeals to sacrifice and grandeur, looked to be more compelling than treacly invitations for people to be a little nicer to one another. However, on closer examination, this loomed as much if not more as a problem of rhetoric—of eloquence, really—than as a problem of content. After all, the boosters, as befitted people who imagined an electronically plugged in, post-Gutenbergian future, neither wrote nor spoke particularly well. It was not so much that they preferred the ten-second TV sound bite and the question-and-answer format to the book or the essay, but rather that they really didn't see what those latter things had been about in the first place, and felt that they were just some New York or European anachronism. "Nobody reads anymore, they have better things to do," Nathan Gardels, the editor of *New Perspectives Quarterly,* told me. And *NPQ* was, of course, a magazine, and a marvelous one at that, perhaps the best political journal to have appeared in the United States in twenty-five years. But its own editor preferred to run interviews, fearing, maybe rightly, that if he were to run anything longer he would lose his audience.

It was true that some of the boosters' slogans were brilliant in their way, but to refer to L.A. as a collage, as *NPQ* so often did, or to America as a "world nation," as Joel Kotkin did, not only seemed a very partial rendering, but had something uncomfortably pat about it. Not surprisingly, most of the boosters who now wrote about the city had been trained as economists or business writers, and their arguments had the trend-besotted quality those fields seem to demand. For the most part, such arguments were at their strongest when considering the economic advantages of life in a post-European America. But, rhetorical flourishes aside, they were on far less solid ground when they abandoned these criteria for their various lofty contentions about America's historic mission. And even then, arguments about what would be desirable for America in the twenty-first century kept segueing into arguments about what was inevitable, and, under the circumstances, how the country could successfully fit into what Joel Kotkin called the "emerging Asia-oriented economic order."

To be sure, that was a prediction worth taking seriously. But it did little to clear up the question of why, beyond the imperatives of money and of demographic *force majeure,* the boosters were so sure that the Third World Los Angeles that was in the process of being born was so obviously to be preferred to the white city whose end was now so plainly in sight. Kotkin might talk of America's "essential message of economic, political and cultural liberty," but, apart from a historic receptivity to immigration and a historic aptitude for entrepreneurship—

two qualities he rather curiously seemed to view as part of the country's nature—it was by no means clear what that message really was, even if Kotkin was right in contending that America's peculiar fondness for shedding its past made it more likely that it could fit into a nonwhite world.

And if the boosters only intermittently understood the full implications of their arguments, the politicians and state bureaucrats spoke in such benign generalities as to be all but incoherent. Even the few worthwhile things they had to say came so swaddled in the off-putting, hypermedicalized language of therapeutic encounter groups and social welfare "professionals"—a world in which there was no wickedness, only "social ills," and no contradictions between people, only failures of communication that could be remedied with the appropriate amount of "openness"—that it was hard to take them seriously. An organization like the California Task Force to Promote Self-Esteem was obviously an easy mark for the satirist; indeed, the cartoonist Garry Trudeau had not been able to resist the temptation, and in his strip, "Doonesbury," he went after the task force with brio for several months. "Why do I know Shirley MacLaine had a hand in all this?" one of Trudeau's characters asks. To which his girlfriend replies, "Wrong, smart guy! Shirley was visiting relatives in ancient Rome that day." But then, how else was one to treat a group that affirmed California to be the state "that more than any other has dared to wonder what it means to be human"?

But it was not simply that the task force's starting point had been the most predictable kind of cultic New Age nonsense, everything that people in the rest of the world wrongly supposed to be the essential spirit of Southern California. That was bad enough, but worse was the pretense on the part of members of Vasconcellos's group to having found the key through which Californians could parse their future.

At least most Californians remained skeptical. Vasconcellos might claim that "we in California (often the leading state, often pioneers)... point the way toward a successful effort to improve our human condition," but, instinctively, at least, even the people most tempted by this type of spiritual self-aggrandizement understood that it only made sense when applied to individuals. That was what the abiding popularity of the innumerable self-help, or, as they were now being called, self-realization groups was based on, this abiding Californian infatuation with tinkering with the self. There was little prospect that such a movement, one, moreover, that was also fed by the almost defiantly anti-communitarian ethos that had reigned in L.A. for so long, could suddenly be transformed into the engine of a new social contract between races and ethnic groups. John Gregory Dunne had summed up the problem when he wrote, "Space in the West, community in the East—those are the myths that sustain us."

But if the boosters' message was simplistically materialistic, and the bureaucrats' naive and bathetic, there remained the Left. And oddly enough, it was among these most extreme of multiculturalists that the vision of a grand future for Los Angeles found its one truly eloquent expression. This was not to say that the radicals were unhampered by their own particular brand of sentimentality. To the contrary, their Manichaean division of the world into a "hegemonic" white power structure guilty of every infamy and an inherently virtuous nonwhite world was the perfect embodiment of wishful thinking. Nonetheless, when they talked about a new America that deserved a more exciting destiny than what the militant black writer Ishmael Reed called "a hum-drum homogeneous world of all brains and no heart," they were (though of course they would have detested the comparison) reminis-cent in their fiery certainty and daring of a General Otis or a Mulholland. The United States, Reed declared with flat, unbending assurance, could become "a place where the cultures of the world crisscross. This is possible because the United States is unique in the world: The world is here."

Men to match its mountains, indeed. There it was, for all its simplicity and hyperbole, rhetoric to make the blood race. Not for the radicals all the antiseptic talk of economic advantage or of recipes for new ways to take your emotional temperature. Here was a future anyone could see the point of wanting to belong to, since it played on both the millenarian Protestantism that was was the oldest form of American radicalism and the belief that in the City on the Hill anything was possible. And if this rhetoric made sense in the United States, for all the obvious historical reasons, it made even greater sense in California, where the flame of exceptionalism still burned so brightly.

And the image that the best polemicists for this view kept returning to was, quite correctly, that of food. Reed had begun his essay "America: The Multinational Society" with an evocation of a Jewish street fair in which a Spanish-speaking family bought Italian ices rabbinically certified as kosher, and where Chinese women ate pizza in front of a Vietnamese-owned grocery store. And although he was in fact describing a scene that had actually taken place on the Lower East Side in New York City, nowhere were such improbable juxtapositions more entrenched as a feature of the urban landscape than in Los Angeles. Reed might as well have been evoking an average day at half the mini-malls in greater L.A. Indeed, the city had, if anything, long since transcended the culinary ecumenicism of the street fair, which, in some ways, was little more than a kind of downscale simulacrum of the world's fair, a Disneyland of the palate, in favor of rawer, more challenging recombinations.

For what had been taking place in the Southland was eccentric to a degree far beyond that implied by a catchphrase like "the mosaic," or even "the ethnic salad," which was the latest image to bemuse the multiculturalists. After all, in a salad the lettuce does not start turning into the tomato by dint of association, nor does the celery intermarry with the radish. And in a mosaic, the various pieces of glass, however well they fit into their integument, still remain distinct from one another. The main reason these comparisons enjoyed such favor was that they seemed like the most viable alternatives to the old idea of the melting pot. They certainly did not conform to the reality of the new L.A. in which, though they were hardly assimilating into some ideal of WASP socialization, as, at least according to legend, the European immigrants of 1900 had done, all these Mexicans, Salvadorans, Persians, and Koreans were having an increasingly more difficult time maintaining their discrete linguistic, ethnic, and even radical identities over the abrading course of generations.

In fact, the more you looked, the more inadequate a notion like diversity became as a frame for thinking about what was going on in Southern California. The truth was drawing closer and closer to embodying the predictions of a Salman Rushdie, whose own books embodied the best and most sophisticated of multiculturalist perspectives, when he said that immigrants and their hosts would not so much assimilate as leak into one another, "like flavors when you cook." Anglo Californians, accustomed as they were to thinking of the world in terms of whites and "minorities," and having in general only the shakiest grasp of the particular characteristics of the countries the immigrants were arriving from, fell easily into the habit of thinking of their new neighbors as Hispanics, Asians, or Middle Easterners. What was more interesting, though, was that the immigrants themselves were coming to accept a similar self-conception. This was an enormous transformation in consciousness, and one that was neither as automatic nor as easily accomplished as it might have appeared to be on the surface.

For the immigrants had not turned up in Los Angeles with any such ideas in their heads, far from it, nor had their initial experiences of life in the region done much more than replicate, however luxurious some of the settings, the sense they had had of life back home. This was part economic necessity—the fact that immigrants, even if they worked for Anglos, otherwise relied on their fellow countrymen in almost every material aspect of life from shopping to finding a job—part language barrier, and since the familiar tastes and customs in the alien world of

Los Angeles (alienness being also in the eye of the beholder) were a consolation, it was tempting to stay in the ethnic ghetto.

In the first generation, they did. If you went to a Salvadoran restaurant patronized by people just in from the South, you *were* in El Salvador, at least until, blinking, you walked out into the mini-mall parking lot and found yourself—that was what it felt like—back in L.A. The same held true in a Korean bar on Olympic Boulevard, an Iranian coffee shop in Westwood, or an Ethiopian diner on Washington Boulevard. And in these places, people tended to talk about their own national identities as if they had never made the trip to the United States. This was not simply because often, though they obviously knew they were in Los Angeles, they were less clear, apart from the fact that they worked there, what this fact implied for the future. It also meant that they would usually identify themselves in roughly the same terms that they might have employed had they remained at home. Thus, Koreans, with their fierce and settled sense of national identity, would usually insist, when asked, that they were Koreans, plain and simple. Only if you pressed them further would they add that they had come from Seoul, Pusan, or Kyongju. In contrast, Mexicans, for most of whom the sense of regional identity was usually stronger than any allegiance to the broader nation, tended to reply to the same question by saying they were from Sonora, or Michoacán, or even a section of one of the states of Mexico, the heights of Jalisco, say, rather than just Jalisco State.

In their insularity, it was possible for Anglos to assume that since they thought of themselves as Americans, and the Europeans they met usually described themselves as coming from France, Germany, or Italy (and, as the reality of the United Europe of 1992 began to sink in, as Europeans), such broad categories had always predominated. In fact, it had only been a few generations since Americans had described themselves as Missourians and Oregonians, Yankees and Southerners. The great-grand-parents of the same Europeans you met in Beverly Hills or Santa Monica had, for their part, thought of themselves more in terms of their provincial identities—as Auvergnats and Lyonnais, Pomeranians and Franconians, or Torinese and Romans—than their national ones. That this process had been accomplished in Europe and in the United States did not mean that it had reached the same terminus in most of the Third World countries the immigrants had come from. Instead, though most Anglos would have been astounded to hear it, where this increasing sense of generalization was taking hold was not in the Third World at all, but right there in Los Angeles, California, U.S.A.

But if the first immigrant generation, for all the eagerness many of its members might have to become American citizens, rarely was able to abandon whatever traditional identity it had come to America with, its children almost invariably withdrew elsewhere. Where a sixty-year-old Mexican might say that he came from the Altos de Jalisco, his forty-year-old son was more likely to describe himself as having come from Mexico, and his twenty-year-old grandson to say that he was a Latino or a Hispanic, depending on his politics. (The Left in L.A. favored Latino, and thought Hispanic to be an artificial association with Spain, even though the term derived from "*Latin* America," a coinage of the French emperor Napoleon III, who had wanted in the mid-nineteenth century to emphasize France's historic connection to the continent). Even a Korean or a Taiwanese adolescent was more likely to think of herself as Asian or Asian-American than choose the more restrictive national origin (even though, for Koreans, this meant being lumped in the same category as their country's hated traditional masters, the Japanese).

Thus, in the space of three generations or less, the immigrants would move from being part of subgroups within their own countries of origin to becoming American minority groups. It was a trajectory as confusing, if not more so, to the people within the immigrant communities themselves as it was to Anglo and black L.A. In Salvador, you were not a Hispanic, you were a Salvadoran. In Asia, you were not Asian, you were Chinese. And yet in Los Angeles, these deepest of selves were simply subsumed in the broader context of a new, overarching Hispanicity or Asianness.

Paradoxically, in leaving their homelands in the Third World to go to L.A., the immigrants had in fact joined the Third World for, in many cases, the first time in their lives. Because the term "Third World" really only made sense in America, or some other rich country; that is, as an antonym to some other world, the white world, say. What else bound such diverse places as Mexico, El Salvador, the Philippines, South Korea, Hong Kong, and Iran, which were so unlike one another in terms of language, culture, history, and national character, if not the weight of some enormous counter-distinction that made even these intricate questions seem secondary? The answer, of course, was that just such a supervening category did exist, in Los Angeles as everywhere else in America, and it was race. But it was important to remember that these were American problems. As new Americans, the immigrants might be stuck with them—part of the price of admission, to use a distinguished Hollywood term—but they would not have been readily understood in Asia, Latin America, and the Middle East, and took some getting used to, even in L.A.

The late Shiva Naipaul once wrote a brilliant essay denouncing the very idea of the Third World, which he deemed to be "a bloodless

universality that robs individuals and their societies of their particular-
ity." He was right in almost every important sense except one, but on
that single point he was almost willfully obtuse. For Naipaul left out the
fact that the idea of the Third World was the inescapable legacy of
European imperialism, a system that had divided peoples—colonizers
and colonized—along the cruel dichotomous lines of white and nonwhite. That was an inheritance no part of the world could so easily
shrug off, least of all the United States, whose great national tragedy had
always been race, just as Europe's had been class. Americans might
prefer the euphemisms of "majority" and "minority," but the meaning
was the same. And where else could the immigrants themselves fall,
once they had arrived, but into this oldest of American fault lines, even
if, ironically, their very presence meant that, in Southern California certainly, the whole idea of a white majority and a nonwhite minority was
rapidly becoming a statistical as well as a metaphysical illusion?

If anything, what was surprising about Los Angeles, and what made it
so different, so very much more hopeful, than other cities and other
regions in the United States, was that for all the prevailing myopia there
were many voices there calling for the country's long racial civil war to
end—even if this meant, as it were, going over to the nonwhite side.
That old Angeleno disdain for the past had conferred a kind of freedom.
It permitted clear-sighted Angelenos to secede from anything, even, it
appeared, from the deepest cornerstone of their own identities. Observing that the world itself was becoming nonwhite, observing the rise of
the Pacific Rim, the demographic explosion in Mexico, and believing
they observed the decline of Europe, the smartest voices in the Southland—from the heirs of General Otis to the heirs of Carey McWilliams
—had joined together. Instead of resisting, of following the line set at a
time when the Southland had set the tone of anti-Asian and anti-Mexican
racial hysteria, that city whose prosperity had derived so crucially from
a Cold War for which the Third World had served as a proving ground
stood poised to clamber aboard.

It was an outcome that had been predicted long before—but by a
Mexican, not an American. In the 1920s, José Vasconcelos (no relation
to the zany assemblyman from Santa Clara), who was later to become
Rector of the National University of Mexico, wrote a book called *La
Raza Cósmica*, "The Cosmic Race." In it, he predicted the advent of
what he called "the fifth race." The destiny of the Americas, Vasconcelos
argued, was to take all the races of the world and meld them together,
as the conquest of Mexico by the Spaniards had mixed together Europeans and Indians. Written in an era when the prestige of racist "purity"
theory was at its height, and as a conscious refutation of the proto-fascist

philosopher Arthur Gobineau, Vasconcelos's book represented the first time the idea of a heterogeneous world had been defended since the very idea of race as a way of dividing people first seized the European imagination.

"The white, the red, the black, and the yellow," Vasconcelos wrote, "America is home to all of them and needs all of them." He closed his book with the premonition that, as he put it, "we will succeed in the Americas, before anywhere else in the globe has come near, in creating a new race, fashioned out of the treasures of all the other races: The final race, the cosmic race." Of course, when Vasconcelos spoke of the Americas, he did not mean the United States. On the contrary, as Samuel Beckett once said when asked by a French journalist if he were English. Vasconcelos imagined the United States as too racist, too Gobineau-like a country to accept such a destiny. His hope was for his beloved Mexico to serve the rest of the continent as model and example. Only if fired by this unifying vision, he argued, could it possibly stand up either to Europe or to the United States.

Vasconcelos was himself no stranger to racial romanticizing. The Fifth Race, he noted confidently, would "be in accordance with the laws of social practicality, sympathy, and beauty, and would lead to the formation of a human type far superior to any that has yet existed." But he was also something of a seer. His description of *La Raza Cósmica*'s capital, the city he dubbed Universopolis, is prescient in its evocation of a place that would be an anthology of the world. The only problem was that Vasconcelos was off in his map reading by about a thousand miles. As a good Mexican nationalist of his time, concerned with exporting what he called Mexico's "ethnic mission" across the continent, Vasconcelos clearly imagined Universopolis as a spruced-up, glorified stand-in for Mexico City. That was not to be. With twenty million people, unspeakable pollution, poverty, and hopelessness, Mexico City was not the future of anything, except, perhaps, dystopia. But what about Los Angeles? That was quite a different matter. Or, as the Mexican writer Carlos Monsivais put it, "The heart of the Mexican Dream is L.A."

For the moment, of course, even in greater Universopolis, the races were not blending nearly so rapidly as the cuisines. A few eccentric Anglos, like the local painter Ed Ruscha, might predict confidently that "a hundred years from now there will be some gorgeous mono-ethnic race living here ... everyone is gradually mixing"—but such voices were rare. Indeed, much of the fashionable talk on college campuses and among radicals was of group rights rather than of individual rights, and of the obligation of members of a particular ethnic or racial group to jealously guard their own culture from outside influences and threats.

But if separation prevailed among intellectuals (a fashionable T-shirt among militant blacks in the summer of 1990 read "It's a black thing, you wouldn't understand," a type of feeling shared by many groups in L.A. besides blacks), on the streets of L.A., from downtown to Compton, Boyle Heights to Malibu, Vasconcelos's vision was proving far more like the shape of things to come.

The food was the first sign, and it was anything but insignificant. Not only were Anglo kids avidly wolfing down fajitas, but that paradigmatic Mexican dish itself was mutating. I learned of this from Nathan Gardels, who, as an early Angeleno reader of Vasconcelos, was in a position to fully apprehend the significance of these food fusions. In a fast-food restaurant in the Valley, near where he lived, Gardels had stumbled across a new offering called the pita-fajita. It was a dish made of the meat of a fajita, usually chicken or beef, but instead of being wrapped in a tortilla it was scooped into a piece of Middle Eastern pita bread. Seemingly a small thing—the decision, perhaps, of the Iranian immigrant who owned the place to cater to the local demand for Mexican food. But as Gardels pointed out to me, in fact such transformations, meldings, and re-creations were taking place everywhere in L.A. "There was the real future of the city," he told me (and though he said it jokingly, he was being entirely serious), "staring up at me from the plastic tray in the form of that pita fajita."

And if culinary miscegenation was roaring along, even its corporeal variant was moving along rather more briskly, though it was more advanced among immigrants than between whites and nonwhites, than many Angelenos supposed. It stood to reason. People from the various new immigrant groups now had the schools virtually all to themselves, and, however much their parents might disapprove, it was a foregone conclusion that they were not going to stick entirely to their own kind. Just as the Irish, Poles, Jews, and Italians who had rubbed shoulders and more in the wake of the European immigration of 1900 had, by the fifties and sixties, begun to intermarry en masse, so the same process was beginning to take place among the recent arrivals in L.A. One could find every sort of nonwhite combination in the city now: Hmong and Salvadoran, Ethiopian and Taiwanese, Mexican and Filipino.

The mind boggled, but then, so did the relatives. For when, say, a Thai married a Persian, it was a safe bet that, among other impediments, neither set of relations would have ever heard of the other family's country. A familiarity with the Buddhist scriptures is really not essential to life in Chihuahua, nor is a familiarity with the Islamic practices of Pakistan one of the things one most associates with Hong Kong Chinese. And why should the various groups have known about each other? After all, they did not know they all belonged to the Third World until after they had arrived in L.A. And yet they were learning. In kitchens all over the Southland, Vietnamese *nuoc mam* fish paste was coming to coexist in the larder with strings of Sonoran chiles, and a refrigerator might well be found to contain leftovers of Iranian *chelo kebab* and also homemade guacamole dip. *La Raza Cósmica*: it could be spotted almost any evening, from Western Avenue in Koreatown to Mexican-American Huntington Park, and from Temple-Beaudry to Chinese Alhambra, sneaking in through the intestinal tract.

But, for that matter, even the Westside was no longer immune, for all its gated communities, streets restricted to neighborhood residents, Westec "armed response" burglar alarm notices on the front lawns, and, inside, the even more formidably buffering protections of the electronic home workplace with its fax machines, computer modem linkups, and cellular phones. One Saturday morning, Tim Rutten took me along to a brunch in Studio City that was being given by his friends, a distinguished psychologist named Marty Berkowitz, and his wife, Jan, a well-known local portrait painter. "They'll probably serve something Jewish," Tim had predicted airily as we drove over to where they lived in a condominium development on the site of the old Fox lot. "You'll like it," he added archly. "It will remind you of New York."

And the Berkowitzes did turn out to be familiar types to me, though they seemed to resemble more the cultivated German Jewish refugees my mother had described knowing during her high school years in Hollywood during the late forties than exiles from Manhattan's Upper West Side. Certainly, the Berkowitzes' Los Angeles could not have appeared more firmly removed from any version of the Third World city that I had been getting to know. In their house, it was Eurocentrism to the max, as teenagers in the Valley used to say, and of the most agreeable kind imaginable.

However, the brunch that Marty Berkowitz had prepared for us turned out, to my surprise, to be both less and more interesting than the Jewish-American standby that Tim had led me to expect. As he led us to the table, Marty Berkowitz smiled crookedly, and waved toward the adjoining kitchen from which wafted smells that were at once familiar and unidentifiable. "I've dreamed up something new this morning," Berkowitz said. "It's an experiment, my own combination of Mexican *huevos rancheros* and Jewish *matzoh brei.*"

"Marty calls it *Dorito brei,*" Jan Berkowitz added indulgently. "Isn't that the perfect name for an L.A. dish?"

It certainly was, in its way, for both Los Angeles and its future. It was also absurd, ill conceived, overly optimistic—as much an idea as a recipe. And yet, like the future itself, there it lay on our plates, its improbable mixture of aromas steaming pungently up at us. Tim and I stole a glance at each other, but as Angelenos had been discovering lately—and in contexts at least as unlikely as this one—there was nothing else to do but go along. After a moment, we picked up our forks and began to dig in.

14. Small World, Big City

·····················

"There are two futures," the great English scientist J. D. Bernal once wrote. "The future of desire and the future of fate, and man's reason has never learned to separate them." By the look of things, man's reason was, if anything, doing an even worse job than usual in Los Angeles in the winter of 1991. For despite the mounting evidence to the contrary, almost everyone in a position to voice an opinion about the city's destiny, from downtown boosters to radical academics, from NIMBY homeowners to newly arrived immigrants, seemed determined to keep faith with the view that, in L.A. at least, it was still desire that determined fate rather than the other way around. No information, no matter how disturbing, appeared capable of altering this entrenched state of mind—at least as long as there was enough space for Angelenos to put between themselves and the real news about what was going to happen to them.

Of course, with the freeways jammed, this meant metaphorical as well as actual space. To maintain an illusion of being able to control their fate, or, failing that, to somehow strip the unwelcome prospect of its force, Angelenos were increasingly indulging in a kind of linguistic damage control. This was a startling phenomenon in a region where verbal precision had never been a quality that many people had prized, and, indeed, that some actively disliked for being what they thought of as a prime example of "eastern" pedantry and elitism. A more normal reaction was the one I had encountered at a fireworks display one Fourth of July in Pacific Palisades, when I had asked the man standing next to me whether he knew the name of the particularly showy and beautiful display bursting in the sky above us. "No, I don't," he'd said, in mild annoyance, "but you know I find that I appreciate an experience more when I don't try to pigeonhole it by giving it a name."

Not naming for him had been an essential part of the idyll he called his life, and he had moved away huffily when I remarked to him that had he been a writer he might have felt somewhat differently. But now, it seemed, as if in order, precisely, to maintain this idyll, it was necessary to pay enormous attention to how things would be named. In the debates, for example, about whether immigrants were "illegal aliens" or "undocumented workers," whether people of Mexican ancestry should call themselves Hispanics or Latinos, or whether L.A. was the leading city of the United States or of the Pacific Rim, the undercurrent of wanting to manage the future as well as understand was rarely absent. Angelenos seemed to assume—and, given L.A.'s origins and its founding myth, they had good reason to do so—that if only they could find the right, that is, the most optimistic, name for what was going on, then they would inevitably get the right, that is, the most optimistic, outcome.

The benefits of this way of thinking, in the short term, at least, were obvious. If, say, you insisted on repeating that L.A. was being overwhelmed by illegal aliens, then you were in fact conceding that the laws of the United States were being defied, that order was breaking down, and that society was impotent to stop any of it. But were you, instead, to describe these new arrivals not as illegal aliens at all but rather as undocumented workers, then their advent, if still not entirely welcome, could come to appear far less threatening—just the story of a lot of newcomers looking for work whose papers were, as it turned out, not entirely in order. Everyone, after all, had had the experience of having an expired car registration or an out-of-date insurance card at one time or another in their lives; it wasn't that important. Certainly, it didn't change your life or the future of your community.

Similarly, if an Angeleno identified the Southland with the United States exclusively, then at least some gloomy presentiments of decline became all but impossible to stave off, at least for anyone who read the business pages. How much more reassuring to speak of the Pacific Rim, to arrogate to Los Angeles, verbally anyway, that region's indisputably bright future. It was a magical practice, but then this reliance on the incantatory had always been the oldest of Los Angeles conceits, and the idea that the words you spoke about the future were themselves a way of making that future come true was hard to abandon, whatever the evidence. It could scarcely have been otherwise in a city where such a certitude was to be found even in cemeteries, where, graven on the tombstones along with the usual pieties, were promises as well.

General Harrison Gray Otis lies buried in such a place, in Hollywood Memorial Park, that now slightly down-at-the-heel cemetery adjoining the old Paramount movie lot, that was founded in 1899 by the developer I. N. Van Nuys and his father-in-law, Colonel Isaac Lankershim. Before the construction of the mammoth Forest Lawn in Glendale, that *ne plus ultra* of Southern California cemeteries that Evelyn Waugh so savagely lampooned in his novel *The Loved One,* Hollywood Memorial was where most of the leading figures in L.A. bought burial plots for themselves. Not only do Otis's remains molder there, not far from those of his daughter, Marion, and his son-in-law and successor, Harry Chandler, but nearby are the crypts of such movie stars as Rudolph Valentino, Douglas Fairbanks, Sr., and Tyrone Power, directors ranging from Cecil B. De Mille to John Huston, and, in the adjacent Jewish cemetery, Beth Olam, the grave of Bugsy Siegel, Los Angeles's most famous, though by no stretch of the imagination its most rapacious, gangster.

As one enters the grounds, there is a curious and unsettling statue of Cupid and Psyche—"explicit" is the word one guidebook uses to describe it—but by far the most interesting monument to be found anywhere in Hollywood Memorial is located further on, directly to the right of the Chandlers' tombs. It commemorates the twenty dutiful employees of the *Los Angeles Times* who were killed when a bomb planted by the McNamara brothers, two celebrated anarchist agitators of the period, blew up the newspaper's offices on October 1, 1910, during the period when the struggle between General Otis and the trade unions was at its height. "The crime of the century," is how the inscription on the base of the monument describes the event. And this grandiloquent epitaph concludes with a solemn promise, made, to all appearances, in the name of the people of Los Angeles, to these fallen heroes, which in many ways reads more like a maintenance contract than a eulogy. "Forever green," reads its exhortation, "be the turf which California through all her perennial summertime will graciously lend among their cherished graves."

A safe engagement to make, on the face of things, or so it must have seemed in those heady days when the aqueduct, still under construction, was snaking its way from poor rooked Inyo County toward the Los

Angeles basin's reservoir at Sylmar. Indeed, not only in Southern Californian but in American terms, this confident assertion has had a remarkably long run. It still would have made sense to most Angelenos as late as the early 1980s. In 1991, however, even those who had successfully weathered the twin psychic knocks of demographic transformation and global economic shift were having a hard time with the weather. They might still maintain their faith, or, for that matter, have faith to spare, in the idea that, whatever form it would take, L.A.'s destiny would be grandiose (even those who favored the *Blade Runner* scenario shared in this, since what could have been more self-regarding, when all was said and done, than to insist that L.A. would be the only *dystopia* that mattered?). But, try as they might to say that desire shaped reality, they were now coming up against the one fact about their lives that all the optimistic spin control on events great and small, the almost vertebral refusal to draw certain obvious conclusions, and, of course, all the desiring in the world, could neither alter nor postpone indefinitely: geography.

And in confronting this actual, rather than wished-for, or imaginative, or man-made, geography of the region they lived in, Angelenos were finally being forced to ask themselves whether their Southern California dream might, just might, not have been a hoax after all. There were ways to accept the idea of the new immigrants, even ways that still permitted you to insist that nothing had changed or that it was all for the best, or to listen to the news, as Anglos in the Southland did in the winter of 1991, and learn that the following year's entering class at UCLA would contain more Asians than any other racial group, and accept that as well as some sort of extension of America's historical identity rather than a remaking of it. But as Los Angeles entered the sixth year of a drought whose end was nowhere in sight, and as they began to understand that the changes this lack of water would bring could not be construed happily, Angelenos, perhaps for the first time, found themselves in a confrontation with their future from which all their dreaming, all their vaunted imaginative resourcefulness, might not excuse them.

The irony was that this reckoning came at exactly the moment when Los Angeles was, as the boosters like to say, "growing up" as a world city, a phrase that implied that L.A was not only the place to be to make money but the place to go for the cultural amenities that went with this version of liberal capitalism. Certainly, the bleak vision of the city that so many intelligent people had favored since the days of Nathanael West and those Hollywood *films noirs* of the 1940s, such as *Double Indemnity,* had given way to great museums like the Getty in Malibu, the Norton Simon in Pasadena, the L.A. County Museum, and the Museum

of Contemporary Art downtown, as well as to far more irenic film por-
traits, such as Steve Martin's *L.A. Story.* But *L.A. Story* began, as any
movie extolling the pleasures of life in the Southland would begin, with
a precredit sequence in which water was everywhere—in the pools
straight out of a David Hockney painting beside which the canonical
blonde babes took the sun, in the fountains of the public plazas, and,
above all, in the sprinklers that watered those lawns that, geographically
speaking, obviously had no business there in the first place. Because no
matter what they might see on the screen, Angelenos had only to leave
the mall or step outside their own front doors to discover that they
lived in a semi-arid desert, a place where, as even Mulholland himself
had recognized, without imported water, and lots of it, no more than a
quarter of a million inhabitants could be provided for comfortably.

When water had been in ample supply, which was to say since the
second decade of the century, there had indeed been no restrictions on
how far Los Angeles could grow. But now, L.A., with its average rainfall
of thirteen inches (New York, by comparison, got almost fifty) and a
regional population fast approaching twenty million, with its own reservoirs empty and the flow through its aqueducts declining steadily, was
forced to confront an idea that was utterly inimical to the spirit of Los
Angeles, that of limits. In the past, the city had always been successful
either by annexing areas that had water, or by bullying other parts of
the state of California, or, for that matter, states as far away as Colorado,
into providing it with more water. But Colorado itself was running
short, and was growing increasingly bitter about Southern California's
demands, while the rest of the state was all but tapped out. The San Luis
Reservoir southeast of San Francisco, a facility originally intended to
hold 1.6 million acre feet of water, now contained a third of that quantity. The other reservoirs were, if anything, in worse shape. Even in the
Sacramento River delta, the area where, when California's reservoir system got into trouble, the Los Angeles Water Management District had
always been able to turn for emergency resupply, the water levels were
drifting lower, the sloughs filling up, and once abundant fish and game
beginning to disappear from a landscape that, as long as people could
remember, had been known for both.

In cities all over the state, from San Francisco in the north to Santa
Barbara in the south, draconian conservation measures already in force
were being steadily tightened. In Marin County, immediately north of
San Francisco, for example, the local authorities had ordered that residential water consumption be reduced to fifty gallons a day, less than
half the average daily use in any normal year. Santa Barbara residents
were in their third year of being forbidden to water their lawns or use

their water to wash their cars, and in nurseries and gardening societies in the area, people could be heard bitterly complaining about the "drought police" who cruised through their neighborhoods looking for violators and imposing stiff fines on anyone they caught watering their flowers. "Sometimes I sneak the hose out," a landscape painter named Patricia Chidlaw admitted to a reporter from *The New York Times,* adding rather wistfully that "seeing things grow enhances the quality of life."

As for farmers, those long-pampered mainstays of the California economy, and, almost as important, of that entrenched California self-image that declared everything to grow more bountifully in the Golden State, they had seen their allotments cut in the previous two years to less than 25 percent of what they had been accustomed to receiving for the past fifty. Some of these cuts were long overdue. It turned out that there were many farmers still growing, often with government subsidies, rice, cotton, and alfalfa in California, three products generally referred to as monsoon crops that hardly seemed suitable for cultivation in a state that, even when it rained as much as it should, never had a super-abundance of water. But other land that farmers now would be obliged to take out of use produced precisely those fruits and vegetables— oranges, grapes, lettuce, apricots—with which California had always been associated. And, as the reports of unemployment in Fresno and barren fields in Kern County started to come in, most knowledgeable people were prophesying worse to come. The incoming Republican governor, Pete Wilson, had scarcely been in office for three months when he was forced to order a contingency plan in which Californians were warned that if matters did not improve soon, an across-the-state water cutback of 50 percent would be imposed.

Predictably, the rest of California tended to blame greater Los Angeles for these problems. Farmers groused that the Southland was stealing the water, just as it had always done, wasting it to fill swimming pools and hot tubs, and using it up in other forms of hedonistic consumption. They had a point, although these ritual denunciations of the sins of the big city tended to leave out the fact that 80 percent of California's water still was allocated to agricultural uses, and at preposterously low prices that, in many instances, had been set a full generation earlier. But many other Californians, who could not have been remotely accused of having the farmers' particular parochial reasons for wanting to shift the blame for the crisis onto L.A., shared this deep grievance against the Southland. L.A. was profligate and had never forced drought cutbacks in usage at anywhere near the level of the rest of the state; L.A. was arrogant; and, it seemed, L.A. richly deserved its comeuppance. It was almost as if the ghosts of the farmers of the Owens Valley were finally exacting a gaunt revenge.

The very growth that had guaranteed the prosperity of greater Los Angeles was proving now to be its undoing. This was not, however, something that anyone with influence in L.A. was in much of a position to think about, since water and growth had always been inextricably linked in the city, not only in Mulholland's and Otis's day but in contemporary times as well. Institutions like the Metropolitan Water Department had been conceived of, from the first, as furthering the interests of land developers. As late as the mid-1980s, their boards were still overloaded with real estate magnates like E. Thornton Ibettson, who had once rashly admitted in public that "I joined the water board to get the water." It was an impeccable move, from his point of view. After all, the more water that was available to greater L.A., the more houses could be built, and the more houses that were completed, the more water would be required. And it was far too simple to argue, as critics of development so often did, that this process was nothing more than a vicious circle. Many people had gotten rich through development, to be sure, but that same process, no matter how unwise and even doomed it now appeared, had allowed many people of modest means to live better than most people in the history of the world had ever dreamed of doing.

This did not mean that the developers were unaware that creating a salable image of Southern California living meant landscaping their properties with flora entirely alien to the ecology of the region. That was why the needed all that water in the first place. If you were going to try to sell a middle-class couple on the joys of life in a new residential community out on some high desert plateau near the Antelope Valley, or in the furthest reaches of San Bernardino in the foothills of the San Gabriels, it was imperative to create lawns as green as the ones you would find in Seattle, or, for that matter, Shropshire. The fact that this was quite a task in the desert was of no account. People had not come to Southern California to live in the desert, even though objectively, that is precisely what they had done in the past and, in record numbers, were continuing to do today.

But the illusion was everything. This was terrain where, as Allegra once put it to me, as we drove away from her house leaving the sprinklers spraying furiously away, "the water has to be in at least two hours a day or everything, but everything, will die."

In the new developments, the water requirements were even greater. At least on the Westside, you were surrounded by other houses, roads, malls, freeways, and public parks, as far as the eye could see. Out in the desert, even the most lush residential enclaves were never far from the barren face of the desert, a particular goad for people who had bought there to want to maintain or even amplify this impression of greenery. In Los Angeles County, a full 35 percent of all water use was devoted to landscaping irrigation in either public spaces or private homes. The figure was higher as you moved away from the center. In comparison, only 22 percent of all the water used went to all forms of industrial and commercial use throughout greater L.A.

But it was one thing to diagnose the problem and quite another to try to figure out what could be done. None of the alternatives were appealing, involving as they did not just change but real transformation in the lives most Angelenos had grown accustomed to. Cities could, for example, choose to spend vast sums of money, as Santa Barbara had undertaken to do, building desalinization plants of a type that were common enough in Israel or Saudi Arabia but were as yet entirely untried in Southern California. A massive effort at conservation, as well as the building of new catchments and reservoirs, would have to take place. And, unquestionably, the price Californians paid for their water, for a whole variety of reasons ranging from the long-standing belief that energy and water would be cheap because they *had* to be cheap—the power of the dream, in other words—to the more mundane matter of the influence of the agricultural and real estate lobbies in the state capital, would have to rise at least threefold. But this was only the beginning, stopgap measures that did not begin to address the roots of the problem.

Everything about Southern California's development, it was beginning to seem, had been based on growth, and yet everything about growth now turned out to exacerbate a water shortage. The highways that most Angelenos now agreed needed to be built or expanded to cope with the gridlock, and the air pollution and waste of energy that inevitably resulted from it, would themselves do irreparable damage to the local water table, as construction lowered and even polluted the aquifer. If subdivisions continued to be built at anything like the present rate— particularly in the outlying areas of greater L.A. that were wholly dependent for their water on supplies from the Colorado River which, in any case, were unlikely to be as available once other claimants like the greater Phoenix conurbation started to need them—there would soon be no way of ensuring the required quantities. But if, as was beginning to happen, local municipalities in the Southland began to stop licensing these new developments, then this slowdown would have a catastrophic effect on the regional economy due to the loss of real estate and construction jobs. And this was hardly what was needed at a time when the Southland was experiencing the steady increase of layoffs and firings in the aerospace industry that had been the most immediate result of the end of the Cold War.

Keep developing and the region would soon run out of potable water; stop developing and literally hundreds of thousands of people, or, more accurately stated, voters, were likely to be put out of work. As George Miller, a California congressman who chaired the House Interior Subcommittee looking into the drought, had remarked plaintively—as if the discovery had somehow offended him as a Californian—there were just "not too many alternatives to water." To his credit, Miller went on to declare himself anything but sanguine about the future, something that could not have endeared him to his campaign contributors. "The largest state in the union," he said, "is on life support. . . . There's Colorado River water we'd like to borrow now and then, and natural gas from the Midwest for the desalinization plants. But I'm deeply concerned that we may be whistling past the graveyard here."

Roughly translated, this meant that the future might not, after all, be anything like what its advance billing had promised. To be sure, this impression of the endlessly redeeming potential of growth—all growth —had always been an illusion, as superficial, in its way, as that first memorable impression of seamless ease that greeted even the most resistant visitor to Los Angeles. But if that time was drawing to a close, if all those heavily marketed images of ambrosial comfort the Southland offered now had to give way to more realistic, not to say uncomfortable, circumstances, in which people put bricks in their toilet tanks to reduce the water used in flushing, rarely washed their cars, and, worse, had to carpool in these grungy vehicles, or took three-minute showers—and these were not trivial uses of water: 16 percent of all the water used in L.A. went to residential toilets, while 12 percent went to bathing and showering—then what on earth was to replace it? Could the new boosters' line really be "Come to the Southland and live a modest life within the region's ecological means"? That didn't sound like L.A., to say the least, any more than did its even more ruthless sibling, "We've got enough people, please go home."

It had been one thing to speak of a perennial summertime that was green and fragrant. To face the reality of one that, as befitted life in the desert, was dry and sere, was something else entirely. Ironically, it turned out that L.A.'s cemeteries were among the few places that would be able to go on as they had been doing, since their lawns were part of the one percent in the city that were watered by reused, unpotable water. But almost everywhere else, what had been for so long—beyond the living memory, in fact, of virtually everyone now residing in the Los Angeles basin, whether native-born or immigrant—taken for a birthright and proof of L.A.'s superior lifestyle was now beginning to seem like evidence of lax and self-indulgent use of a scarce and valuable resource. By the fall of 1990, even the development-minded Mayor Bradley had admitted that things had to change and that Los Angeles would actually have to impose *limits* on itself for the first time in its history. A few months later, mandatory rationing was announced, an event as cataclysmic in its implications as any of the revolutions that had been transforming the world of late—the fall of the Berlin Wall, say, or the rise of nonwhite Los Angeles.

Before too long, the lawns had begun to go brown all over greater Los Angeles. The first priority, it had turned out, was to conserve a lot of the water that was being used in landscaping. Not surprisingly, the L.A. City Council tried at first to cushion the blow, and when it banned the watering of private lawns between 10 A.M. and 5 P.M. it made an exception for what it referred to rather euphemistically as "professional gardeners." What that really meant, of course, was the illegal aliens and the contractors who employed them. What else was new? The questions of cheap water and cheap labor were hardly unconnected, and it was natural that an attempt would be made, now that the ecological bill was coming due, not to let its effect fall too heavily or in such a way as to challenge the system of immigrant labor on which the region now so obviously depended. No businessman in L.A. really wanted the immigrants to leave. And if such imperatives also had the collateral effect of further de-democratizing household work by, in effect, making it legal to hire someone to look after your lawn, but inconvenient if not manifestly illegal to look after it yourself, such a result was barely remarked upon, things in L.A. having gone most of the way in that direction long before.

And, of course, the illegals would suffer a great deal anyway. By the winter of 1991, when you drove along Sawtelle Boulevard in West L.A., that horizontal hiring hall for Hispanic gardeners and yardmen, you might very well run across the same faces at two in the afternoon that you had seen at six in the morning—a wait that would have been exceptional in the days before Los Angeles began to grapple with its drought. Men who, when I had first met them on my arrival in the city a year earlier, had spoken of getting two or three offers of work in the course of a day now considered themselves lucky if they could earn even a few hours' wages. "The ground, she is not as beautiful now," one man confided to me mournfully as we stood in the parking lot at the corner of Pico watching the noontime traffic move by in its usual fits and starts. And though I waited with him for the remainder of the day, and wound up paying him for his time as if I had hired him for my yard rather than interviewed him, he did not receive a single offer of the work he was most skilled in. I last saw him, chipped trowel in hand, walking disconsolately off toward the freeway underpass where he was due to meet the ride that would ferry him back to East Los Angeles.

If the testimony of contractors, nurserymen, and landscapers on the Westside was even remotely accurate, this Mexican gardener's experience was anything but untypical. Employers spoke of letting not only their occasional, read illegal, workers go, but of firing permanent employees too. Even those greenhouse owners who were managing to get by said they were now stocking fewer and fewer plants that required much water, that is, the various flowers and plants that, however exogenous they were to the Southland, had formed the bulk of their inventory for more than three quarters of a century. Instead, they were trying to persuade their customers to buy desert plants that, while a common sight in Arizona, had never found much of a clientele on the Westside of L.A. "Everything is bound to be browner in years to come," one self-styled "lawn designer" told me matter-of-factly. He laughed mirthlessly and added, "In other ways as well."

Another grandiose expectation shot to hell. It seemed to be the season for it, even in a Southern California that everyone liked to pretend had no seasons, only period of Santa Ana winds and leaping, unpredictable fires. In *L.A. Story,* a cynical Englishman sneers that "if you turned the sprinklers off, you'd have a desert," and Victoria Tennant, the film's heroine, retorts that "I think they've turned a desert into their dreams." That was what most Angelenos had thought, and, at the beginning of the drought, few had believed that it posed more than a fleeting impediment to the upward curve of their comfort. But if Mulholland's solution was no longer any good, if you didn't get to choose your future after all, then what was it that really separated Los Angeles from the declining cities of the northeastern United States, or even from Tijuana? In the minds of many, not just one cynical landscaper, the ecological and the demographic crises began to get confused. It was one thing to live in a green city perplexingly full of brown people, but a brown city full of brown people? That was something else again.

And yet with every passing month, those patches of brown seemed to pervade the L.A. cityscape a little more authoritatively. First the landscaping along the freeways went, as the state of California ordered its own agencies, Caltrans not least among them, to cut back. Then came the corporate plazas, which soon lost their incongruous tropicality. But it was among individual homeowners, in front yards, and back gardens, and hedges and borders, that the change was most pronounced. Those lawns were L.A., not only because of the fantasy of a perennial summer but because homeownership was the real draw of life in the Southland and always had been. These houses usually constituted the bulk of a person's material assets, but they were something of a mystical necessity as well, the dream that fueled even the sizable number of middle-class Angelenos who now lived in apartments or condominiums.

But however powerful this fantasy, the actual lawns were starting to suffer. In disgust, some people were simply allowing their front yards to fray and turn brown. Others managed to conceal the extent of the change. But even when outward signs of the deterioration were not immediately visible, it was usually possible, on closer examination, to see what accommodations were being made with the drought. A lawn might not extend all the way to the property line. Another sure give-away was a vogue for Zen gardens among people with no previous interest either in Buddhism or in Japanese aesthetics, or else the appearance of a cactus bed in the backyard border of a person previously known as an ardent rose fancier. The only solution from which Angelenos seemed so far to have excused themselves was the radical decision taken by at least one homeowner in Santa Barbara of spray painting his lawn green.

Of course, none of this meant that L.A. had really started to resemble Baja California. Increasingly, however, what the city no longer resembled was its pristine, green self. Most Angelenos went on claiming that they did not notice the daily, incremental changes, until the brief period at the beginning of March when, though it was too late to do much good, it rained all over the Southland. Then, with the same shock with which you suddenly register the aging of a friend you see too often to observe realistically, Angelenos admitted what was going on. As Walter Gomperz, a spokesman for the Metropolitan Water District, put it, as he tried to explain why the drought was not over, "Cars sitting outdoors are getting washed off, and lawns are getting watered, and may even turn green." Then, pausing, he told the assembled reporters, "I vaguely remember green."

Among a few Angelenos, the drought had brought to the fore nastiness that the city's seemingly unstoppable prosperity had held in check. An ugly racist undercurrent seemed to have touched even some people who, when I first met them, had proclaimed themselves staunch and unswerving L.A. boosters. I heard cracks about the city being a place of "brown skins, brown lungs, and brown front yards." These, thankfully, were rare. Less so was a tendency among Anglos to speculate about whether the arrival of the new immigrants represented not something unprecedented but rather the accelerated clarification of an outcome already all but predetermined by history and geography; specifically, by the Pacific Ocean, which the advent of air travel had turned into little more than a lake, both for the capitalist and for the immigrant, and, of course, by the region's long overdue settling of accounts with Mexico and Central America.

There were even a few Angelenos, like the scriptwriter and novelist Josh Greenfield, who had always found the comparison with the Third World irresistible. "It always struck me that way," Greenfield had told me, when I first spoke to him early in my stay in Los Angeles. "Just look at the walls, at every house on the Westside surrounded by walls as if it were in Lima or Cairo." At the time, I took the remark to be fanciful, a derogation of the town's morals, the way people spoke of the Washington of Ronald Reagan and Oliver North as a banana republic, rather than about its physical essence. Even now, as I neared the end of my time in the city and had come to see his point, it seemed unlikely that the view would have found many takers. But what was common was some inchoate sense that, at a certain moment during the twentieth century, the United States had stopped being an extension of Europe, and had, for better or worse, struck out on its own, an increasingly nonwhite country adrift, however majestically and powerfully, in an increasingly nonwhite world.

Sometimes, people expressed this view without fully realizing what they were saying. One afternoon, I sat with Nathan Gardels in the lobby of the Mondrian Hotel, a postmodernist folly on Sunset in West Hollywood, arguing amiably about the future of Los Angeles. He had been extolling the new world city, and I, as much for the sake of provoking him as anything else, launched into a litany of denunciation, evoking the schools that did not work, the traffic jams, the economic inequities, the pollution. Obviously, Nathan had heard all this before, but the answer he gave, when, at last, I let my little jeremiad trail off into silence, was anything but the one I had expected. "You may be right," he said, "but what you have to remember is that people here live a lot better than they do in the Philippines, or South Korea, or Taiwan, let alone Mexico or Salvador."

I was astonished. "Since when," I asked, "did the best way of thinking about the United States become to compare it to countries in the Third World?"

Nathan's face stiffened, and he fell silent. For a long moment, I thought he wouldn't answer, or that, if he did, he would either brush off our entire exchange or else turn it into a joke. But then, musingly, he did reply. "I don't really know," he said. "Maybe it was after the defeat in Vietnam, or earlier, after the 1965 immigration reform. It's hard to say. But what I do know is that every time I go to Europe nowadays, there is a moment when I think to myself, 'Very little of what I'm seeing here has all that much to do with the future of Southern California.' "

"And in Mexico City or Seoul?" I inquired, sure now of the answer I would receive.

"Exactly," he said, smiling. "There I might as well be in some version of home. I don't mean the one we've made here in L.A., of course; if that were true, you wouldn't see people lined up in front of the U.S. Embassy all day and all night trying to get a visa to come here. But something familiar, just the same."

All he was sure of, he told me as we parted, was that, whatever else would happen in Southern California, L.A.'s European period—assuming, that is, it had ever really had one, and, perhaps, America's, which had, as well—was ending along with its dream time. Unlike the boosters, Nathan placed no value on what was happening, or so he insisted. As for me, as I watched him get into his car at the hotel entrance and drive cheerfully off, I found that I agreed with him. I also found, though it was a dry, hot day, that the thought made me shiver.

The following morning, I drove to the airport, my journey to Los Angeles at an end. Of course, I went surface, as Allegra had instructed me to do. We had stood in front of her house in mid-Wilshire, trying not to part too awkwardly. So far, her roses had survived the drought. "You know the way," she had repeated. "Only tourists take the freeways at this hour. They're sure to be jammed."

Just as she had predicted, traffic all the way out was light. Not having to wrestle with it gave me time to look for one final, intense moment at all those signs in Hankul and Spanish, Cantonese and Tagalog, Thai and Farsi, that had been my companions during my time in L.A. There they were, those emblems of the new California, of the new America as well, at once a confused jumble whose meaning I could not make out and the clearest of markers toward the future. Then the airport rose up in the distance, and my attention began to flag.

At LAX, I was engrossed in the details of returning the car, of wrestling with the crowds, and finally of settling into my seat on the plane. It was only later, as Los Angeles, enveloped in its usual smog, began to recede from view, and I could see nothing down below but the high desert as yet untouched by development, and, with the drought, now unlikely to be, that I began to try to sort out what I thought about L.A., trying to fix this last impression of space and emptiness, the skull beneath the city's skin, in my mind for good. But of course, I couldn't, and as we landed in New York this whole period of time seemed almost ungraspable.

I did not speak to Allegra for some time. A month later, though, she called me. "What do you think of Los Angeles now?" she asked.

Not quite knowing what I was saying, I found myself reciting a line of poetry that had been in my mind a lot when I first went to Los Angeles but which I had not thought about for some time.

"We must love one another or die," I said.

There was a silence on the other end of the line. Allegra recognized the quote, and, almost automatically, corrected me.

"We must love one another and die," she said.

We must love one another or die.

Index

· · · · · · · ·